FROM
EDEN
TO
EXILE

FROM
EDEN
TO
EXILE

UNRAVELING MYSTERIES
OF THE BIBLE

ERIC H. CLINE

NATIONAL GEOGRAPHIC

WASHINGTON, D.C.

ISBN-13: 978-1-4262-0084-7

The Scripture quotations contained herein are from the New Revised Standard Version Bible, copyright 1989 by the Division of Christian Education of the National Council of Churches of Christ in the U.S.A., and are used by permission. In addition, some material in this book previously appeared in oral and/or written form by the present author and appears here with the permission of Modern Scholar/Recorded Books (www.modernscholar.com).

Library of Congress Cataloging-in-Publication Data:

Cline, Eric H.
  From Eden to exile : unraveling mysteries of the Bible / by Eric H. Cline. -- 1st ed.
    p. cm.
  Includes index.
  ISBN 978-1-4262-0084-7 (hardcover : alk. paper)
  1. Bible. O.T.–Evidences, authority, etc. 2. Bible. O.T.–History of Biblical events. 3. Bible. O.T.–Antiquities. 4. Bible. O.T.–Criticism, interpretation, etc. 5. Judaism–History–To 70 A.D. 6. Jews–History–To 70 A.D. I. Title.
  BS1180.C64 2006
  221.6'7--dc22
                              2007003122

Founded in 1888, the National Geographic Society is one of the largest nonprofit scientific and educational organizations in the world. It reaches more than 285 million people worldwide each month through its official journal, NATIONAL GEOGRAPHIC, and its four other magazines; the National Geographic Channel; television documentaries; radio programs; films; books; videos and DVDs; maps; and interactive media. National Geographic has funded more than 8,000 scientific research projects and supports an education program combating geographic illiteracy.

For more information, please call
1-800-NGS LINE (647-5463)
or write to the following address:

National Geographic Society
1145 17th Street N.W.
Washington, D.C. 20036-4688 U.S.A.

Visit us online at www.nationalgeographic.com/books

For information about special discounts for bulk purchases, please contact National Geographic Books Special Sales: ngspecsales@ngs.org

Printed in U.S.A.

Interior Design: Cameron Zotter

CONTENTS

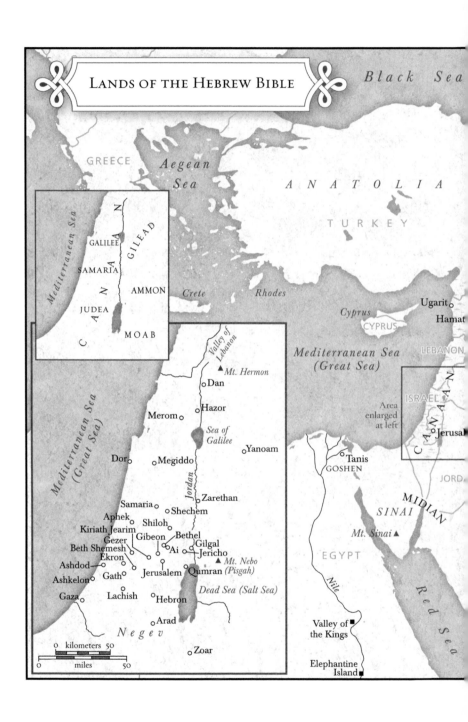

LANDS OF THE HEBREW BIBLE

Black Sea

GREECE

Aegean Sea

ANATOLIA

TURKEY

Mediterranean Sea

GALILEE

GILEAD

SAMARIA

AMMON

JUDEA

MOAB

Crete

Rhodes

Cyprus

CYPRUS

Ugarit

Hamat

Mediterranean Sea (Great Sea)

LEBANON

ISRAEL

Area enlarged at left

Jerusal

CANAAN

Valley of Lebanon

▲ Mt. Hermon

Dan

Hazor

Merom

Sea of Galilee

Yanoam

Dor

Megiddo

Tanis

GOSHEN

JORD

Jordan

Zarethan

MIDIAN

SINAI

Samaria

Shechem

Aphek

Shiloh

Kiriath Jearim

Gezer

Gibeon

Bethel

Mt. Sinai ▲

Beth Shemesh

Ai

Gilgal

Ekron

Jericho

Ashdod

Jerusalem

Qumran

▲ Mt. Nebo (Pisgah)

EGYPT

Ashkelon

Gath

Gaza

Lachish

Hebron

Dead Sea (Salt Sea)

Nile

Arad

Negev

Valley of the Kings

Zoar

Red Sea

0 kilometers 50

0 miles 50

Elephantine Island

INTRODUCTION

"The greatest challenge for anyone trying to 'solve' a Biblical mystery
is that the Bible interweaves the historical and the theological, the mystical
and the verifiable—often in one sentence."
—Molly Dewsnap Meinhardt, *Biblical Archaeology Society*

There are many mysteries in the Bible. Some cannot be explained and must remain as mysteries or even miracles—at least for now, if not forever. Other mysteries can be discussed rationally within a historical and archaeological framework. A number of these, including the Garden of Eden, Noah's ark, Sodom and Gomorrah, Moses and the Exodus, Joshua and the Battle of Jericho, the Ark of the Covenant, and the Ten Lost Tribes, are of great interest to many people. It is on these seven mysteries that we will concentrate here.

While doing the research for this book, I became amazed and, frankly, appalled by the amount of pseudoscientific nonsense that has been published on these topics, especially on the Internet but also in book form. The vast majority of this work has not been produced by professional scholars but rather by amateur enthusiasts, some of whom we will meet in the following chapters. These enthusiasts—most of whom are self-trained and self-employed, and some of whom publish only, or primarily, on the Internet—all work outside of academia. As such, they are not held to the same standards of rigor, peer review, and scrutiny as professional scholars employed by colleges, universities, and other institutions of higher learning. Indeed, the work of such enthusiasts frequently meets the criteria of "junk science," especially when it, as Ron W. Pritchett has explained, "advocates a cause, pays little attention to the investigative process, ignores contrary evidence, and advertises a high moral purpose."

Quite frequently, the public embraces such enthusiasts, for they are entertaining and passionate, for the most part. And, unfortunately, when it comes right down to it, it seems that a good but erroneous story trumps good but boring data every time: The enthusiast might be completely wrong, but he or she is frequently a charismatic storyteller who never lets the facts get in the way of a good story. As a result, such stories frequently reach a larger audience than the more detailed and often dry work of the archaeologists, ancient historians, and biblical scholars. On television shows or in media articles devoted to these stories, real scholars are often reduced to the role of mere commentators and "nattering nabobs of negativism," to use the words of former Vice President Spiro Agnew and William Safire in a new context. Frequently, these experts come off as spoilsports—"an effete corps of impudent snobs"—refuting the exciting nonsense being spewed by those who have no formal training in history or archaeology and who are, as they say, taking on the establishment.

That is not to say that the work of such enthusiasts is always without merit or completely flawed. Some of them may have good evidence or logical clues that they are following, but then come to faulty or erroneous conclusions. Sometimes they are simply guilty of wishful thinking or of reading too much into the evidence. Other times they are guilty of setting off on their investigations with an a priori set of assumptions, such as the infallibility of the Bible, which does not inspire confidence in the impartiality of their investigations. They frequently do not seem to know, or care, that there are larger debates within the fields of biblical studies, ancient history, and archaeology that will (or should) affect their studies, ranging from biblical criticism and source theory to the validity and accuracy of radiocarbon dating.

The materials written and published by some scholars on these topics can also be problematic, especially the most fervent of the evangelical biblical maximalists, who see the Hebrew Bible as infallible, and the biblical minimalists, who see the Hebrew Bible as a late (that is, Persian or Hellenistic) fabrication. Some biblical maximalists—particularly those working outside of mainstream academia—seem to be closer to the enthusiasts in setting out with their own a priori set of assumptions, which are often stated outright in the mission or message statements on their Web sites. Others dilute their good and careful analysis of archaeological material and ancient literary sources with uncritical thinking or blatant proselytizing. In addition, both the maximalist and minimalist camps harbor individuals who abuse and occasionally distort the information.

Thus, one of the reasons I have written this book is to sound both a word of warning and a call to arms, because I believe that the general public deserves—and wants—better. It is high time that professional archaeologists, ancient historians, and mainstream biblical scholars take back their fields from the amateur enthusiasts, pseudoscientists, uninformed documentary filmmakers, and overzealous biblical maximalists and minimalists who had, for the most part, free rein to do what they wish, without any regard to scientific method or an unbiased investigation for the truth. In return, though, we as academics owe it to the general public to deal with these mysteries in a serious way and to publish our findings. Even if our investigations come up empty, it is frequently the journey—including the benchmarks established and information imparted along the way—that is most valuable and sometimes even more interesting than the end result.

I will say right up front, however, that what I cannot do is solve all of these mysteries—nobody who adheres to the facts can do that. All that I can do is unravel some of the threads that make up these mysteries, present the current state of our evidence and what professional scholars are thinking about these topics today, highlight the most likely situation, and provide enough information so that the reader will be able to better assess future claims made by another author or a television program. But I doubt that alone is enough reason for anyone to want to read on. So are there other reasons to explore these topics? The answer, I believe, is a resounding "yes."

For one thing, these mysteries are not ancient history. They are still very much around today, showing up every few weeks or months in newspaper headlines and as references in stories about all kinds of otherwise unrelated events. Sodom and Gomorrah, Armageddon, the walls of Jericho, Adam and Eve, the Garden of Eden, the Tower of Babel—references to these topics constantly appear in media around the world, and not just in tabloids sold at supermarket checkout stands. To know a little about these topics is to be culturally literate; to know more about them is to have an informed opinion.

Moreover, these topics still resonate and are both used and abused in connection with current events. Plenty of people read the Bible as history—even though we cannot correlate and confirm its specific details until the events of the first millennium B.C. (as we shall see in chapter 7)—and they use these biblical narratives to frame today's headlines, especially news from the modern Middle East. Did Joshua really fight the Battle of Jericho and drive the Canaanites out of the land, as stated in the biblical account of the Israelite conquest of Canaan? If so, who was there first and to whom does the land really belong today? The Palestinians, via their ostensible ancestors, the Canaanites and Jebusites, or the Israelis, via their ostensible ancestors, the invading Israelites? The debate over who has first rights to the Holy Land may be completely moot if Professor Israel Finkelstein of Tel Aviv University is correct about the original Israelites and their role in Canaan. His "Invisible Israelites" model, which we will touch upon in chapter 5, suggests that long ago the Israelites and the Canaanites once occupied the land at the same time because they were the same people. This would mean that there was never an Israelite conquest of Canaan—and that, in turn, means that the current cycle of violence in modern Israel and Palestine is less like two nations at war and more like a sibling rivalry or a family reunion gone bad.

Similarly, does it matter whether the Ark of the Covenant is located in a cave on a mountain in Jordan or underneath the Temple Mount in modern-day Jerusalem or even in a church treasury in Aksum, Ethiopia? It matters very much to political and religious authorities. And what about the Ten Lost Tribes? Does it matter that the Lemba in Africa or the B'nai Menashe in India claim to be members of the lost tribes of Israel? It certainly does, especially when we consider that the emigration and airlifting of Ethiopian Falasha Jews to Israel from 1977 to 1991 occurred in part because of a similar possibility. The biblical stories become real when people adopt them as their own, regardless of their historical accuracy.

Therefore, in the following pages, I will investigate the seven intriguing mysteries of the Bible mentioned earlier. I will put each of them into their proper historical and archaeological contexts and describe what many archaeologists, ancient historians, and biblical scholars are currently thinking. I will be exploring these mysteries primarily as an archaeologist and an ancient historian. I am not a theologian, so I will not be looking at the theological questions that are present in some of these mysteries; I will leave that to others. I am also not specifically an expert in literary criticism or textual analysis. However, as an ancient historian, I frequently use many of the same tools, although not to the extent that the specialists do. I often tell my students that ancient history is essentially "texts plus archaeology," and to interpret the texts correctly means using the tools of literary criticism and textual analysis.

My own methodology, therefore, is the standard historical method followed by most historians. I generally hope to have several—preferably at least three—independent bodies of evidence when attempting to answer a question or confirm a fact about something in the ancient world. In the case of most of the mysteries that we will investigate in this book, the data will come from the biblical account, extra-biblical literary texts, and archaeology.

In each of the following chapters, I will first present a brief recapitulation of the biblical account relevant to the mystery at hand. Within the ensuing discussion section, I will present the additional available evidence—both textual and archaeological—and will briefly evaluate some of the suggestions that have been proposed to explain each mystery. I will also include a section on the historical context of the biblical mystery in question, because by putting each mystery into its probable (or definite) historical context, we can see if it is possible to explain it logically.

In the concluding section for each chapter, I will attempt to weigh the pros and cons of each topic and to discuss any possible historical kernel of truth upon which the mystery may rest. And, finally, I will suggest what I believe to be the most likely solution to each mystery, if there is one. We will need to keep in mind, though, that there is a wide range of reactions and responses to these mysteries even among archaeologists, ancient historians, and biblical scholars themselves—from those who say that the Bible can be proven to those who say that there isn't a single word of truth in it—so my suggested solution to each of the biblical mysteries will be just that, no more and no less.

I must also point out that each of the chapters in this book could easily be expanded into a book itself—or could be a chapter with a different title and orientation. For instance, the chapter on Sodom and Gomorrah could just as easily have been recast as a chapter entitled "Abraham and Ur," which is, in fact, how it was originally conceived. In addition, I am keenly aware that in each chapter I am only able to present the basic facts; we could easily spend dozens more pages in each case, discussing the best literary approach to take when analyzing the biblical text, or why a certain archaeological theory is no longer held to be valid—or we could even go off on long tangents when examining the myriad of smaller topics that will be raised on virtually every page. A truly comprehensive discussion of every topic in this book would take many years, dozens of volumes, and numerous scholars working together—and probably would end up being something that only a handful of people would read.

In addition, each of these topics has had quite literally hundreds, if not thousands, of books and articles written about it. Readers, and especially students, not to mention my esteemed academic colleagues and erudite book reviewers, should be aware that for every book, article, and argument that I cite here, there are dozens more that I either do not have the room to mention or have chosen not to include for one reason or another. I apologize in advance if anyone's favorite book or article has been left out.

I am neither a biblical maximalist nor a biblical minimalist. As a humanist, I do not believe in the complete accuracy and infallibility of the Bible, but I also do not see any reason to abandon the Bible entirely. Instead, I treat the Bible as I would any other ancient literary source: a text to be tested, prodded, compared, analyzed, and essentially wrung dry of all that it will yield. I let the information, observations, and interpretations coming from archaeology, ancient history, and biblical studies interact with—and sometimes against—each other as much as possible, and I use a common-sense approach in applying the data from these disciplines to a reconstruction of the ancient world, attempting to neither overinterpret nor underinterpret the available facts.

Having worked in ancient history for a quarter of a century, I know that firm conclusions are frequently hard to come by. I have had to become comfortable with ambiguity and with the necessity of presenting and discussing data that seems to, and sometimes actually does, conflict with other data. Furthermore, since the study of biblical texts has a long history and will continue to evolve, I accept it as a given that some of the evidence that might allow neat solutions to the problems and mysteries may not have yet been discovered. I can only present the evidence as we have it today. If that means we might have to accept less than conclusive answers for the moment because we don't have all of the evidence yet, then so be it. At the very least, the journey of discovery promises to be extremely interesting.

THE GARDEN OF EDEN

Where was the Garden of Eden?
Is it even possible to find it?

In trying to determine where the Garden of Eden might have been located, we have an immediate problem, because while the biblical description is quite detailed, it is also fairly succinct. We are told only that:

> The Lord God planted a garden in Eden, in the east; and there he put the man whom he had formed. . . . A river flows out of Eden to water the garden, and from there it divides and becomes four branches. The name of the first is Pishon; it is the one that flows around the whole land of Havilah, where there is gold; and the gold of that land is good; bdellium and onyx stone are there. The name of the second river is Gihon; it is the one that flows around the whole land of Cush. The name of the third river is Tigris, which flows east of Assyria. And the fourth river is the Euphrates. (Genesis 2:8-14)

We have little to corroborate the biblical account just presented, because there are no other independent sources of textual evidence for the Garden of Eden. Unfortunately, as we noted in the introduction, most ancient historians and archaeologists generally want several separate sources of evidence before they will believe something to be factually substantiated, and that is simply not possible in the case of the Garden of Eden.

This is not the only time we will run into this problem, especially when dealing with topics found in the first 11 chapters of the Book of Genesis. These early chapters—which include accounts of the Creation, the Garden of Eden, Adam and Eve, and the biblical Flood—are very different from those that follow, in large part because of the nature of the evidence surrounding the stories. It is always difficult to determine how much material in the Bible can be taken as true history, in our definition of the term today, and how much material is instead presented to illustrate an ethical or moral point.

Many scholars would agree that it is only when we get into periods marked by the invention of writing (that is, after 3000 B.C.) that we have any hope of corroborating the biblical accounts. This means that the stories presented in the first chapters of Genesis may be more difficult to corroborate than stories that appear later in Genesis and certainly much harder to corroborate than stories that appear in the other books of the Hebrew Bible.

Thus, we must deal with the biblical description of the Garden of Eden on its own, and make of it what we will. Fortunately, two of the four rivers mentioned in the biblical account are well known: the Tigris and Euphrates rivers in Mesopotamia (modern Iraq). We should note that the original biblical text doesn't actually name the third river as "Tigris"; instead the text says "Hiddekel." However, we know from elsewhere in the Bible (for example, Daniel 10:4) that this is a reference to the Tigris River, so most modern translations of the Bible simply call it the "Tigris" to reduce potential confusion. Similarly, the Euphrates is referred to in the original biblical text as "Prat," the Hebrew rendition of the Babylonian and Assyrian words for the river that was located next to the city of Babylon (the Euphrates). Again, most modern translations of the Bible simply say "Euphrates" without further explanation.

The other two rivers are less well known, and herein lies the problem of determining where the Garden of Eden was located. The Bible says that the Gihon River surrounded the land of Cush, while the Pishon River flowed around the land of Havilah. Some researchers identify the land of

The Renaissance view of Eden probably bore little resemblance to the actual vegetation found in the original Garden of Eden.

Havilah as southern Arabia, but this is merely a hypothesis. As for the land of Cush, although we know that it was really in Africa, the Bible seems to connect it with Mesopotamia (Genesis 10:8). However, as Alessandro Scafi notes in *Mapping Paradise: A History of Heaven on Earth*: "From the time of Augustine [fifth century A.D.] to the Renaissance, the most learned scholars in all Europe, Africa and Asia, agreed that the Gihon and the Pishon were the Nile and the Ganges, an idea put forward by the first-century [A.D.] Jewish historian Flavius Josephus." After the Renaissance, speculation began anew.

In short, the biblical account is ambiguous and open to interpretation. As a result, both ancient and modern authors have located the Garden of Eden everywhere from Iran and Mongolia to South America and even Jackson County, Missouri (according to Joseph Smith, Jr., founder of the Church of Jesus Christ of Latter-day Saints, better known today as the Mormon Church).

———————

MOST SCHOLARS WHO have written recently about the Garden of Eden, however, usually place it in or around ancient Mesopotamia—anywhere from the Persian Gulf to southern Turkey. This makes some sense from a textual point of view, because not only does the biblical account say that the garden lay "in the east" (meaning to the east of Israel), but it also mentions the Tigris and Euphrates Rivers in connection with the Garden of Eden. In fact, the Greek meaning of the very word "Mesopotamia" is "the land between the [two] rivers," a reference to the Tigris and Euphrates Rivers.

No earlier tales from ancient Mesopotamia can provide us with an exact parallel for the Garden of Eden story, but the Sumerians who lived in this region during the third millennium B.C. apparently did have the word "Eden" in their language. Scholars have suggested that the Sumerians adopted this word from an even earlier people—the Ubaidians, who lived in the region from approximately 5500 to 3500 B.C.—and many of them think the word should be translated as "fertile plain." Moreover, there is one Sumerian paradise myth about a land of plenty called "Dilmun," which scholars today suggest may well be modern-day Bahrain in the Persian Gulf. The myth, known as "Enki and Ninhursag," describes Dilmun as being turned into a paradise when the Sumerian god Enki gave it the gift of water:

> The land Dilmun is pure, the land Dilmun is clean;
> The land Dilmun is clean, the land Dilmun is most bright.
>
> . . .
>
> Her well of bitter water, verily it is become a well of sweet water,
> Her furrowed fields and farms bore her grain,
> Her city, verily it is become the bank-quay house of the land Dilmun. . . .

There are also creation stories from this area that have striking similarities to the story found in Genesis. The most famous of these is the myth called *Enuma Elish* (*When on High*), which has long been noted for its biblical parallels. It begins as follows:

> When on high the heaven had not been named,
> Firm ground below had not been called by name,
> Naught but primordial Apsu, their begetter,
> [And] Mummu-Tiamat, she who bore them all,
> Their waters commingling as a single body;
> No reed hut had been matted, no marsh land had appeared,
> When no gods whatever had been brought into being,
> Uncalled by name, their destinies undetermined—
> Then it was that the gods were formed within them.

This myth is sometimes referred to as the Babylonian Genesis because of the obvious parallels to the account in the Hebrew Bible, and yet it is hundreds of years older than the Bible. Scholars generally agree that the Hebrew Bible as we have it today was compiled from various sources, which were written down as early as the tenth or ninth century B.C. and

The Mesopotamian Tree of Life may be the inspiration for the tree that figures prominently in the story of the Garden of Eden.

as late as the sixth or fifth century B.C. Even the earliest parts of the Bible, such as the source called J by biblical scholars, do not date earlier than the tenth or ninth century B.C., hundreds of years after *Enuma Elish* was written.

In fact, surprising as it may seem to some, it is Mesopotamia that had a tremendous impact on later biblical Israel—for this area, during the course of more than 9,000 years, from 10,000 B.C. to 1500 B.C., gave rise to inventions, techniques, ideas, stories, and even laws that were still in use centuries later in Israel and Judah. It is in Mesopotamia, for instance, that we find Hammurabi's Law Code, which gave us "an eye for an eye, a tooth for a tooth" hundreds of years before the Bible. It is in Mesopotamia that Abraham and the Patriarchs had their origins. And it is in Mesopotamia that we find earlier accounts—Sumerian, Babylonian, and Akkadian—of the Flood and of Noah's ark. In these accounts, Noah is instead named Ziusudra, Atrahasis, and Utnapishtim, and the Flood is sent not because humankind is evil and has sinned but because humankind is too noisy and is keeping the gods awake.

Enuma Elish in particular is a good example of what I would call a transmitted narrative: a story that was handed down from generation to generation and culture to culture in the ancient Near East. One of the best ways to explain both the similarities and the differences between the details in this myth and the biblical story found in Genesis is to suggest that the original Mesopotamian story (or the concepts contained within it) may have been passed down from the Sumerians in the third millennium B.C. to the Babylonians, Assyrians, and the peoples of Ugarit and Canaan in the second millennium B.C. and then to the Israelites, eventually making its way into the Hebrew Bible in the first millennium B.C. Additional examples of such transmitted narratives include portions of the *Epic of Gilgamesh* and Hammurabi's Law Code, both of which, as we shall see, are probably reflected in the Hebrew Bible.

IN TRYING TO LOCATE the Garden of Eden by using archaeological evidence, of principal interest to us is the fact that the first plants and animals were domesticated some 10,000 to 12,000 years ago in a wide swath of land stretching across what is now modern Iraq, northern Syria, and southern Turkey. This took place during the so-called neolithic revolution (a reference to the revolutionary ideas that resulted in the origins of agriculture).

This general region—encompassing Mesopotamia and beyond—has been dubbed the Fertile Crescent by archaeologists. It was here that sheep, goats, cattle, and even dogs were first domesticated, and it was here that the idea of actually growing wheat, barley, einkorn, and other grains was first put into practice, as opposed to just picking the wild varieties at random each year.

This area may have also become somewhat of an agricultural paradise for the local residents following the invention of irrigation during the fourth millennium B.C. Archaeologists have long understood that sometime during the period of 4000 to 3000 B.C., the various towns and villages in this region gradually turned to irrigation agriculture. From this, it is thought, the first city-states, then kingdoms, and eventually even empires emerged as a result of the need to work together to create such large-scale projects. Whether or not this hypothesis is correct, it is clear that the region was literally made to bloom in the centuries before the Sumerian civilization arose near the end of the fourth millennium B.C.

SINCE BOTH THE INVENTION of agriculture and the invention of irrigation occurred in the region of Mesopotamia, we should not be surprised that some scholars have suggested the original Garden of Eden might have been located in or near this area.

Persian Gulf Region—For instance, based on a variety of environmental, geological, and archaeological data, Juris Zarins, professor of anthropology at Southwest Missouri State University, has suggested that the original location of the Garden of Eden is now underwater, at the head of the Persian Gulf, near Bahrain. It was into this gulf that the Tigris and Euphrates Rivers spilled their water in antiquity. Nearby, the Karun River–which bears a similar name to the Bible's Gihon River–flows southwest through Iran toward the Persian Gulf. Landsat images suggest that other rivers, now long dried up, flowed through the region as well.

According to Zarins, geological and archaeological evidence suggest that this area was subjected to changes in water level, resulting in the expansion and contraction of the Persian Gulf coastline over time. The southernmost part of Mesopotamia was finally flooded for good sometime between 5000 and 4000 B.C. as part of a worldwide event scientists call the Flandrian Transgression. This transgression caused gulf waters to rise and cover large sections of what had once been dry land in Mesopotamia. It is this region that formed the southeastern portion of the Fertile Crescent, and it is in this region that we find the Sumerians in the fourth and third millennia B.C.

Several decades before Zarins, the esteemed archaeologist and biblical scholar Ephraim A. Speiser, who was a professor and chairman of the

Department of Oriental Studies at the University of Pennsylvania, made a similar suggestion. In a brief article entitled "The Rivers of Paradise," Speiser hypothesizes that the Garden of Eden lay near the head of the Persian Gulf, where the Tigris and Euphrates Rivers came together, although he did not suggest that the garden was presently underwater. After examining the biblical text in detail, as well as additional factors such as the local geography in Mesopotamia, Speiser states that "the biblical text, the traditions of ancient Mesopotamia, the geographic history of the land at the head of the Persian Gulf, and the surviving building practices in that marshy country point jointly to an older garden land, richly watered, and favored by religion and literature alike—the kind of Paradise, in short, that local tradition still locates at the confluence of the Euphrates and the Tigris."

Arabian Peninsula—A second possibility for the location of the Garden of Eden, which has been suggested on the basis of scientific data, is the nearby Arabian Peninsula. The late James Sauer, a professor at the University of Pennsylvania and Harvard University, wrote, "With the use of remote sensing technology, Boston University geologist Farouk El-Baz has traced a major, partially underground, sand river channel from the mountains of Hijaz to Kuwait, which he has named the Kuwait River." Sauer cautiously suggests that this river, which dried up sometime between 3500 and 2000 B.C., might be linked with the biblical Pishon River, since the account also mentions bdellium (an aromatic resin) and onyx (a semiprecious stone), both of which are found in Yemen, on the Arabian Peninsula.

For Sauer, however, the key lies in the biblical phrase "the gold of that land is good," for the only large deposit of gold in the area is found at the site of Mahd edh-Dhahab ("cradle of gold") near the headwaters of this Kuwait river. He concludes, "No other river would seem to fit the Biblical description" and that "the Kuwait river could well be the Pishon of the Bible." We should note, however, that it seems to be this same "fossil river" that Zarins also suggests could be the Pishon River, but he uses it to place the Garden of Eden underwater in the Persian Gulf, rather than on the Arabian Peninsula.

Iran—More recently, British archaeologist David Rohl claims to have located the Garden of Eden in Iran, near the modern city of Tabriz. Rohl has a degree in ancient history and Egyptology from University College London, and believes that scholars have wrongly dated portions of ancient history. Although his earlier work was concerned with the second and first millennia B.C., Rohl has moved backward in time and is now working on material connected with Genesis and the books of the Hebrew Bible.

Utilizing the work done by an earlier scholar named Reginald Walker, Rohl suggests that the biblical Gihon and Pishon Rivers are respectively the Aras (or Araxes) River—which reportedly was previously known as the Gaihun River—and the Uizhun River in Iran. Rohl posits that when these rivers are combined with the Tigris and the Euphrates Rivers, the headwaters for all four rivers are in the approximate region of the Garden of Eden. He also identifies "Noqdi," an area east of his Eden, as the biblical land of Nod, where Cain was exiled after killing his brother, Abel.

Rohl first proposed this hypothesis in his 1998 book, *Legend: The Genesis of Civilisation,* but his suggestions have not caught on with the scholarly establishment. His argument is not helped by the fact that it depends upon speculations regarding the transmission of place-names for both the various rivers and nearby related areas from antiquity to the present. In the end, while Rohl's suggestion is not out of the question, it seems no more probable than any other hypothesis, and less likely than those suggested by Speiser, Zarins, and Sauer.

Egypt—Two years after Rohl's hypothesis was first published, Gary Greenberg, a criminal defense attorney based in New York City, suggested in his book *101 Myths of the Bible* that the Garden of Eden was located in Egypt. At first, this seems to make some sense, since Egypt lies in Africa, and most physical anthropologists and other scientists believe

Was the Garden of Eden located in Egypt, perhaps in or near Heliopolis, pictured above? Such a suggestion has recently been made.

that humans originated in Africa and migrated outward from there, long before the Sumerians—or their legends—ever existed.

Greenberg believes that the Garden of Eden was actually located at Heliopolis, on the banks of the Nile River in Egypt, where Egyptian tradition places the Tree of Life. He hypothesizes that the Garden of Eden story derives from the Egyptian (Heliopolitan) Creation myths. Eden, he says, was originally the "Isle of Flames"—the first land referred to in these Egyptian Creation myths—which was situated at Heliopolis.

However, Greenberg's hypothesis depends in large part upon his argument that the four rivers mentioned in the biblical account were all originally tributaries of the Nile and that only later, when the Judeans were carried off to Babylon in the sixth century B.C., were the names of two of the rivers changed from branches of the Nile to the two Mesopotamian rivers (the Tigris and the Euphrates). Greenberg suggests that whoever changed the names of the rivers was "someone familiar with Babylonian traditions but not knowledgeable about African geography" and that the "flames associated with the original isle were transformed into fiery swords wielded by cherubs."

Like Rohl's hypothesis, Greenberg's suggestion cannot be dismissed outright, but it seems a stretch to postulate that ancient authors or editors changed the names of rivers and tributaries and moved these rivers and other details from Egypt to Mesopotamia. As a result, Greenberg's suggestion has not received wide acceptance from the scholarly establishment. Given the rest of the textual and archaeological evidence, Mesopotamia seems a much more likely location, despite the early origins of humanity in Africa.

Turkey–In 2001, Michael S. Sanders, a self-taught "Biblical Scholar of Archaeology, Egyptology and Assyriology," announced that he had located the Garden of Eden in Turkey. In January 2001, Sanders was quoted in the Canadian *National Post,* the *Chicago Sun-Times,* and the *Daily Mail* as saying his research indicates that all of the earliest Bible stories occurred in what is now Turkey, and not in the Persian Gulf as previously believed. "The Garden of Eden, the Flood, the Tower of Babel, the story of Abraham–all took place in a relatively small area between the Black Sea in the North and the Ararat Range in the East," he stated.

Using photographs taken by NASA satellites, Sanders identified the four rivers of Eden as the Murat River, the Tigris, the Euphrates, and the north fork of the Euphrates. "It is just remarkable that there are actually four rivers in this region in Turkey," he said, adding that this "proves the Bible's description of the Garden of Eden is completely, and literally, accurate." As we shall see in the following chapters, since 1998 Sanders also claims to have pinpointed the location of the Ark of the Covenant, the Ten Commandments, Solomon's Temple, Sodom and Gomorrah, and the Tower of Babel. Such additional claims may or may not affect our appreciation of his assertions regarding the Garden of Eden, as will the observation that Sanders has apparently made his identification based primarily on NASA photographs and an a priori assumption that the Bible is "completely, and literally, accurate." Even if Sanders were correct, we would need more facts on the ground before we could decide whether he has proven his case.

IT IS HARD TO PUT THE Garden of Eden into historical context, for it belongs to the realm of prehistory, if not myth or legend. In fact, much of the material found in the first 11 chapters of Genesis—especially the stories— seem to be more literary than historical. Even biblical scholars refer to Genesis 1-11 as the Primeval History and separate it from chapters 12-50, the Patriarchal Tales. Robert Alter, translator of *The Five Books of Moses*, observes: "The Primeval History, in contrast to what follows in Genesis, cultivates a kind of narrative that is fablelike or legendary, and sometimes residually mythic." We should also note the words of renowned scholar Ephraim Speiser, who wrote in his commentary on Genesis that "it should be borne in mind that the Primeval History is but a general preface to a much larger work, a preface about a remote age which comes to life in Mesopotamia and for which that land alone furnishes the necessary his-torical and cultural records."

It is conceivable, however, that there is a historical kernel of truth at the base of the Garden of Eden story, because, as Speiser notes, "To the writer of the account in Gen. 2:8 . . . the Garden of Eden was obviously a geographic reality." If there is some historical truth to the account, it would seem to be the fact that the region of Mesopotamia was home to the Fertile Crescent, which stretched in an arc from the Persian Gulf to southern Turkey and saw the origins of agriculture and the first domestication of animals from approximately 10,000 B.C. onward. It may well be that both the various Mesopotamian myths and the stories in the Hebrew Bible have their origins in the simple fact that it was this region that first saw the flowering of agriculture, both back during the original neolithic revolution around 10,000 B.C. and then again during the introduction of irrigation during the fourth millennium B.C.

So where is, or was, the Garden of Eden? The available evidence is rather thin, and so this may be the least satisfying of our quests. However, there is—or at least there was before the beginning of the second Gulf War in 2003—a battered sign standing at the site of Querna in Iraq, where the Tigris and the Euphrates join near the modern (and ancient) cities of Basra and Ur, welcoming travelers to the "Original Garden of Eden." Is this merely wishful thinking? Is it merely coincidence that this is the same general region where Speiser suggested that the Garden of Eden would have been?

Bearing in mind that every suggestion that has been made to date is merely a hypothesis, I think that those suggestions that take into account both the textual evidence of earlier Mesopotamian literature and the archaeological data concerning the origins of agriculture and the domestication of animals in the Fertile Crescent, as well as the introduction of irrigation, are most likely to be on the right track. Thus, I would follow Speiser and suggest that the Garden of Eden, if it existed, is most likely to have been located somewhere in the region of Mesopotamia and the Fertile Crescent, perhaps even near the site of Querna, just as the battered sign says.

However, if Zarins is correct that portions of Mesopotamia were flooded at some point, then his proposal that the Garden of Eden lies in this general region but under the headwaters of the Persian Gulf is reasonably plausible. Sauer's suggestion of the Arabian Peninsula as the location of the Garden of Eden is also conceivable, while Rohl's suggestion of Iran, Sanders's suggestion of Turkey, and Greenberg's suggestion of Egypt follow in descending order of plausibility. Joseph Smith's suggestion of Jackson County, Missouri, lags far behind, but is kept company by numerous other similarly implausible suggestions that we will not discuss here.

In the end, we are left with a final compelling question: How can anyone really hope to find the Garden of Eden, especially given what has been said about the Primeval History within the Book of Genesis? Even if the garden once was a real place, and even if we know the general location for where it might have been, how would we know its physical parameters, since there were no ancient signs or inscriptions at the entrance to the garden (for writing hadn't been invented yet)?

So how will we know if we have really found it? The answer is that we won't. As Victor Hurowitz, professor of Bible and ancient Near Eastern studies at Ben-Gurion University, once said: "I doubt we'll ever find Eden outside the pages of the Bible."

NOAH'S ARK

Did the Great Flood take place as depicted in the Bible?
Can Noah's ark be found?

The tale of the biblical Flood and of Noah's ark is familiar to most readers in the Western world and to many others as well. As the story in the Hebrew Bible goes, God instructed Noah to build an ark, since the world was about to be flooded as punishment for the sins and evil of humankind. We read as follows:

> Now the earth was corrupt in God's sight, and the earth was filled with violence. And God saw that the earth was corrupt; for all flesh had corrupted its ways upon the earth. And God said to Noah: "I have determined to make an end of all flesh, for the earth is filled with violence because of them; now I am going to destroy them along with the earth." (Genesis 6:11-13)

Noah was a righteous man, however, so God decided to save him and his family, along with two of every kind of living creature. Therefore, God commanded Noah to build the ark, and instructed him on its dimensions and the number of floors there should be, and who could come on board:

> Make yourself an ark of cypress wood; make rooms in the ark, and cover it inside and out with pitch. This is how you are to make it: the length of the ark

three hundred cubits, its width fifty cubits, and its height thirty cubits. Make a roof for the ark, and finish it to a cubit above; and put the door of the ark in its side; make it with lower, second, and third decks. For my part, I am going to bring a flood of waters on the earth, to destroy from under heaven all flesh in which is the breath of life; everything that is on the earth shall die. But I will establish my covenant with you; and you shall come into the ark, you, your sons, your wife, and your sons' wives with you. And of every living thing, of all flesh, you shall bring two of every kind into the ark, to keep them alive with you; they shall be male and female. (Genesis 6:14-19)

We are told that the Flood lasted for 40 days and 40 nights (6:17), and that floodwaters covered the earth for 150 days. All living things drowned, with the exception of Noah and the people and animals that were with him in the ark (Genesis 7:11-24).

The biblical story next tells us that Noah's ark "came to rest on the mountains of Ararat" (Genesis 8:4). We must note that the Bible does not say the ark came to rest specifically on top of Mount Ararat, as many people assume, but rather on the "mountains of Ararat." These mountains are most likely in the region of ancient Urartu, near modern-day Armenia. Mount Ararat in Turkey—where people have been searching for Noah's ark on and off for the past century—was apparently given that name only within the past few centuries at most, according to scholars. Because of this, some enthusiasts and explorers have suggested and investigated other possible locations for the ark, including Iran, as we will see.

The biblical account continues on, explaining that once the ark rested on the mountaintop, Noah released various birds in an effort to determine if the Flood waters had receded and if dry land had appeared. And so we are told that Noah sent out a raven, which flew around until the waters dried up, and that he also sent forth a dove three times, waiting one week in between each try. The third time the dove did not come back, which Noah interpreted to mean that dry land had begun to appear. So he opened up the ark and he, his family, and all of the animals disembarked (Genesis 8:1-20).

The animals go two by two into Noah's ark in this 13th-century depiction.
But was there one pair or seven pairs of each animal?

Then he offered up a sacrifice of thanksgiving for being saved, and the story ends on a happy note, at least for Noah and his family:

> Then Noah built an altar to the Lord, and took of every clean animal and of every clean bird, and offered burnt offerings on the altar. . . . God blessed Noah and his sons, and said to them, "Be fruitful and multiply, and fill the earth." (Genesis 8:20–9:1)

LONG AGO, BIBLICAL SCHOLARS demonstrated that there are at least two versions of the creation story within the Book of Genesis. Similarly, scholars have long noted that the biblical account of Noah and his ark actually consists of two different stories that have been woven together. As a result, details within the Bible's account contradict themselves, as many scholars have pointed out, including Richard Elliott Friedman, professor of Hebrew and comparative literature at the University of California at San Diego and author of *Who Wrote the Bible?*

For instance, we are told that the Flood lasted for 40 days (Genesis 7:17) but also that the floodwaters covered the earth for 150 days (7:24). Which was it—40 or 150 days? Or did it rain for 40 days but then take an additional 110 days for dry land to appear? And how many animals was Noah told to take into the ark? One pair of each kind of animal (6:19)? Or seven pairs of each kind of clean animal and one pair of each kind of unclean animal (7:2)? And did he release a raven which "went to and fro until the waters were dried up from the earth" (8:7), or did he release a dove three different times before "it did not return to him ever again" (8:8-12)? Or was it both?

There are additional examples as well, as other scholars have demonstrated in great detail, which show that whoever put the Hebrew Bible together in the form we know it today was using at least two versions of the Flood story. However, we are left with numerous questions. When was each of these versions originally created? And by whom? These are difficult questions to answer, but we already possess some of the data that will eventually allow us to answer them.

In 1872, George Smith was working in the basement of the British Museum. By day he was a bank official; by night he was an assistant in the Assyriology section of the museum, sorting and translating clay tablets excavated from the ancient site of Nineveh. One evening he began translating the contents of a tablet and found, much to his astonishment, that it told the story of a great Flood and a man who had survived it by building a boat and bringing his family and assorted animals on board. Rather than landing on Mount Ararat, however, this man's boat came to rest on a mountain called Nisir.

Quickly sorting through the rest of the tablet fragments in the basement, Smith found more pieces and was able to determine that it was, indeed, a story about the Flood, but that it didn't feature a man named Noah. Moreover, he was missing a big piece of the original tablet, right in the middle of the story. When he announced his discovery, the British media went wild, and the London *Daily Telegraph* offered him a thousand British pounds (a large sum in those days) if he would go to Iraq in search of the missing fragment. This appeared to be a nearly impossible challenge, but Smith accepted.

He proceeded to Nineveh, finally arriving after an arduous and dangerous journey. Rather than beginning fresh excavations of this ancient site, he began digging instead through the "back dirt" piles left by the previous British excavators. These piles of earth accumulate during every excavation, because the dirt that the archaeologists dig through and remove must be put somewhere (in fact, enormous back dirt piles can be seen today at the site of Troy in Turkey and at the site of Megiddo in Israel, to mention two famous instances). Frequently, these back dirt piles, especially those from earlier excavations, contain hundreds of objects that have been missed by the early archaeologists and their huge teams of local workers.

Sure enough, within just a few days of beginning his search at Nineveh, George Smith found more than 300 fragments of clay tablets on the excavation's back dirt pile, including the missing piece of the story. He was able to read the entire account now, confirming his earlier announcement that this Mesopotamian story of the Flood was amazingly similar to the story told in the Bible. And yet there were a number of differences, which left Smith and his fellow scholars with the task of explaining the relationship between these two stories. One possibility, embraced by many people, was that this Mesopotamian tablet confirmed the biblical account and was proof that the great Flood had actually taken place.

What many of these people did not realize (and many still do not) is that there are several even earlier versions of the same story, all from ancient Mesopotamia. The oldest known version of the Flood account comes from the Sumerians, a civilization that flourished in what is now modern Iraq during the late fourth and third millennia B.C. In that story,

*Clay tablets from ancient Mesopotamia describe a great flood,
but do not mention anyone named Noah.*

which dates to some time during the third millennium B.C., the hero is
named Ziusudra. A later copy of this original Sumerian Flood story was
found on a clay tablet in the city of Nippur in Mesopotamia (modern Iraq)
and dates to about 1740 B.C. It includes the following lines:

All the destructive winds (and) gales were present,
The storm swept over the capitals.
After the storm had swept the country for seven days and seven nights . . .
And the destructive wind had rocked the huge boat in the high water,

The Sun came out, illuminating the earth and the sky.

Ziusudra made an opening in the huge boat,

And the Sun with its rays entered the huge boat.

The king Ziusudra

Prostrated himself before the sun god;

The king slaughtered a large number of bulls and sheep.

Around the beginning of the second millennium B.C., a new version of the story emerged, with the name of the hero changed to Atrahasis. Then around 1800 B.C. or maybe a bit later, someone took a group of separate, earlier stories and wove them together to form one great work, the *Epic of Gilgamesh*. Gilgamesh was a king who ruled in the Sumerian city of Uruk sometime during the years 2700 and 2500 B.C., but he was not present in the original versions—including the original Sumerian tale—of the Flood. Thus, the earlier stories were rewritten where necessary in order to introduce Gilgamesh into the epic narrative. For example, the epic inserts Gilgamesh into the Flood account by having the survivor of the Flood tell him the story. This time, however, the hero is not Ziusudra or Atrahasis but a man named Utnapishtim, who says to Gilgamesh: "I will reveal to you a mystery, I will tell you a secret of the gods."

The *Epic of Gilgamesh* became a favorite tale, and was told and retold, copied and recopied over the centuries. A fragment of the epic was even found at Megiddo in Israel, probably dating from the late second millennium B.C. A copy was also found at Nineveh in the library of the Neo-Assyrian king Ashurbanipal, who ruled in the seventh century B.C.—and that was the tablet George Smith read in the basement of the British Museum on that fateful day in 1872.

Each of these Flood stories, whether from the Sumerians, Akkadians, or Babylonians, is extremely similar to the one told in the Hebrew Bible about Noah and his ark. They all explain that God (or the gods) decided to flood the world and drown its inhabitants. However, one man was saved, along with his family and whatever animals he was able to take with him on board. He—whether named Ziusudra, Atrahasis, Utnapishtim, or

Noah—sailed for a period of time until the ark eventually came to rest on top of a mountain. The hero then sent out several birds, which came back one after the other, until the waters receded and the bird in question did not return. The humans disembarked, released the animals, made sacrifices in gratitude, and then went forth and multiplied.

For example, in the *Epic of Gilgamesh*, Utnapishtim tells Gilgamesh that the god Ea instructed him to build a ship and outfit it as follows:

> These are the measurements of the barque as you shall build her: let her beam equal her length. Let her deck be roofed like the vault that covers the abyss; then take up into the boat the seed of all living creatures. . . . On the fifth day I laid the keel and the ribs, then I made fast the planking. The ground-space was one acre, each side of the deck measured one hundred and twenty cubits, making a square. I built six decks below, seven in all, I divided them into nine sections with bulkheads between. . . . I loaded into her all that I had of gold and of living things, my family, my kin, the beast of the field both wild and tame, and all the craftsmen.

As we can see, this is much like the story of Noah and the ark. The length of time the Flood lasted and what happened after it ended are also very similar to the biblical account; although we are told in these earlier Mesopotamian stories that the rain lasted for only six days and six nights, even in that short span of time "all mankind had returned to clay." What is perhaps even more interesting is that the *Epic of Gilgamesh* tells us that the gods themselves were frightened by the Flood: "The gods are terrified by the deluge, they flee and mount to the heaven of Anu; the gods cowered like dogs in an enclosure." This is certainly an unusual way to describe one's gods, but it is consistent with the Mesopotamian worldview in which the gods and their society were viewed as similar to humans (including a fear of thunder and lightning, in this case), except that they were endowed with eternal life.

Yet even if the similarities between the various stories are quite unmistakable, it is sometimes the differences that are the most interesting, particularly when the biblical version has had a new moral or ethical twist added to it. For example, the reason God sent the great Flood in the Hebrew Bible is well known: It was because humankind was corrupt and violent and needed to be punished. However, the Old Babylonian version, dating to the early second millennium B.C., gives a very different reason for the sending of the Flood:

> You know the city Shurrupak, it stands on the banks of the Euphrates? That city grew old and the gods that were in it were old. There was Anu, lord of the firmament, their father, and warrior Enlil their counselor, Ninurta the helper, and Ennugi watcher over canals; and with them also was Ea. In those days the world teemed, the people multiplied, the world bellowed like a wild bull, and the great god was aroused by the clamor. Enlil heard the clamor and he said to the gods in council, "The uproar of mankind is intolerable and sleep is no longer possible by reason of the babble." So the gods agreed to exterminate mankind.

This account is not unique; in all the various versions of the Flood story that were floating around Mesopotamia a good 900 years before the Hebrew Bible was written, including the *Epic of Gilgamesh,* the gods agreed to exterminate the human race not because mankind was corrupt and evil but because there were too many people, they were being too noisy, and the gods could not get to sleep. In the Bible the Flood is sent for a moral reason, but in the original Mesopotamian versions, morals and spiritual concerns are nowhere to be found and the reasons the Flood is sent are comparatively mundane.

This is an interesting twist that we find over and over again when comparing a biblical story to the versions that were circulating in the ancient Near East hundreds of years earlier: Although there are obvious similarities, the most significant changes are the moralistic or ethical endings or twists that were added to the original story to illustrate a point the biblical writers wanted to make. Thus, according to the biblical account, Noah was saved because he was a righteous man. But no particular reason is given in the earlier Mesopotamian versions for why Ziusudra, Atrahasis, or Utnapishtim were spared:

> Ea . . . warned me in a dream. He whispered their words to my house of reeds, "Reed-house, reed-house! Wall, O wall, hearken reed-house, wall reflect; O man of Shurrupak, son of Ubara-Tutu; tear down your house and build a boat, abandon possessions and look for life, despise worldly goods and save your soul alive. Tear down your house, I say, and build a boat."

The similarities continue when the ark finally comes to rest on a mountaintop. Just as Noah eventually landed on the mountains of Ararat and disembarked with all of his family and animals, so Utnapishtim landed on Mount Nisir and similarly disembarked. The biblical story tells us that Noah released a raven and then a dove three times to determine if the waters had receded and if dry land had begun to appear. In the earlier Babylonian and Sumerian stories, the survivor of the Flood also released birds, but in these versions, it was a dove, followed by a swallow, and then a raven—and it was the raven that did not come back and presumably found dry land.

The Hebrew Bible then says, "Noah built an altar to the Lord, and took of every clean animal and of every clean bird, and offered burnt offerings on the altar" (Genesis 8:20). The *Epic of Gilgamesh* describes a similar scene, but in a way that no modern society would ever consider doing. "I brought a sacrifice on the mountain top," says Utnapishtim. "Seven and seven cult jars I arranged. Beneath them I strewed reeds, cedarwood and myrtle. The gods smelled the odor, the gods smelled the sweet odor. The gods like flies gathered around the sacrifices."

What do we make of all this? If each of these stories simply stated that a Flood took place and one man and his family survived, we might conclude that a worldwide Flood really did occur and that the biblical account can be confirmed by these earlier Mesopotamian stories. And, indeed, many people today do take these stories at face value and reach exactly that conclusion—in part because almost all civilizations, from the Greeks to Native Americans, have some sort of Flood legend.

What makes these stories much more than a simple confirmation of the biblical account, however, is that not only is the plot essentially the same, but many of the minute details are similar as well, and yet centuries—and sometimes millennia—separate one version from another. Thus, scholars tend to favor the suggestion that these stories are an example of a transmitted narrative. In fact, most scholars today think the story of Noah's ark is one of the best examples of such a narrative. Originating in ancient Mesopotamia and making its way from the Sumerians to the Babylonians and then to the Canaanites and the Israelites, the tale of Noah and his ark has not only spanned generations, it has also spanned civilizations, with only a few details changed before finally ending up in the Hebrew Bible.

———

In 1929, Sir Leonard Woolley, a British archaeologist, was excavating at the site of Tell el Muqayyar, in what is now modern Iraq. His workmen had dug through a level of river silt between eight and twelve feet thick that had been laid down by a flood that occurred in antiquity. The levels immediately above and below the river silt contained pottery, indicating that people had been living at the site—which Woolley identified as ancient Ur—both before and after the flood hit. As the story goes, upon viewing this deposit, Woolley's wife casually remarked, "Well, of course, it's the Flood." Woolley's subsequent announcement that he had found evidence for the biblical Flood made the front page of newspapers around the world that year.

Later, Woolley retracted his statement, having concluded that, while what he had found was indeed the remains of a flood, it was only a local flood and not one of biblical proportions. Since Woolley's discovery, evidence for other floods has been uncovered at a number of additional sites in Mesopotamia, including Nineveh and Kish, but none of them seem to indicate that the flood was anything more than a local catastrophe, with each occurring at a different time than the others.

In 1998, a much more relevant discovery was announced by William Ryan and Walter Pitman, two geologists at Columbia University, who published evidence for a great flood emanating from the Black Sea, located north of Turkey. They presented data that indicated the sea had broken through its barriers and flooded a large area in Turkey (and perhaps even farther south) around 7,500 years ago, in approximately 5500 B.C.

Whether Ryan and Pitman are correct in their interpretation of this data has been hotly debated in the years since their book appeared. In 1999, Bob Ballard, the discoverer of the *Titanic,* turned up evidence of an ancient shoreline deep below the surface of the Black Sea—one complete with shells from freshwater and saltwater mollusk species whose radiocarbon dates support Ryan and Pitman's theory that a freshwater lake was inundated by the Black Sea some 7,500 years ago. Whether this flood would have been large enough to come to the attention of the Sumerians and other ancient peoples remains a matter of debate. But, at the moment, the evidence seems fairly convincing that, at the very least, a large area around the Black Sea would have been affected by the sudden rise in water.

Unfortunately, beyond these two instances, there is no other good archaeological or geological evidence for the existence of the biblical Flood or for Noah and his ark, despite numerous claims to the contrary by amateur sleuths and scholars each year. These claims run the gamut from theories involving meteors from outer space to the simultaneous eruption of geysers across the world to the sudden collapse of a heavy cloud cover. None has been accepted by the scientific community as an adequate explanation.

The closest we might come to some sort of additional archaeological or geological evidence for a biblical Flood is to suggest that all the Flood stories found around the world are essentially a folk memory of the end of the Ice Age, when much of the ice covering various parts of the continents melted and water levels around the world rose. But even this is sheer speculation, because it is by no means clear that this occurrence would have given rise to

Sir Leonard Woolley excavated the site of Tell el Muqayyar in Iraq,
which he identified as Ur of the Chaldees.

worldwide stories of such a Flood. Similarly, the Flandrian Transgression, which caused a sudden rise in sea level sometime between 5000 and 4000 B.C. and flooded the southernmost portions of Mesopotamia, probably occurred too slowly to be remembered as the Flood.

MOST EXPEDITIONS GOING in search of Noah's ark focus primarily on the area of Mount Ararat (Agri Dagi) in northeastern Turkey, even though it is not at all certain that this location is where they should be looking. Ancient writers such as Josephus, the Jewish general turned Roman historian, were also unclear as to where to search and variously suggested that the ark came to rest in what is now southern Armenia, Iraq, central Asia Minor, and even Saudi Arabia. Although many of the modern expeditions have claimed success, none has succeeded in producing tangible evidence or even reasonable hypotheses sufficient to persuade the scholarly and scientific establishments.

Early Expeditions—William Stiebing, emeritus professor of history at the University of New Orleans, has been keeping track of the numerous expeditions that have gone in search of Noah's ark. Stiebing has published a list of these expeditions, which he has updated in various publications over the past 20 years. Stiebing's list includes perhaps the earliest official expedition, led by the British explorer Sir James Bryce in 1876. According to Stiebing, Bryce claimed to have found "a large piece of hand-tooled wood at the 13,000-foot level of Mt. Ararat."

One interesting expedition concerned a group of Russian soldiers who supposedly found the ark after it was spotted from the air in 1915, but claimed the Russian Revolution of 1917 occurred before they could return home and report their findings. Another infamous set of claims came from Fernand Navarra, who in 1955 said that he had found a five-foot-long piece of wood in a crevasse on Mount Ararat. The wood was initially dated to 3000 B.C. by a Spanish laboratory, but was subsequently redated to between A.D. 260 and A.D. 790, plus or minus 90 years, via carbon-14 dating methods. Thus, the wood—and other pieces found in the same location on Mount Ararat in 1969—was deemed much too recent to be from Noah's ark. Stiebing suggests that Navarra's findings may be from "the remains of some wooden structure (perhaps a chapel, a replica of the Ark, or a hut for climbers) built near the snow line . . . during the Middle Ages."

Since then, various expeditions and claims have been made every couple of years—including two led by ex-astronaut James Irwin (of Apollo 15) in the 1980s—but none of the claims have been verified and none of the expeditions have panned out.

Wyatt's Ark—Perhaps the most infamous set of claims and series of expeditions were those made by Ron Wyatt, a nurse anesthetist from Nashville with an interest in archaeology, who first traveled to Turkey in 1977 to examine a "boat shaped object" that had been reported on in *Life* magazine. By 1979, Wyatt claimed that he could see evenly spaced indentations all the way around the object, which "looked like decaying rib timbers," as well as "horizontal deck support timbers" also present at consistent intervals. Eventually, by June 1991, Wyatt claimed that he could see "an object that when observed . . . bore the shape of a very large 'rivet' head, with a washer around it."

Two months later, in August 1991, Wyatt and three of his ark-seeking companions were taken hostage by Kurdish separatist rebels and held for three weeks before being released. This put a stop to their expeditions. To this day, Wyatt's claims are embraced by enthusiastic admirers but few, if any, scholars.

Cornuke's Ark—In July 2006, Bob Cornuke, a former police investigator and SWAT team member turned "biblical investigator, international explorer, and best-selling author," led the most recent expedition in search of Noah's ark. Cornuke originally served as a security advisor and provided protection for ex-astronaut James Irwin and his team as they searched for the remains of Noah's ark in Eastern Turkey during the 1980s—in the same region where Ron Wyatt and his colleagues were later kidnapped and terrorized by Kurdish separatist rebels. After Irwin's death, Cornuke founded the BASE (Bible Archaeology Search and Exploration) Institute and began his own series of explorations.

Media reports announced that Cornuke's 2006 expedition team had discovered boat-shaped rocks at an altitude of 13,000 feet (4,000 meters) on Mount Suleiman in Iran's Elburz Mountains. The same media reports also stated that photographs taken by expedition members showed a rock outcrop shaped like the prow of a boat emerging from a ridge. Cornuke stated that the rocks looked "uncannily like wood. . . . We have had [cut] thin sections of the rock made, and we can see [wood] cell structures."

Cornuke's claims failed to convince most experts, though. Kevin Pickering, a geologist at University College London who specializes in sedimentary rocks, said, "The photos appear to show iron-stained sedimentary rocks, probably thin beds of silicified sandstones and shales, which were most likely laid down in a marine environment a long time ago." Moreover, Robert Spicer, a geologist at England's Open University who specializes in the study of petrification, said: "What needs to be

Mesopotamian ziggurats, such as this 4,000-year-old one at Ur, were religious structures that may have given rise to the story of the Tower of Babel.

documented in this case are preserved, human-made joints, such as . . . mortice and tenon, or even just pegged boards. I see none of this in the pictures. It's all very unconvincing."

IT IS DIFFICULT, if not impossible, to put the biblical story of the Flood and Noah's ark into historical context, since these events took place well before the beginning of recorded history, which is considered to be circa 3000 B.C., when writing was invented in both Mesopotamia and Egypt.

We should take this opportunity to mention the story of the Tower of Babel here, even if it seems to be a bit of a tangent, because it appears immediately after the story of Noah's ark in the Book of Genesis (11:1-9). More important, the tower's description fits the archaeological remains of the second millennium B.C. religious structures that we call ziggurats, which were built in Babylon, Uruk, Ur, and elsewhere in Mesopotamia.

Thus, the Babel tale may serve as one point where a portion of Genesis could be reflected in the actual archaeological record.

The original story of the Tower of Babel may well have been invented in order to explain why there were so many different languages in the world as well as to highlight the importance of Babylon. In the biblical version, the tale has been tweaked and is generally considered by scholars to be a judgment against humankind because of its hubris and sin. The biblical account says:

> Now the whole earth had one language and the same words. And as they migrated from the east, they came upon a plain in the land of Shinar and settled there. And they said to one another, "Come, let us make bricks, and burn them thoroughly." And they had brick for stone, and bitumen for mortar. Then they said, "Come, let us build ourselves a city, and a tower with its top in the heavens, and let us make a name for ourselves; otherwise we shall be scattered abroad upon the face of the whole earth." The Lord came down to see the city and the tower, which mortals had built. And the Lord said, "Look, they are one people, and they have all one language; and this is only the beginning of what they will do; nothing that they propose to do will now be impossible for them. Come, let us go down, and confuse their language there, so that they will not understand one another's speech." So the Lord scattered them abroad from there over the face of all the earth, and they left off building the city. Therefore it was called Babel, because there the Lord confused the language of all the earth; and from there the Lord scattered them abroad over the face of all the earth. (Genesis 11:1-9)

Archaeologists and ancient historians generally place the "plain in the land of Shinar" in the region of the Tigris and Euphrates Rivers, in Mesopotamia. There, the city of Babylon rose, made famous especially by Hammurabi (circa 1792–1750 B.C.), who issued his famous Law Code (which we shall discuss in chapter 4). The city lasted for more than a thousand years, rising and falling in prominence; it is in this city that Alexander the Great died in 323 B.C.

One of the most visible structures, and enduring monuments, in the city of Babylon was the pyramid-shaped ziggurat. The ziggurat was built in several stages with increasingly smaller sections placed one on top of the other, reaching so high that it appeared to have "its top in the heavens," just as the Bible describes. Such ziggurats, which were built in many major Mesopotamian cities during the second millennium B.C., served a religious function. (As an aside, it has been suggested that the ziggurat at Babylon was also the real location for the Hanging Gardens of Babylon—one of the Seven Wonders of the Ancient World—since draping plants and other vegetation off each of the stages of the ziggurat would have resulted in a veritable hanging garden.)

Linking the Tower of Babel to the ziggurat that stood in Babylon during the second millennium B.C. may seem to be a stretch in trying to place the biblical story of the Flood and of Noah's ark into historical context—and indeed it is. However, the point is simply that it is possible to explain some mysteries that appear in the biblical account, insofar as they may be historical memories of things Babylonian or Sumerian that filtered down through the centuries to the Israelites and eventually made it into the Bible.

IT IS CLEAR FROM the textual evidence that there are a number of major similarities and minor differences between the Flood story in the Hebrew Bible and those found in the earlier civilizations of Mesopotamia, which all predate the writing of the Bible by at least eight or nine centuries. So where does that leave us?

The vast majority of scholars agree that the Flood tales told by the earlier Sumerian and Babylonian civilizations—especially the version found in the *Epic of Gilgamesh*—probably represent the historical kernel at the base of the biblical story of the Flood and Noah's ark. The question then becomes whether there is any truth to the stories of Ziusudra, Atrahasis, and Utnapishtim—the survivors of the earlier floods. Unfortunately, it is impossible to answer this question.

The story of the Tower of Babel, depicted here in Pieter Bruegel's famous 1563 painting, may have been written to explain why there are so many languages in the world.

Of course, there are many, many Flood stories found in other civilizations across the world, from Alaska to Australia, but they are all from much later periods. Even the earlier stories from other civilizations, such as the Greek myth of Deucalian and the Flood, are most likely also borrowed from the Near East during periods of cultural contact that took place long after the initial stories were written, such as the Orientalizing period in Greece during the early first millennium B.C. Around that time several stories, including the Mesopotamian *Epic of Gilgamesh* and the Hittite *Myth of Kumarbi,* made their way West, eventually influencing Homer's *Iliad* and *Odyssey* and Hesiod's *Theogony.*

In terms of archaeological evidence, Noah's ark has not yet been found, despite recent claims to the contrary. There are indications, however, that a number of floods varying in size and intensity occurred in

Mesopotamia and elsewhere in the ancient world, including in the Black Sea region.

What, then, does all of this say about the existence of Noah and his ark? Did they ever exist? Can we ever find their remains? I can only answer the last of these questions. I would argue that whether or not a great Flood took place, it is unlikely we will ever find the remains of Noah's ark . . . and if we do, it will be by accident, when we are looking for something else. Such a discovery will only happen if the ark has been fortuitously petrified or otherwise accidentally preserved—and the odds are stacked against such a chance circumstance having occurred.

The truth of the matter is that any such searches for Noah's ark are unlikely ever to be successful. Even if the ark did exist, it would be tremendously old by now and its wooden parts would have been long ago reduced to dust, leaving few traces behind. The most we could hope for would be discovering something like the Sutton Hoo ship in England from the seventh century A.D.; the disintegrated wood and corroded nails from this vessel left a perfect imprint on the damp soil. Only if the ark had come to rest in the sands of Egypt, which contain perfectly preserved pharaonic boats by the Pyramids, or at the bottom of an ocean or a sea where there is little oxygen and organic material is perfectly preserved—such as in the Black Sea, where Bob Ballard's expeditions have found ships sunk up to their gunwales and perfectly preserved in anoxygenic mud—would we even be able to hope that Noah's ark, or portions of it, have been preserved.

The most unlikely place to find Noah's ark is probably on top of a mountain, such as Mount Ararat in Turkey, where most expeditions go looking for it, or even on the mountains of Ararat, where the Bible says the ark landed. It is a very long shot to hope that the ark has been preserved in glacier ice like the woolly mammoths in Siberia or like "Ötzi the Iceman," the 5,000-year-old man (dating to 3200 B.C.) found frozen, reasonably intact, and quite well preserved on the Italian-Austrian border in the Alps during the mid 1990s.

In the end, we are still left with a series of major questions: Why are so many people looking for Noah's ark, while not a single person is looking for Utnapishtim's ark or Ziusudra's ark or Atrahasis's ark? Why are we so interested in the biblical story and yet almost nobody has heard of the earlier Babylonian and Sumerian versions, which are almost identical? Why is no one searching for Mount Nisir, but numerous expeditions search on Mount Ararat, or the mountains of Ararat, looking for Noah's ark nearly every year? Are these mountains in fact one and the same or are they different? If we find one, are we likely to find the other? Or are we doomed to watch one optimistic expedition after another fail? These are questions for which I, and everyone else for that matter, have yet to find answers.

SODOM AND GOMORRAH

Did Sodom and Gomorrah exist?
If so, where were they?

The destruction of the cities of Sodom and Gomorrah as told in the Hebrew Bible is sudden, dramatic, and final. In the Book of Genesis we are told:

> Then the Lord rained on Sodom and Gomorrah sulphur and fire from the Lord out of heaven; and he overthrew those cities, and all the Plain, and all the inhabitants of the cities, and what grew on the ground. Abraham . . . looked down towards Sodom and Gomorrah and towards all the land of the Plain, and saw the smoke of the land going up like the smoke of a furnace. (Genesis 19:24-28)

Earlier in Genesis, the biblical writers explain that "the people of Sodom were wicked, great sinners against the Lord" (13:13). A little later we are told: "Then the Lord said, 'How great is the outcry against Sodom and Gomorrah and how very grave their sin! I must go down and see whether they have done altogether according to the outcry that has come to me; and if not, I will know'" (18:20-21). The text then goes on to describe Abraham's negotiations with the Lord regarding how many "good" men it would take to save Sodom (18:22-33). Gomorrah is not mentioned again until the destruction of both cities is presented in Genesis 19.

Even though it is said that these cities were sinful numerous times in both the Hebrew Bible and the New Testament, there are few details in the original story about what specifically went on in Sodom and Gomorrah; exactly how the town's inhabitants gave offense is never described. In Genesis itself, there is only a brief mention of an attempt by some men of Sodom to have sex with three guests—actually angels in disguise—who were visiting Lot (19:1-11). The men's attempt obviously goes against the biblical custom of treating strangers as honored guests, but this is hardly sufficient reason for God to destroy both towns. The closest we get to a full explanation in the Hebrew Bible is a reference later in the Book of Ezekiel, which says: "Behold, this was the iniquity of thy sister Sodom, pride, fullness of bread, and abundance of idleness was in her and in her daughters, neither did she strengthen the hand of the poor and needy" (Ezekiel 16:49).

However, the New Testament Book of Jude—written sometime after the period of the Apostles, probably in the first or second century A.D.— says: "Likewise, Sodom and Gomorrah and the surrounding cities . . . indulged in sexual immorality and pursued unnatural lust, [and] serve as an example by undergoing a punishment of eternal fire" (Jude 1:7). It is from this account—as well as from later religious authorities, writers, and artists, continuing right up to the present day—that our mental picture of Sodom and Gomorrah has been derived, perpetuating the common perception today that the inhabitants' sins included homosexuality (sodomy), rape, and other kinds of sexual immorality.

So did Sodom and Gomorrah exist? If so, where? Can they be, or have they been, located today? While our questions are simple, our quest for answers may be frustrated by a lack of textual and archaeological data. Before we attempt to answer these questions, though, we should take a quick look at the events immediately preceding the destruction of Sodom and Gomorrah, as told in the Hebrew Bible.

ACCORDING TO THE biblical account, long after Noah had survived the great Flood, his distant descendant Abraham was born and raised in a city known

Typical beehive-shaped homes in the village of Haran, Turkey, probably look much the same today as they did during the time of Abraham.

as Ur of the Chaldees (Genesis 11:26-27). The city was located in the land of Shinar, which is believed to be lower Mesopotamia, or modern Iraq.

We are told that Abraham's father decided to leave Ur of the Chaldees and migrate with his family to the land of Canaan. First, however, he settled in the vicinity of Haran. The biblical account says, "Terah took his son Abram and his grandson Lot, son of Haran, and his daughter-in-law Sarai, his son Abram's wife, and they went out together from Ur of the Chaldeans to go into the land of Canaan; but when they came to Haran, they settled there" (Genesis 11:31). (Note that Abraham and Sarah were still known as Abram and Sarai at that time, because God had not yet changed their names to Abraham and Sarah, an event described in Genesis 17:1-22.)

Haran is generally thought to be located in southeastern Anatolia (modern Turkey). To get there, Abraham's father would have followed the course of the Euphrates River, which was an international trade route at that time. It is certainly possible that he settled in either northern Syria or southern Turkey, since there are villages in the region today that still look much like they did 4,000 years ago.

It was only after his father's death that Abraham migrated from Haran to Canaan. According to the biblical account, he was already 75 years old when he undertook this journey in the company of his wife, Sarah, and his nephew, Lot, as well as their families, flocks, and tents (Genesis 12:4-5). The journey was, however, by no means direct. We are told that Abraham first passed through Canaan, stopping at Shechem and the hill country "with Bethel on the west and Ai on the east" before proceeding to the Negev and then to Egypt. Eventually, he returned to Canaan and the area between Bethel and Ai before finally settling in Hebron (Genesis 12:5-13:18). And it was while Abraham was on these journeys that we are told he and Lot witnessed the destruction of Sodom and Gomorrah.

ABRAHAM'S NEPHEW, Lot, settled with his flocks in the land of Jordan, specifically in Sodom, one of the "Cities of the Plain." Most archaeologists and biblical scholars think that the Cities of the Plain are located in modern-day Jordan, in part because a passage in Genesis reads:

> Then Abram said to Lot, "Let there be no strife between you and me, and between your herders and my herders; for we are kindred. Is not the whole land before you? Separate yourself from me. If you take the left hand, then I will go to the right; or if you take the right hand, then I will go to the left." Lot looked about him, and saw that the plain of the Jordan was well watered everywhere like the garden of the Lord, like the land of

Egypt, in the direction of Zoar; this was before the Lord had destroyed Sodom and Gomorrah. So Lot chose for himself all the plain of the Jordan, and Lot journeyed eastwards; thus they separated from each other. Abram settled in the land of Canaan, while Lot settled among the cities of the Plain and moved his tent as far as Sodom. (Genesis 13:8-12)

The text that follows in the next chapter of Genesis is thought to lend credence to the idea that Sodom and Gomorrah were located on the eastern (the modern Jordanian) side of the Dead Sea. Here, the Bible specifically refers to a battle fought in "the Valley of Siddim—that is, the Salt Sea" (14:3). Most scholars believe the Valley of Siddim was in the region of the Dead Sea, for the Hebrew name for the Dead Sea is actually *Yam Hamelach,* which translates as the "Salt Sea." According to the biblical account, King Bera of Sodom and King Birsha of Gomorrah took part in this battle, along with the kings of three other nearby cities (Admah, Zeboiim, and Bela/Zoar), as part of a rebellion against their overlord, King Chedorlaomer of Elam (14:2-9). We are given no other clues, however, as to the location of the Valley of Siddim, apart from the description that it was "full of bitumen pits" (14:10).

After the battle, the king of Sodom went to meet Abraham at the Valley of Shaveh (14:17), for Abraham had rescued—and perhaps ransomed—the king and all of his people, including Lot, after they had been captured in the war against King Chedorlaomer. Unfortunately, this reference to the Valley of Shaveh does not help us to further locate Sodom itself, because although the Valley of Shaveh is identified as "the King's Valley" and is thought to be near Jerusalem, we are not told how far it was from Sodom or Gomorrah.

The only other tidbit of biblical information that may be of any help in locating Sodom is found in the Book of Ezekiel (16:46), where Sodom is said to lie south of Jerusalem. It is not specified, though, how far to the south, and whether it is directly to the south or to the southeast or southwest.

The other texts we have are probably not useful, since they date to centuries later, during the Hellenistic and Roman periods. These include

The existence of ruins such as at Bab edh-Dhra may have led ancient people to create tales explaining the sites' presence.

the accounts of Diodorus Siculus, the Greek historian who wrote during the first century B.C.; Strabo, the geographer who wrote during the first century B.C. and into the first century A.D.; Philo of Alexandria, who also spanned the end of the first century B.C. and the beginning of the first century A.D.; Flavius Josephus, the Jewish general turned Roman historian who wrote during the first century A.D.; and Tacitus, the Roman historian who wrote during the first and second centuries A.D. Each of these authors—and numerous other ancient writers as well—discuss the geography of the Dead Sea, the cities of Sodom and Gomorrah, and the possible means by which they were destroyed, but all these observations are mere speculation and must be considered with caution, if at all.

IN THE 1970s, a flurry of excitement took place when it was announced that texts found at the site of Ebla in Syria dating to the third millennium B.C. mentioned the five Cities of the Plain, including Sodom and Gomorrah, listed in the same order as in the Hebrew Bible. These readings, however, were soon shown to be faulty. The tablets were written in a previously unknown language, referred to by researchers as Eblaite or Eblaitic, which took some time to properly decipher and translate. In the end, the city that had first been identified as "Gomorrah" (*é-ma-ra*^{KI}) in the Ebla tablets turned out to be a probable reference to ancient Emar, a major town on the Euphrates River. As for the city first identified as "Sodom" (*si-da-mu*^{KI}), its real identity has not been ascertained, but it is thought to be somewhere in northwest Syria—nowhere near the Dead Sea, and completely unrelated to the account found in the Bible. So apart from the biblical text itself, we are left with no contemporary references to Sodom, Gomorrah, or the other Cities of the Plain.

Thus, even after looking carefully through the biblical account, we are still at a loss for clues regarding the location of Sodom and Gomorrah. Although the two cities, or their kings, are mentioned in numerous books of the Bible (including Genesis, Deuteronomy, I and II Kings, Isaiah, Jeremiah, Lamentations, Amos, Matthew, Mark, Luke, Romans, and Revelation), as we have already seen, there are only a few passages that hint at their location. Many of the geographical descriptions that are frequently cited come from much later writers, such as Flavius Josephus and Strabo. Yet this has not deterred modern-day explorers and adventurers from eagerly searching for the ruins of these two cities.

If we are seriously searching for Sodom and Gomorrah, however, we must look primarily at two Early Bronze Age sites that have been presented as most likely to lie at the root of the tale. These are the sites of Bab edh-Dhra and Numeira, dating to the third millennium B.C., and located at the southeastern end of the Dead Sea in modern-day Jordan. The two sites have been excavated by highly respected archaeologists R. Thomas Schaub, a professor at Indiana University of Pennsylvania, and the late Walter E. Rast, who was a professor at Valparaiso University.

As Rast and Schaub have noted, Bab edh-Dhra was first discovered during a survey of the Jordan Valley in 1924. The survey was led by William Foxwell Albright, a famous biblical scholar and archaeologist in

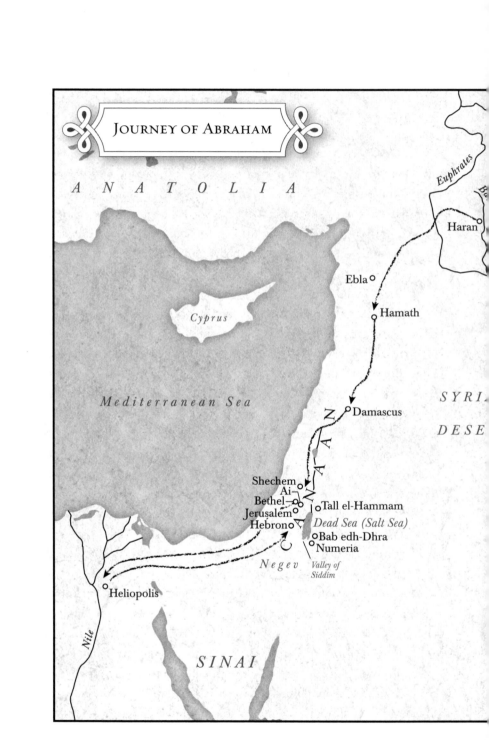

JOURNEY OF ABRAHAM

ANATOLIA

Euphrates

Haran

Ebla

Hamath

Cyprus

Mediterranean Sea

Damascus

SYRIA

DESE

C
A
N
A
A
N

Shechem
Ai
Bethel
Jerusalem
Hebron

Tall el-Hammam

Dead Sea (Salt Sea)

Bab edh-Dhra
Numeria

Negev

Valley of
Siddim

Heliopolis

Nile

SINAI

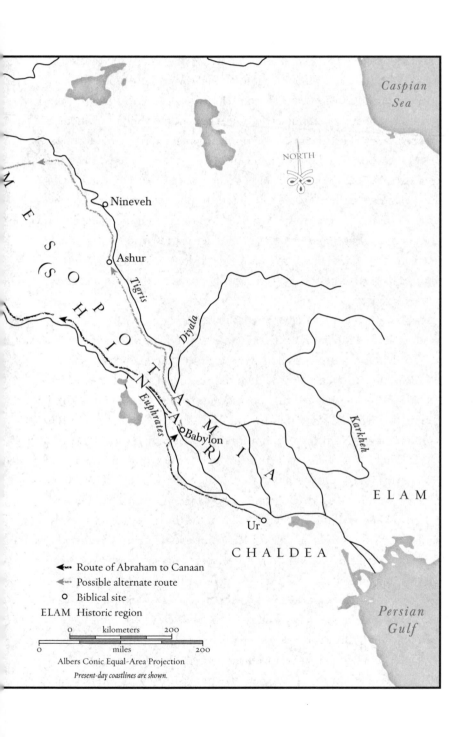

Caspian
Sea

NORTH

M E S O ° Nineveh
(S
O
P

Ashur
O
T
A
M
I
A
R)

Tigris

Diyala

Euphrates
Babylon

Karkheh

E L A M

Ur

C H A L D E A

Persian
Gulf

◄ Route of Abraham to Canaan
◄ Possible alternate route
○ Biblical site
ELAM Historic region

0   kilometers   200
0   miles   200
Albers Conic Equal-Area Projection
Present-day coastlines are shown.

his own right, who spent much of his career teaching at the Johns Hopkins University. Since then, several teams of archaeologists have excavated at the site, with Rast and Schaub beginning their project in 1975.

In all, the excavations at Bab edh-Dhra reveal an Early Bronze Age town established in approximately 3300 B.C. and occupied for about a thousand years. The town was thriving and prosperous, with a fortification wall surrounding it during much of its history, and houses, a temple, and an altar inside the walls. A large cemetery was located nearby. The town apparently suffered some sort of catastrophe about 2300 B.C., at the end of the Early Bronze III period. Archaeologists found evidence that portions of the walls and gate areas were destroyed by fire. Piles of collapsed and fallen mud bricks were uncovered along with large deposits of ash and charcoal. The site itself was totally abandoned within a century and never reoccupied.

Rast and Schaub also conducted archaeological surveys of the surrounding area. They found a second ancient site, Numeira, which they proceeded to excavate, as well as the remains of three additional sites—Safi, Feifa, and Khanazir—which they did not excavate. They reported that Numeira was inhabited for about a century and was then destroyed at approximately the same time as nearby Bab edh-Dhra, around 2300 B.C. Interestingly, Numeira also shows evidence of having been destroyed by fire: There is a thick layer of debris everywhere and the bodies of several men were found, perhaps killed in the collapse of a building. One of the excavators, Michael Coogan, wrote, "The entire area was covered by the ashy debris of the final destruction of the town," which was nearly half a meter deep in places. Walter Rast himself wondered whether the destruction could have been caused by "some sort of disaster—perhaps an earthquake which set off fires in all parts of the town? Whatever the cause, it was certainly a tragedy: The skeletons of two adult males were found embedded in burnt debris next to the tower."

In June 1980, Rast and Schaub tentatively suggested that the five sites they had discovered might be identified with the five Cities of the Plain listed in the Bible. In the *ASOR Newsletter* (published by the professional archaeological association known as the American Schools of Oriental Research), they wrote:

> In addition to the expedition's archaeological goals of giving explanations for the ancient cultures, there is an interesting historical problem in connection with the sites. This concerns the question whether the sites being excavated presently, and several other contemporary sites to the south, may be the remains of the ancient cities of Sodom, Gomorrah, and the related cities of the Bible. This is an interesting problem, given the location of Bab edh-Dhra and Numeira in an area which has much to commend it as the general location for these cities. . . . The result is that we are in the process of proposing that these Early Bronze sites may indeed represent the remains of the ancient cities.

Rast and Schaub reached this conclusion in part because they had also been able to survey the floor of the southern end of the Dead Sea during a drought in 1979, when the waters had receded significantly. They reported that there were no other cities located near the southern end of the Dead Sea after 3000 B.C. In other words, they could not locate any other candidates to be identified as Sodom and Gomorrah. That is not to say that additional ancient remains might not lie in the area, buried under meters of ancient alluvium and invisible today, but even this is unlikely. As Rast pointed out, virtually none of the settlements in this region were located on the flat plain itself but were instead situated on the slightly elevated areas nearby, just like Bab edh-Dhra and Numeira, and these would still be visible—or at least easily excavated—today.

————————

RAST ALSO MENTIONED that another way to investigate the story of Sodom and Gomorrah is to look at the geology of the area around the Dead Sea. Many of the others who have been searching for these lost cities have taken this approach, combing the region for evidence of earthquakes and earthquake activity, for bubbling tar pits and ancient bitumen, and for huge amounts of salt (to explain the story of Lot's wife turning into a pillar of salt when she turned to look at the destruction of Sodom and Gomorrah).

Near Masada—Ron Wyatt, the nurse anesthetist and amateur archaeologist from Nashville whom we met in chapter 2, announced in 1989 and 1990 that he had seen "formations" that "looked to him like city walls and buildings, only whitish in color" and had found "round balls of encapsulated sulfur (brimstone)" near the site of Masada on the western edge of the Dead Sea. These he linked to the story of the destruction of Sodom and Gomorrah. In fact, the Web site run by his organization states: "The account of [the] destruction of Sodom, Gomorrah and '*all the plain*' was not a fairy tale. It was an historical event that occurred exactly as the Biblical account presented it."

Wyatt's declaration has not, however, been taken seriously by scholars, in large part because of his lack of formal training in both archaeology and geology, but also because of his additional claims over the years to have found Noah's ark, the Ark of the Covenant, Mount Sinai, the route of the Exodus, the method by which the Egyptian pyramids were built, and so on. Most important, Wyatt's geological claims have been severely questioned and ultimately dismissed by Dr. Elizabeth H. Gierlowski-Kordesch, associate professor of geology at Ohio University. She concludes that Wyatt's claims are baseless and that he is guilty of practicing "junk science"—a science that, as stated earlier, "advocates a cause, pays little attention to the investigative process, ignores contrary evidence, and advertises a high moral purpose." As for his "cities" and balls of "brimstone," she states:

> The geological formations that Wyatt mistakes for ancient cities are simply lake sediments that accumulated when the Dead Sea was larger and deeper, back in the Late Pleistocene period (an epoch ranging from 700,000 to 10,000 years before the present). . . . The layering visible today is similar to those of sediments and sedimentary rocks found everywhere—no surprise there. . . . Wyatt's main "proof" that these geological

*Looking at the landscape surrounding the Dead Sea, it is easy to envision
the biblical destruction of Sodom and Gomorrah.*

formations are the remains of Sodom and Gomorrah is the presence of
round sulfur balls. . . . These sulfur nodules contain portions of the surrounding sediment (gypsum is hydrated calcium sulfate) and the degraded
organic remains of animals buried in the sediments (sulfur is an important component of living tissue). This type of post-depositional chemical
feature within lake sediments is a common phenomenon in ancient lakes
around the world.

Under the Dead Sea—Similarly, Michael S. Sanders, the self-taught "Biblical
Scholar of Archaeology, Egyptology and Assyriology" already men-
tioned—and who likewise claims to have located the Garden of Eden, the
Ark of the Covenant, the Ten Commandments, Solomon's Temple, and
the Tower of Babel—has also gone searching for the lost cities of Sodom
and Gomorrah. In the November 18, 1998, edition of Britain's *Sunday
Times,* Sanders suggested that "new satellite photographs from NASA, the
American space agency, may show that Sodom and Gomorrah not only

existed, but also that they were probably destroyed in a catastrophe about 5,000 years ago, and that their ruins were engulfed beneath the salty waters of the Dead Sea."

Sanders's evidence includes "sulphur balls" like those Ron Wyatt claims to have found, and NASA satellite photographs showing "anomalies" on the seafloor. He stated that there are "three clear and startling anomalies, which could be architectural ruins, deep beneath the surface of the northern end of the Dead Sea." Sanders's expedition was subsequently featured in a prime-time special on NBC in the United States and Channel 4 in England, in which he and his team used a two-man Delta mini-submarine to explore the depths of the Dead Sea to examine these "anomalies" and search for other evidence of the lost cities.

The expedition was questioned even before it began by respected Israeli geologist David Neev, in part because the team was searching at the northern end of the Dead Sea, while, as Neev noted, the biblical account clearly states that the cities were located at the southern end. Although Sanders and his team located a series of salt-encrusted mounds on the floor of the Dead Sea, which he claimed to be man-made remains, his findings have been ignored by both archaeologists and geologists for the same reasons that Wyatt's claims have been disregarded.

Ancient Earthquakes—There are many other people with more serious credentials who have gone in search of these two cities. For instance, as early as 1936, a geologist named Frederick Clapp published a theory in the *American Journal of Archaeology* (as well as in the *Bulletin of the American Association of Petroleum Geologists*), stating that an ancient earthquake may have created pressure underground, which in turn forced bitumen to explode out through cracks in the earth—much like an initial strike on an oil deposit sends a geyser of oil into the sky. Clapp theorized that a stray spark or even a kitchen hearth in Sodom or Gomorrah could have ignited the red-hot bitumen, turning the two cities into raging infernos. His theory received a lukewarm reaction from archaeologists and biblical scholars, although it was received more favorably by the general public.

More recently, in 1995 David Neev of the Israel Geological Survey—who would criticize Michael Sanders's Dead Sea expedition a few years later—and Kenneth (K. O.) Emery of the Woods Hole Oceanographic Institute published a book in which they also suggest that the destruction of Sodom and Gomorrah was caused by an earthquake as well as by climatic problems. Their hypothesis was quickly attacked by biblical scholars and geophysicists alike, but their suggestion cannot be dismissed out of hand. That same year, Graham Harris and Anthony Beardow published an article in the *Quarterly Journal of Engineering Geology* entitled "The Destruction of Sodom and Gomorrah: A Geotechnical Perspective." As they and others have pointed out, the Dead Sea is known to be a seismically active region. Numerous earthquakes have been reported there, especially since the advent of modern technology and recording equipment.

In the article, Harris and Beardow also suggested (apparently independently of Neev and Emery) that Sodom and Gomorrah were destroyed by an earthquake, specifically linking the destruction of the cities to "a liquefaction failure of alluvial fan and flood-plain deposits." When such a failure takes place, the soil acts like a liquid rather than like solid ground and can sink or even pull apart. This means that the cities could have been literally swallowed up by the earth, and Harris and Beardow surmise that they were. However, they identify Bab edh-Dhra not with Sodom, but with the smaller town of Zoar—where, according to the biblical account, Lot fled—because it is in an area "underlain by a fan of Nubian sandstone" and was thus immune to the process of liquefaction.

Most recently, in 2001, the BBC ran the breathless headline, "Scientists Uncover Sodom's Fiery End," citing a retired British geologist named Graham Harris—the same scientist who had previously teamed with Anthony Beardow. In this case, the BBC reported the hypothesis that "flammable methane pockets lie under the Dead Sea shores; the earthquake would have ignited them, the ground would have turned to quicksand, and a massive landslide would have swept the cities into the water." The network even stated, "Experiments carried out at Cambridge University have backed up this account." However, the report did admit that "more conclusive evidence is still needed; not unless the remains of Sodom and Gomorrah are found under the Dead Sea's salty waters will the theory be proved."

In searching for the location—and existence—of Sodom and Gomorrah, we are really investigating the larger question of whether Abraham and the Patriarchs existed, since nearly the entire biblical tale is told through the eyes of Abraham. It was Abraham who reportedly negotiated with the Lord before the destruction of Sodom (Genesis 18:22-33); it was Abraham who "looked down towards Sodom and Gomorrah and towards all the land of the Plain, and saw the smoke of the land going up like the smoke of a furnace" (Genesis 19:27-28); and it was Abraham whom God remembered when he "sent Lot out of the midst of the overthrow, when he overthrew the cities in which Lot had settled" (Genesis 19:29).

Maxwell Miller and John Hayes, two eminent biblical scholars and professors at Emory University in Atlanta, Georgia, have pointed out that Abraham and his wanderings fit with what was happening during the early second millennium B.C. This is the date generally given for Abraham and the Patriarchs, not least because it accords well with the biblical chronology: The Bible says that the Exodus took place 480 years before Solomon began to build his Temple and that the Israelites had been in Egypt for 430 years before the Exodus occurred (I Kings 6:1 and Exodus 12:40).

Since it is generally thought that Solomon began building his Temple at about 970 B.C., this would place the migration of Joseph and the Israelites into Egypt at about 1880 B.C. and would therefore place Abraham, Joseph's great-grandfather, approximately a hundred years before that at about 1980 B.C. During this time in the ancient Near East, between approximately 2000 and 1800 B.C., there were mass migrations of peoples and a breakdown of the powerful city-states that had flourished during the third millennium. Thus, until recently, numerous scholars were in general agreement that the stories of Abraham's migration from Mesopotamia to Canaan, and the later migration of Jacob into Egypt, make sense when viewed in light of the

Sodom and Gomorrah probably looked nothing like later artists envisioned them, as in this 15th-century French painting, but were more like typical Near Eastern villages or small towns.

political and demographic changes that were taking place in these regions during the early second millennium B.C.

However, not all scholars think that Abraham lived sometime between 2000 and 1800 B.C. (the Middle Bronze Age). For instance, it has recently been suggested that Abraham and the Patriarchs actually date to the Early Iron Age, the early years of the first millennium, and that the writers of the Hebrew Bible simply placed them more than a thousand years earlier in order to concoct a history of ancient Israel. It has also been suggested

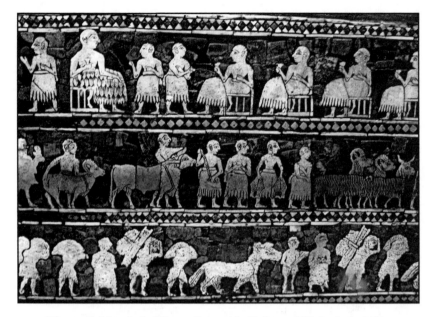

The so-called Standard of Ur was discovered by Sir Leonard Woolley in the 1920s.
It dates to about 2500 BCE, several centuries before Abraham.

that there were no Patriarchs—that Abraham, Isaac, and Jacob never existed—and that they were simply created as part of an invented history to illustrate particular stories. The debates concerning Abraham and the Patriarchs are currently among the most contentious in biblical archaeology, rivaled only by those concerning David and Solomon, and to date, there is no resolution in sight.

As an aside, we should note that Ur of the Chaldees, described by the Hebrew Bible as the birthplace of Abraham, is usually identified with the ancient site of Ur that was excavated by Sir Leonard Woolley in Mesopotamia during the 1920s, which we mentioned in connection with possible evidence for the Flood. There is no proof, however, that these two sites are one and the same. Although the city of Ur was already old by the time of Abraham, having been established well before 2800 B.C., the Chaldeans do not appear in Mesopotamia until hundreds of years after the traditional time of Abraham and his father in the early second millennium B.C.

The biblical writers' reference to Abraham's father's city as Ur of the Chaldees is, therefore, clearly anachronistic. This point is accepted by virtually all scholars, without argument. The biblical writers probably made this reference because they were putting the Bible into its current form during the late seventh century B.C., when Ur was indeed ruled by the Chaldeans. If, however, Abraham is dated to the early first millennium B.C., closer to the seventh century B.C., then the reference might make more sense, although it would still be anachronistic given the earlier context the writers set Abraham into. As a result, a few scholars have suggested that Abraham's "Ur" might be a completely different site not yet located by archaeologists and that perhaps we should be looking much closer to Haran, in northwestern Mesopotamia.

IN ATTEMPTING TO SOLVE the mystery of the location and destruction of Sodom and Gomorrah, we have several questions to address: First, did Sodom and Gomorrah even exist? Second, if they did, were Rast and Schaub correct in suggesting Bab edh-Dhra and Numeira as the two cities? Third, could Abraham and Lot really have been eyewitnesses to the destruction of Sodom and Gomorrah, as the biblical account states?

In addressing the first question, we must note that there are scholars who caution not to read too much into the story itself, who say that sometimes a story is just a story, a literary creation in which the events described have little or no connection to the real world. In other words, they call the very tale of Sodom and Gomorrah itself into question.

Other scholars have suggested that the story of Sodom especially, as well as the linking of Sodom and Gomorrah, may well come from a Canaanite tradition and be both pre-Israelite and non-Israelite in origin. Could this be? Is it possible that this is a fable or even a memory of a past event that the biblical writers inherited and turned into an ethical story—just like, as some suggest, the story of the Flood? In this case, Abraham would have been inserted into a Near Eastern story, one in which he did not play a role and was not an eyewitness.

Still other scholars have suggested that the story should actually be dated much later than the second millennium B.C., to the Iron Age, instead of the Bronze Age. They state that Abraham and the Patriarchs are much more at home in the first millennium B.C., a time when there really were domesticated camels being used in caravans, as the Bible states, and other biblical details of social and cultural life were present.

But what if Sodom and Gomorrah did exist? If so, then our two best candidates to date, archaeologically speaking, are Bab edh-Dhra and Numeira. However, these two ancient sites were destroyed about 2300 B.C., several hundred years before the generally accepted time of Abraham, making it difficult for him to be the eyewitness that the biblical account says he is.

Is it conceivable that Abraham was not an eyewitness, especially if he lived later, and that the biblical writers merely inserted him into a Near Eastern story? It is certainly possible, especially if the story was adapted from the Canaanites. It is also possible that Abraham never existed at all, for we still have no archaeological evidence for Abraham or any of the Patriarchs having lived and breathed in the ancient Near East. However, we must keep in mind the archaeological dictum that "absence of evidence does not necessarily mean evidence of absence." Just because we haven't found proof of Abraham's existence yet doesn't necessarily mean he is merely a fictional character.

What if Bab edh-Dhra and Numeira are not Sodom and Gomorrah? This may actually be the most logical solution, despite the fact that the archaeological surveys conducted by Schaub and Rast did turn up three other Early Bronze Age sites in the same vicinity. There are no signposts among the ancient remains at Bab edh-Dhra or Numeira welcoming the visitor to Sodom and Gomorrah. Indeed, Schaub and Rast only cautiously suggested the link—in part because of the other three ancient cities nearby and in part because of the lack of later sites in the area—and emphasized that it could not be proven.

In the end, the fact that the two ancient sites of Bab edh-Dhra and Numeira were destroyed several hundred years before the generally accepted time of Abraham (if not a thousand or more years earlier) suggests that Abraham could not have seen their destruction with his own eyes. The destruction of these ancient sites, if they are indeed to be identified with Sodom and Gomorrah, could have only been a story told either to Abraham or to the later writers of the Bible. Moreover, there is no longer any particular reason to insist that Bab edh-Dhra and Numeira are definitely Sodom and Gomorrah, especially if we wish to have Abraham both as an eyewitness and living in the Middle Bronze Age. Tom Schaub, the excavator of Bab edh-Dhra and Numeira, has recently determined that "short-lived carbon-14 dates we have received from Numeira place the destruction of that site around 2600 b.c., earlier than the dates we have for Bab edh-Dhra's demise." He says further, "I think this raises serious doubts about some of the biblical identifications that have been made."

Perhaps the best explanation, or at least the one most acceptable to the most people, has been suggested by Professor Joe Greene of Harvard University's Semitic Museum. In *The Oxford Companion to the Bible,* he writes: "The presence of these ruins [i.e., Bab edh-Dhra and Numeira], abandoned long before the advent of the Israelites in Canaan, may have given rise much later to local legends that their destruction resulted from divine wrath. At a subsequent stage these legends may have become attached to stories of the wanderings of Abraham and Lot in Canaan." Such an etiological explanation, as it is called in biblical scholarship, is based on the idea that many stories, myths, and legends from the ancient world may have been originally concocted to try to explain something out of the ordinary, such as the long-abandoned but possibly still visible ruins of Bab edh-Dhra and Numeira.

Perhaps it would be wise to untether Sodom and Gomorrah from Bab edh-Dhra and Numeira and search elsewhere for them. But where? Steven Collins, a professor at Trinity Southwest University's College of Archaeology, rejects the identification of Sodom and Gomorrah with Bab edh-Dhra and Numeira and suggests instead that biblical Sodom is located at a site named Tall el Hammam in Jordan, which he is currently excavating.

Yet Tall el Hammam is more often identified as biblical Shittim, the final place the Israelites camped before beginning their conquest of Jordan under the command of Joshua—and Collins has not yet produced any compelling archaeological evidence to substantiate his identification of the site as Sodom. Which leads us right back to where we began.

Thus, the location, and indeed the very existence, of Sodom and Gomorrah remains a mystery. It may be that a team of archaeologists, such as the one led by Collins, will definitively locate the cities. Until then, we can only speculate on the additional hypotheses that will be suggested in the meantime. Frankly, though, we would probably be better off listening to Neil Asher Silberman, the respected archaeological writer and current director of the Ename Center for Public Archaeology and Heritage Presentation in Belgium. Having learned of Harris and Beardow's "earthquake and liquefaction" theory, Silberman said: "This is Noah's Ark stuff. The real challenge for biblical archaeologists today is not to search for long-lost cities, but to understand why the ancient Israelites formulated these powerful myths."

MOSES AND THE EXODUS

Did the Exodus take place?
If so, when?

According to the Hebrew Bible, during the reign of an unnamed Egyptian pharaoh, a man named Moses led the Israelites out of slavery in Egypt, embarking upon a 40-year Exodus that would eventually result in freedom and a new life in a Promised Land of milk and honey in the region of Canaan. The story of Moses and the Exodus of the Hebrew slaves has become one of the most famous and enduring tales of the Bible, repeated each year during both the Jewish celebration of Passover and the Christian observation of Easter.

For us, the story begins in the Book of Genesis with Abraham's great-grandsons, the 12 sons of Jacob. We are particularly interested in Joseph, who was sold by his brothers into slavery because they were jealous of the attention he received from their father. Joseph was taken to Egypt, where after seeing his fortunes rise and fall, he eventually ended up in prison. There, he began to interpret dreams and came to the attention of the pharaoh, the king of Egypt, who released Joseph from prison and made him his right-hand man (Genesis 37-41).

At that point in time, according to the biblical account, a famine ravaged both Canaan and Egypt, but Joseph had stocked the royal granaries and storerooms in anticipation of the coming time of need. Because of the famine, Jacob and his other sons—and their families, flocks, and belongings—all eventually migrated to Egypt. There, after much commotion and intrigue, they were reunited with Joseph and settled down to live (Genesis 42-50). They remained in Egypt for 430 years (Exodus 12:40).

Our interest in the tale picks up again almost immediately with the birth of Moses and his journey downriver in a basket, after which point Moses ends up in the hands of Pharaoh's daughter and receives a privileged childhood at the royal court. Thus begins the Book of Exodus, and it is this portion of the text that we will be concerned with for the remainder of the chapter.

Under the pharaoh who "did not know Joseph" (Exodus 1:8), the Hebrews began to suffer as never before in Egypt. The Bible states: "Therefore they [the Egyptians] set taskmasters over them to oppress them with forced labour. They built supply cities, Pithom and Rameses, for Pharaoh. But the more they were oppressed, the more they multiplied and spread, so that the Egyptians came to dread the Israelites. The Egyptians became ruthless in imposing tasks on the Israelites, and made their lives bitter with hard service in mortar and brick and in every kind of field labour. They were ruthless in all the tasks that they imposed on them" (Exodus 1:11-14).

This same pharaoh was responsible for ordering that every son born to the Hebrew slaves should be killed (Exodus 1:15-22). This order set in motion the events that led to Moses being placed in a wicker basket and eventually being raised incognito in the pharaoh's own court. He was named Moses because, as Pharaoh's daughter said, "I drew him out of the water" (Exodus 2:1-10).

While he was still a young man, Moses accidentally killed an overseer who was mistreating some of the Hebrew slaves. He fled from the wrath of the pharaoh to the country of Midian, where he married and had a son. Eventually, when the pharaoh died, Moses returned to Egypt, where a new pharaoh—also unnamed—was persecuting the Hebrews even more than before (Exodus 2:11-25).

According to the biblical account, the Hebrews left Egypt with 600,000 fighting men and their families but only two midwives, pictured here on a first-century A.D. sarcophagus.

Moses had to be persuaded to return to Egypt, because he had a good life in Midian. It took a burning bush and a wooden staff being turned into a snake to convince him, but eventually he went back to rescue his people, taking his wife and young son with him (Exodus 3:1–4:20).

With the help of his brother, Aaron, Moses convinced the Israelites to leave Egypt (Exodus 4:27-31). However, it proved a bit more difficult to persuade the pharaoh to actually let them go. In fact, the Bible says that it took a number of miracles and the famous ten plagues before the pharaoh decided that it was in his best interest to do so (Exodus 5:1–12:32). The plagues included frogs, locusts, boils, flies, hail, and the killing of the Egyptian firstborn children. These plagues have been the focus of innumerable efforts by scientists and charlatans, scholars and quacks, to locate in the physical world and to identify with real life episodes that could correlate with them. Such efforts have not been particularly successful or convincing.

*The parting of the Red Sea has been a favorite topic for artists and filmmakers alike,
including Gustave Doré in this 19th-century engraving.*

The pharaoh finally agreed to let the Hebrew slaves go after suffering
the death of his own firstborn son. Still, he regretted his decision almost
immediately and ordered his soldiers to give chase. We are told: "The
Israelites journeyed from Rameses to Succoth, about six hundred thousand men on foot, besides children. A mixed crowd also went up with
them, and livestock in great numbers, both flocks and herds. They baked
unleavened cakes of the dough that they had brought out of Egypt; it was
not leavened, because they were driven out of Egypt and could not wait,
nor had they prepared any provisions for themselves" (Exodus 12:37-39).
(This passage in particular has inspired the tradition of serving matzoh at
Passover, instead of leavened bread.)

The Bible then states, "The time that the Israelites had lived in Egypt was four hundred and thirty years. At the end of four hundred and thirty years, on that very day, all the companies of the Lord went out from the land of Egypt" (Exodus 12:40). As we shall see, this chronological point—that 430 years had elapsed since Joseph and his brothers had first migrated into Egypt—plays an important role as one of the two biblical linchpins that provide a possible date for the Exodus (and for the dates of Joseph and Abraham).

The rest of the story, starting with the parting of the Red Sea and the drowning of Pharaoh's army, and continuing with the Israelites wandering through the desert for 40 years before entering the Promised Land, is well known and need not be repeated here. We will deal with some of this story in the next chapter, when we take a look at Joshua and the Battle of Jericho.

THERE ARE NUMEROUS questions associated with this story, virtually none of which has been satisfactorily answered to date by archaeologists, ancient historians, or biblical scholars. For instance, did the Exodus take place at all? If it did, when it did occur? Was it an event, occurring at a single moment in time, or was it a process, occurring gradually over two centuries or more? Who was the pharaoh (or who were the pharaohs) ruling Egypt at the time? How many people were involved? And how do we explain the various parts of the story, including the ten plagues, the parting of the Red Sea ("Red Sea" is a mistranslation of the original Hebrew words *Yam Suf*, which actually mean "Reed Sea" or "Sea of Reeds"), the Ten Commandments, and so on? We can now try to answer some of these questions by exploring the biblical story in more detail, taking into consideration the relevant extra-biblical historical and archaeological evidence.

The Story of Joseph—Let us begin by considering precisely when during the history of Egypt and Canaan Joseph and his brothers could have migrated to and lived in Egypt for several centuries. The possible historical context and kernels of truth underlying this portion of the tale are matters of great debate among scholars, and have been for a long time.

The Book of I Kings (6:1) says that the Exodus took place 480 years before Solomon began building the Temple in Jerusalem, and the Book of Exodus (12:40) says the Israelites had lived in Egypt for 430 years before they left during the Exodus. These are the two linchpins for the biblical chronology. Using these two numbers, and assuming that Solomon began building the Temple soon after he came to the throne in approximately 970 B.C., as many believe was the case, we arrive at the biblical date of 1880 B.C. for the migration of Joseph and his brothers from Canaan to Egypt.

This almost works well with what we know of Egyptian history during this period, for we know that foreigners invaded, occupied, and ruled over much of Egypt from approximately 1720 to 1570 B.C. These were the infamous Hyksos, Semites who came from the region of Canaan, and it is tempting to link the biblical story of the Hebrew migrations with the archaeological and historical record of the Hyksos invasion. Certainly, this period in Egyptian history is one of the few times a foreigner like Joseph, who was himself Semitic, could possibly have risen to govern at the right hand of Pharaoh. There are even well-known wall paintings at Beni Hasan in Upper Egypt, dating to the 19th century B.C., that depict a caravan of Semitic-looking people (probably Canaanites from the northern Transjordan area) being led by their chief, whose name is recorded as Abishar.

And yet the biblical chronology places Joseph and his brothers 150 years too early to be associated with the Hyksos, for the Hyksos did not arrive in Egypt en masse until circa 1720 B.C. But perhaps the biblical chronology is wrong. If we argue that the biblical writers could not possibly have known the exact number of years before various events occurred and that the Israelites were perhaps in Egypt for only 280 years before the Exodus took place—or that the Exodus took place 330 years before Solomon began building his Temple—then we could have the historical record agree with the biblical record. But that would be choosing which parts of the biblical story we want to believe and ignoring or amending the parts we don't like or are not convenient. This is known as cherry-picking, and it is exactly what many amateur sleuths do while investigating these biblical problems and mysteries, often without even realizing it.

The Story of Moses' Birth and Childhood—In chapter 2 of Exodus, we are told the story of the birth of Moses and how he came to be raised in the court of the Egyptian pharaoh:

> Now a man from the house of Levi went and married a Levite woman. The woman conceived and bore a son; and when she saw that he was a fine baby, she hid him for three months. When she could hide him no longer she got a papyrus basket for him, and plastered it with bitumen and pitch; she put the child in it and placed it among the reeds on the bank of the river. His sister stood at a distance, to see what would happen to him. The daughter of Pharaoh came down to bathe at the river, while her attendants walked beside the river. She saw the basket among the reeds and sent her maid to bring it. When she opened it, she saw the child. He was crying, and she took pity on him. "This must be one of the Hebrews' children," she said. Then his sister said to Pharaoh's daughter, "Shall I go and get you a nurse from the Hebrew women to nurse the child for you?" Pharaoh's daughter said to her, "Yes." So the girl went and called the child's mother. Pharaoh's daughter said to her, "Take this child and nurse it for me, and I will give you your wages." So the woman took the child and nursed it. When the child grew up, she brought him to Pharaoh's daughter, and she took him as her son. She named him Moses, "because," she said, "I drew him out of the water."

While this is both a dramatic and a feel-good story, we must realize that it is not unique among the annals of ancient stories. It is what scholars call a foundation myth, a story told about someone who rose from obscure origins to become a leader of his or her people. The most famous of these is probably the myth of Romulus and Remus, who reportedly

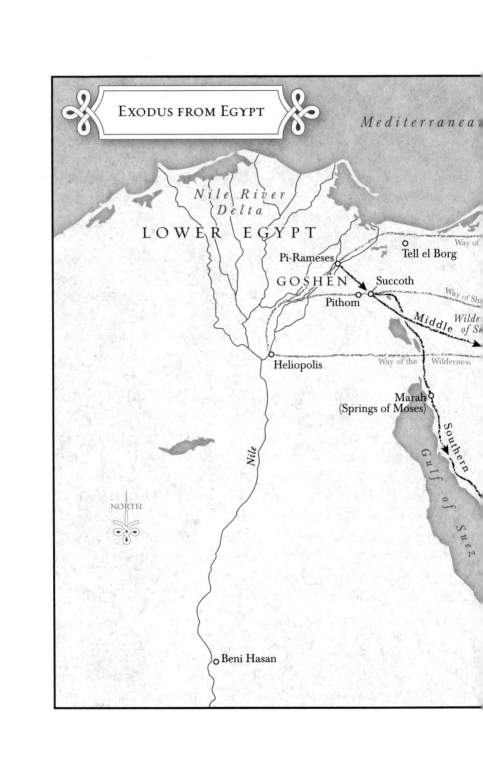

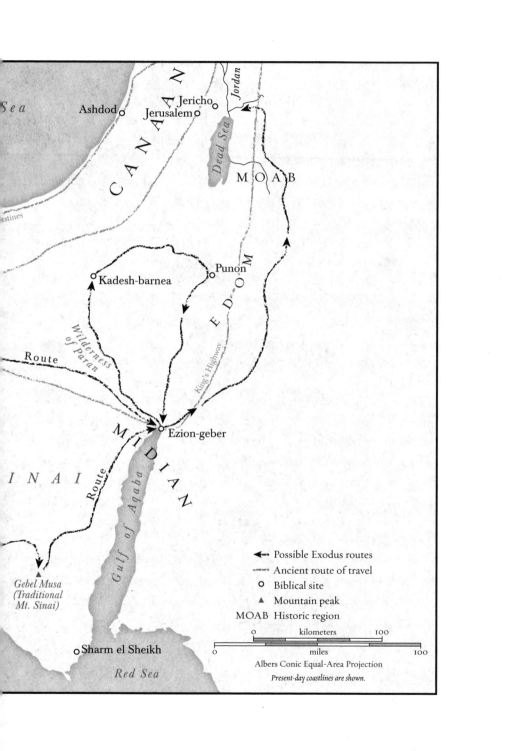

Sea

Ashdod ○

Jericho ○
Jerusalem ○

Jordan

C A N A A N

Dead Sea

M O A B

astines

Kadesh-barnea ○

Punon ○

E D O M

Route

Wilderness
of Paran

King's Highway

Ezion-geber ○

M I D I A N

I N A I

Route

Gulf of Aqaba

Gebel Musa
(Traditional
Mt. Sinai)

◀━ Possible Exodus routes
╌╌╌ Ancient route of travel
○ Biblical site
▲ Mountain peak
MOAB Historic region

Sharm el Sheikh ○

kilometers
0   100

Red Sea

0   miles   100

Albers Conic Equal-Area Projection
Present-day coastlines are shown.

founded the city of Rome in the eighth century B.C. They, it was said, had been raised by a wolf and then a herdsman, but were actually the scions of a royal family and descendants of Aenaeus, the famous Trojan who had escaped the destruction of his city during the Trojan War and made his way to Italy toward the end of the second millennium B.C.

Similarly, the Greek historian Herodotus tells the story of the Persian ruler and conqueror Cyrus the Great, who lived and ruled during the sixth century B.C. Cyrus, it was said, was actually the grandson of the ruler Cyaxares, but because his grandfather had a series of dreams that Cyrus would overthrow him, Cyrus was sent away as a newborn. Cyaxares had ordered that he be killed, but Cyrus was instead raised by a kindly cowherd and his wife. (The wife's name, we are told, roughly translated as Cyno or "female dog," which gave rise to the alternate story that he had been raised by wild dogs.) Cyrus eventually learned of his royal heritage and became a great ruler. Although he did take over the throne from his grandfather, as the dreams had predicted, it was a peaceful transition.

These stories indicate a larger tradition of tales in which children destined to rule are raised in obscurity and in initial ignorance of their royal roots. However, both date to centuries later than Moses and his story. Romulus and Remus date to the eighth century B.C.; their story was made famous by the Roman historian Livy who wrote centuries later, during the time of Augustus in the first centuries B.C. and A.D. Cyrus dates to the sixth century B.C.; the story of his birth and childhood has come to us via Herodotus, who wrote during the fifth century B.C.

Of even greater interest to us, therefore, is the legend of Sargon, the great Akkadian king who ruled in Mesopotamia during the third millennium B.C., at least a thousand years before Moses was born. The similarities to the story of Moses are readily apparent:

I am Sargon, the mighty king—king of Akkad.
My mother was a high priestess; I did not know my father.
My father's brother occupies the mountains.

Azupiranu is my city, situated on the bank of the Euphrates.

My mother, the high priestess, conceived me; in secrecy she bore me.

She placed me in a reed basket; she sealed my opening with bitumen.

She gave me to the river, from which I could not come forth.

The river carried me; to Aqqi the water-drawer it brought me.

Aqqi the water-drawer brought me forth when he dipped his bucket.

Aqqi the water-drawer raised me as his adopted son.

Aqqi the water-drawer made me his gardener.

While I was a gardener, Ishtar loved me and

I reigned as king for [. . .] years.

Unfortunately, the only copies we possess of the *Legend of Sargon* date to the Neo-Assyrian and Neo-Babylonian periods, during the early to middle first millennium B.C. We do not know how far back in time the legend extends—that is, whether it goes back to the actual time of Sargon, who ruled circa 2334 B.C. Thus, we do not know whether it can be seen as another example of a Mesopotamian story that was adopted and reused by the writers of the Hebrew Bible, although it certainly seems likely.

For the time being, we can only say that the story of Moses' birth and childhood is probably a foundation myth, similar to those of Sargon of Akkad, Romulus and Remus of Italy, and Cyrus the Great of Persia. Now, having ascertained that it is probably a foundation myth, we can legitimately ask how much truth there is to the story and how much we can believe. Unfortunately, the answer is that we do not know and probably never will.

Who Was the Pharaoh of the Exodus?—The Hebrew Bible never names the pharaoh of Egypt at the time of the Exodus. Nor does it name the earlier pharaoh, the one who did not know Joseph. In fact, one of the few clues we are given for identifying the earlier pharaoh, who began the initial persecution of the Hebrew slaves, is that he built the supply cities Pithom and Rameses (Exodus 1:11-14).

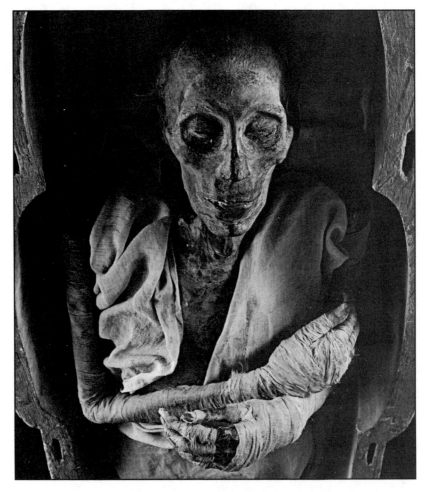

The mummy of Ramses II shows no indication that he drowned in the Red Sea,
evidence one might look for in corroborating the Exodus account.

We know from Egyptian historical and archaeological evidence that it
was Seti I who ruled from 1291 to 1278 B.C. and began building the cities
Pithom and Rameses, which were located in the Nile Delta. So perhaps
we can work from this point to identify the pharaoh of the Exodus, since
these are the two cities mentioned in the biblical account. This should be
fairly simple, because the text further states that, when the pharaoh died,

it was his son who took his place, and it was during the son's reign that the Exodus took place. Therefore, if we have correctly identified the first pharaoh as Seti I, then we can easily identify his son, Ramses II, who ruled from 1279 to 1212 B.C.

However, if we wish to follow the chronology in the Bible, such an identification—which is the one most frequently found in both scholarly and popular books—does not work. As we have noted, the Bible places the Exodus at approximately 1450 B.C., based on the statement in I Kings 6:1 that the event took place some 480 years before Solomon built the Temple in Jerusalem. This date of 1450 B.C. falls at the end of the reign of Pharaoh Thutmose III, when Egypt was an extremely powerful force in the Near East, and is nearly 200 years before Ramses II came to the throne.

Thus, something must be wrong. Either the biblical chronology is incorrect, and the Exodus did not take place when the Bible says that it did; or it was not the supply cities of Pithom and Rameses that the Hebrew slaves were busy building in Egypt; or Egyptologists are incorrect about who was ruling over Egypt at the time that Pithom and Rameses were built (i.e., it wasn't Seti I). We can dismiss the third possibility right away, leaving the possibility that either the biblical chronology is incorrect about when the Exodus took place or the biblical account is incorrect about which cities in Egypt were being built by the Hebrew slaves at the time of Moses. Either way, we apparently have a problem with the biblical account.

Of course, there are additional possibilities as well, but in the end we are faced with the fact that we do not really know who was ruling over Egypt at the time of the Exodus. We will leave this question for the moment and consider it again later, when we address the actual date for the Exodus in further detail.

How Many People Left Egypt?—We are told in the Bible that when the pharaoh finally agreed to let the Hebrew slaves leave Egypt, "the Israelites journeyed from Rameses to Succoth, about six hundred thousand men on foot, besides children. A mixed crowd also went up with them, and livestock in great numbers, both flocks and herds" (Exodus 12:37-38). This passage gives many archaeologists and biblical scholars pause, because having "six hundred thousand fighting men" leave Egypt presents the potential problem of having too many people involved in the Exodus.

Maxwell Miller and John Hayes—two eminent biblical scholars at Emory University whom we introduced in chapter 3—have pointed out that if "six hundred thousand fighting men" left Egypt, then altogether there would have been about 2.5 million people who left Egypt at that time, since most of the "fighting men" would have had wives, and most of the couples would have had several children. Add in the assorted others the Bible says were also present, and we have easily 2.5 million people taking part in the Exodus. As Miller and Hayes note, if this were the case, the Israelites would have formed a line 150 miles long, marching ten across, and would have taken "eight or nine days to march by any fixed point."

A line of escaped slaves 150 miles long certainly makes the crossing of the Red Sea very problematic, for Moses would have had to keep the water parted for nearly nine days for all his people to cross safely. Moreover, as Miller and Hayes note, we can only begin to imagine the logistics involved in keeping 2.5 million people alive in the desert for 40 years, especially if they are reduced to eating manna and quail upon occasion. However, it is unlikely that the Egyptians would have had that many Hebrew slaves in the first place, no matter when the Exodus took place (and if they had, the slaves probably would have revolted even earlier!).

The more likely suggestion is that we should not take the number in the biblical account at face value, and indeed most archaeologists, historians, and biblical scholars do not. It is frequently suggested that perhaps there are simply a few too many zeroes in the account. It would make a great deal more sense if, rather than having six hundred thousand Hebrews of fighting age leave Egypt, there were only 60,000, or 6,000, or perhaps even 600. It may also be that the Hebrew words usually translated as "thousand" could mean "family" or "clan," in which case we would be talking about 600 families or clans, which would be even more logical.

When Did the Exodus Take Place?—As we have mentioned, the biblical account says: "The time that the Israelites had lived in Egypt was four hundred and thirty years. At the end of four hundred and thirty years, on that very day, all the companies of the Lord went out from the land of Egypt" (Exodus 12:40). We have also already noted that this chronological point—that 430 years had elapsed since Joseph and his brothers had first migrated to Egypt—plays an important role as one of the two linchpins that provide a possible date for the occurrence of the Exodus and for the dates of Joseph and Abraham.

However, the second chronological linchpin is actually more important for determining the date of the Exodus. The following statement made in I Kings tells us that the Exodus occurred 480 years before Solomon began building the Temple in Jerusalem: "In the four hundred and eightieth year after the Israelites came out of the land of Egypt, in the fourth year of Solomon's reign over Israel, in the month of Ziv, which is the second month, he began to build the house of the Lord" (I Kings 6:1). Since it is generally believed that Solomon began building the Temple soon after he came to the throne in approximately 970 B.C., this would place the Exodus at approximately 1450 B.C. (and Joseph's move to Egypt at approximately 1880 B.C.), as we have mentioned several times already.

Not all scholars are prepared to accept these dates at face value, however, in part because the number 40—which goes into 480 twelve times—was a symbolic number in the ancient world, representing the length of a generation. Moreover, as we have mentioned, 1450 B.C. would place the Exodus right at the end of the reign of Thutmose III, one of Egypt's most famous and feared pharaohs, who ruled from 1479 to 1450 B.C. We know from other sources that Thutmose III was in firm control of Canaan, having fought a major battle at the site of Megiddo (biblical Armageddon) in 1479 B.C. It is extremely unlikely that he would have allowed the Israelites to flee from Egypt to that region, or that his successors would have allowed them to wander around for 40 years before settling down, particularly since Egypt retained firm control of the region even after the reign of Thutmose III.

According to the biblical account, the Hebrews spent 40 years wandering in the desert, with little shade or food. The wood from acacia trees like these were used to construct the Ark of the Covenant.

Thus, many scholars have suggested an alternate date of 1250 B.C. for the Exodus. This date, which is favored by most secular archaeologists, allows as much as 40 years for the Israelites to wander around in the desert before entering Canaan, but still arriving in time to be mentioned by Pharaoh Merneptah on his Israel Stele, a granite slab with the first extra-biblical inscription to mention Israel, which dates to 1207 B.C. (the fifth year of Pharaoh Merneptah's reign). It shows that the Exodus had to have happened by the time of the inscription, since an entity (or people) called "Israel" was definitely present in the land of Canaan.

The inscription was discovered in February 1896 by Sir William Matthew Flinders Petrie within Merneptah's mortuary temple, located near the Valley of the Kings across the Nile River from the modern town of Luxor. On the stele, Merneptah indicates that he came into contact with and conquered a people known as "Israel," located in the region of Canaan:

> The kings are prostrate, saying: "Mercy!"
>
> Not one raises his head among the Nine Bows.
>
> Desolation is for Tehenu; Hatti is pacified;
>
> Plundered is the Canaan with every evil;
>
> Carried off is Ashkelon; seized upon is Gezer;
>
> Yanoam is made as that which does not exist;
>
> Israel is laid waste, his seed is not;
>
> Hurru is become a widow for Egypt!
>
> All lands together, they are pacified;
>
> Everyone who was restless, he has been bound.

Such a late date (of 1250 B.C.) would also allow the Hebrew slaves to have built the cities of Pithom and Rameses (begun during the reign of Seti I and completed during the reign of Ramses II) before leaving Egypt. This again would allow us to retain at least some of the biblical account.

There is, however, also a third possibility, since it is conceivable that the Exodus was a process rather than an event and that it took place over several centuries, from 1450 B.C. to 1250 B.C. This would require the Hebrews to have left Egypt in a series of small groups rather than in one large group, perhaps as small groups of pastoralists or even as escaped slaves leaving by ones and twos, as Baruch Halpern, professor of ancient history at the Pennsylvania State University, has suggested.

Although this would almost completely negate the biblical account, it is quite possible that this is what actually took place. On the other hand, we would then wish to have some sort of textual mention of the Israelites' existence in Canaanite or Egyptian records. But there are none we can point to before Merneptah's Israel Stele in 1207 B.C., unless the Israelites are the social group called the Habiru mentioned by the Egyptians as causing trouble in Canaan during the 14th and 13th centuries B.C.

Finally, there is a fourth possibility that the Exodus did not take place at all and was made up by later writers, as a number of scholars have recently suggested. We shall take up this point in a moment, but if this last possibility is the correct one, it is most likely that the story was concocted during the seventh century B.C., if not later.

This brings us back to square one. Either we can believe completely in the biblical account and date the Exodus to approximately 1450 B.C.; or we can discount some of the numbers and details involved in the biblical account and look more toward historical and archaeological data that suggest the Exodus took place in approximately 1250 B.C. Or we can argue that there was a gradual migration that took place over the course of two centuries, from 1450 to 1250 B.C.; or we can argue that the entire story was fabricated at a later date. At the moment, there is no way to decide which of these possibilities is correct, so the jury is still out as to when the Exodus took place, if indeed it did at all.

Which Route Did the Israelites Take?—The Bible tells us that after the Hebrew slaves left Egypt, having crossed the Red (Reed) Sea and escaping the pharaoh and his army, they spent the next 40 years wandering in the desert before they entered the "land of milk and honey," or Canaan. It was during this period that Moses climbed Mount Sinai—the exact location of which is still debated today—and received the Ten Commandments (which we will return to in just a moment).

One of the primary questions we must ask is what route would (or could) Moses and the Hebrews have followed during their initial flight from Egypt and then during their subsequent wanderings? Could they have taken a northern route, traveling along the Mediterranean coast? Did they take a middle route, through desolate wilderness and desert?

Or did they swing farther south, down toward the bottom of what we call the Sinai peninsula today?

All these routes are possible, and yet the northernmost route—the Way of the Land of the Philistines (known to the Egyptians as the Ways of Horus)—is most likely out of the question, because the Egyptians had a series of forts along this route. The middle routes, such as the Way of Shur and the Way of the Wilderness, are unlikely as well for a variety of reasons, although they cannot be completely eliminated. The route that makes the most sense for the Israelites to have taken is the one that leads south down the western coast of the Sinai, going about two-thirds of the way to modern Sharm el Sheikh before swinging inland, and then eventually heading north again along the eastern coast of the Sinai. Therefore, in recent years, most archaeologists and historians who believe in the veracity of the biblical account, whether in whole or in part, have argued that the Israelites wandered around the southernmost part, and then went back up the eastern coast of the Sinai before they finally entered the land of Canaan proper.

At this point we should also bring up the question of the location of Mount Sinai, where Moses reportedly received the Ten Commandments and other laws. Unfortunately, despite the best efforts of both profession-als and amateurs, we are no closer to a positive identification of Mount Sinai than we were 200 or more years ago, when people first started searching. Suggested locations have been in the Sinai itself—including the most famous location by St. Catherine's monastery—and in Jordan, Saudi Arabia, Yemen, and other sites around the modern Middle East.

Although the most likely suggestion for the location of Mount Sinai seems to be in the southern Sinai itself, we will never be able to posi-tively identify this particular mountain unless archaeological and/or inscriptional evidence is found. Even then, the question could remain as to whether the evidence represents a modern or ancient forgery and/or misidentification. Unless and until such evidence is found, it is fruitless to spend much ink, let alone time, money, and effort, on such a search. Indeed, the discerning reader will note, when perusing the available

*The location of the Mount Sinai where Moses received the Ten Commandments is still debated.
Tradition places it at the summit of Gebel Musa, the site of St. Catherine's Monastery.*

literature, that not a single search for Mount Sinai has been mounted in recent years by professional archaeologists—that is, a university-sponsored, scholarly team.

The Ten Commandments and the Other Laws of Moses—However, we can comment upon and put into historical context the Ten Commandments themselves. The commandments are described in Exodus 20:1-17 and repeated in Deuteronomy 5:6-21. They are known as "absolute laws," which forbid actions and deeds absolutely. Thus, we are told in no uncertain terms that we shall not kill, we shall not steal, we shall not bear false witness against our neighbors, and so on.

Such absolute laws have never been found in any of the earlier civilizations in the ancient Near East or Mesopotamia. The nearest parallel that may be noted is in an Egyptian source—the so-called Negative Confession from the Egyptian Book of the Dead. It includes statements such as "I have not done evil. . . . I have not killed. I have not commanded to kill.

I have not made suffering for anyone." Even these, however, are a far cry from the absolute laws found in the Hebrew Bible, which as far as we know, are unique to Israelite society.

The Ten Commandments were not the only laws that Moses received from God. The biblical account says that Moses also received more than 600 other laws that included extensive legal and cultic instructions and regulations. These are spelled out in Exodus 21-23 and repeated in Deuteronomy 6-8. Some scholars include the laws found in Leviticus as well. These laws, instructions, and regulations were issued with the understanding that they were to be followed by the people from that time on. And indeed, these laws have governed the Jewish people ever since, and have had a major impact upon Christianity and Islam as well. Many of these laws, which include instructions on how to remain kosher, are still followed by people today.

The vast majority of these laws, specifically those found in Exodus and repeated in Deuteronomy, are written as so-called conditional laws—that is, they are written using "if . . . then" clauses and address specific circumstances when certain conditions apply. What is particularly interesting is that in a number of cases, they sound identical to laws found in earlier Near Eastern law codes, including the Sumerian and other law codes of Ur-Nammu, Eshnunna, and Lipit-Ishtar but most especially Hammurabi's Law Code.

As we have mentioned, Hammurabi was the ruler of Babylon from 1792 to 1750 B.C., perhaps about the time of Abraham and the Patriarchs. Hammurabi's Law Code was inscribed on an eight-foot-tall black pillar made of diorite. (The original is now on display in the Louvre Museum in Paris.) Copies, perhaps inscribed on similar stone pillars known as steles, were undoubtedly set up in the empire's major cities. The laws themselves may have been read to the inhabitants, since only an estimated one percent of the population could read and write.

At the top of the pillar is a scene of Hammurabi standing on top of a mountain, receiving the Law Code from Shamash, the sun god, who was also the god of justice at the time—a striking similarity to the story of

Moses on Mount Sinai. Below this scene, the prologue to the Law Code and then the laws themselves are inscribed—all 272 of them, written in cuneiform. (Cuneiform is a writing system that utilized wedge-shaped signs made by pressing the end of a reed stem into wet clay; the word "cuneiform" itself was coined by British and European epigraphers and comes from the Latin *cuneus,* meaning "wedge.")

Hammurabi's laws are separated into different sections, each concerned with a different aspect of the Law Code. In all, the laws cover virtually every aspect of society, but of perhaps the greatest interest to us today are the cases concerning personal injuries, especially those that spell out the "eye for an eye, tooth for a tooth" verdicts, hundreds of years before the biblical writers elected to put the same punishments into the Hebrew Bible. For instance, Laws 196-200 in Hammurabi's Law Code state: "(196) If a man has destroyed the eye of a member of the aristocracy, they shall destroy his eye; (197) If he has broken another man's bone, they shall break his bone. . . . (200) If a man has knocked out a tooth of a man of his own rank, they shall knock out his tooth." We can readily note that these laws are essentially identical to—but a good deal older than—the laws found in Exodus, which read: "If any harm follows [for example, in a fight], then you shall give life for life, eye for eye, tooth for tooth, hand for hand, foot for foot, burn for burn, wound for wound, stripe for stripe" (21:22-23).

We should not be completely surprised that there are similarities between the conditional laws in the Bible and those in much earlier law codes of the ancient Near East. As the late Samuel Noah Kramer, a research professor at the University of Pennsylvania and at one time the world's foremost expert on the ancient Sumerians, once wrote, there are numerous items or ideas invented by the ancient Sumerians—not just stories or narratives—that have made their way down to us today, many of them via biblical Israel and Judah. These include advances in pottery, agriculture, medicine, laws, and so on. As we have mentioned, it seems likely that some of these ideas could have been handed down from generation to generation, and even from culture to culture. There is no reason why law codes could not be suggested as another potential instance of a transmitted idea, especially when we can see noted similarities between portions of the Hebrew Bible and material from the earlier Mesopotamian civilizations.

In addition, the similarities between these conditional laws should not be surprising considering that both common sense and historical observations tell us at least two things. First, similar peoples living in similar situations in similar areas frequently need similar laws, regardless of when they live (assuming that a radical transformation, such as an industrial revolution, has not occurred in the meantime). Thus, the Sumerians, Akkadians, Babylonians, Assyrians, Canaanites, and Israelites, who all lived in approximately the same area of the world, all needed similar laws if they were to survive in an orderly manner, regardless of whether they lived in the third or the second millennia B.C. Second, newcomers (or invaders) will frequently adopt customs, laws, and other aspects of culture from the inhabitants already living there, as many anthropologists, archaeologists, and ancient historians have noted.

Thus, we may easily suggest that the similarities between law codes in the ancient Near East can be explained by one culture adopting (and revising) the laws of an earlier culture that had already been determined to work in that particular area. The Israelites could have adopted laws from the Canaanites, who had earlier adopted them from the Akkadians and Babylonians, who had adopted them from the Sumerians. Each culture would have its own idiosyncrasies and would need to tweak the laws to better fit their own society, but the majority of the laws could remain essentially the same, since "an eye for an eye, a tooth for a tooth" worked as well for the Babylonians following Hammurabi's Law Code as it did for the Israelites following the Law of Moses.

———

WHEN TURNING TO archaeological evidence, there is little data from which to draw conclusions about the Exodus. Numerous sites have been excavated that could potentially be related, such as the site of Tell el Borg

No archaeological evidence for the Exodus has yet been found—and remains unlikely because, like Bedouin encampments today, the Israelites probably set up tents rather than permanent structures.

in the North Sinai, which James Hoffmeier, professor of Old Testament and ancient Near Eastern history and archaeology at Trinity Evangelical Divinity School, is currently excavating. But virtually nothing else has been found to shed specific light on the historicity of the Exodus—all is inference so far. This is a disturbing fact, especially for those who believe in the veracity of the biblical account, but it is undeniable.

On the other hand, we might ask what we are expecting to find. If the Israelites were camping, they would have used tents with postholes, rather than permanent structures, just as the Bedouin of today do. An archaeologist searching for the Exodus is probably not going to find houses and walls and remains of permanent structures. The most anyone could hope to find would be holes in the ground where tent pegs had once been placed, which would be almost impossible to find.

Still, as Israel Finkelstein, professor of archaeology at Tel Aviv University, and Neil Asher Silberman, director of the Ename Center for

Public Archaeology and Heritage Presentation in Belgium, have pointed out, "Modern archaeological techniques are quite capable of tracing even the very meager remains of hunter-gatherers and pastoral nomads all over the world." Furthermore, "repeated archaeological surveys in all regions of the [Sinai] peninsula . . . have yielded only negative evidence, not even a single shred, no structure, not a single house, no trace of an ancient encampment. . . . There is simply no such evidence at the supposed time of the Exodus."

Similarly, numerous and repeated efforts—both archaeological and otherwise—to identify the famous ten plagues that tormented the Egyptians have been neither particularly successful nor convincing. The same goes for the parting of the Red (Reed) Sea, which has proved elusive to identify and explain, despite innumerable attempts, many of which have been featured on network and cable television channels. Again, when it comes to the parting of the sea, we might ask what evidence an archaeologist might hope to find, unless it is the water-logged remains of Pharaoh's drowned charioteers, along with their horses, chariots, and weapons. Regardless, nothing has come to light.

———————

ONE OF THE FAVORITE suggestions by scholars and enthusiasts alike is that the parting of the Red Sea and the ten plagues were caused by the eruption of the Santorini volcano, located about 70 miles north of the island of Crete in the Aegean Sea. In other words, we should link the Exodus to the Santorini eruption. As tempting as this might be—and indeed this theory is postulated over and over again on television documentaries (most recently on the History Channel as part of *The Exodus Decoded* by Simcha Jacobovici)—it is extremely unlikely that the two can be linked, primarily because of chronological problems.

The original suggestions to link the two events came back when scholars believed the Santorini volcano had erupted in 1450 B.C. or thereabouts. If one follows the biblical chronology for the Exodus, arriving at the same date of 1450 B.C., it is clear that the two events could be close enough in time so that the one could be used to explain the other. For instance, the tsunami caused by the volcanic eruption (which we know took place, from archaeological evidence on Crete and elsewhere) may well have caused the waters in the Red Sea to first retreat and then come back with a vengeance, thus allowing Moses and the Hebrew slaves to cross but drowning the pursing Egyptian army.

But in the early to mid 1980s, the Santorini eruption was redated on the basis of carbon-14 dating and ice-core dates to approximately 1628 B.C. Even though it remains a matter of debate, virtually no scholars argue for the 1450 B.C. date anymore. In fact, even if we disagree with the 1628 B.C. date, the earliest date that the volcano erupted would have been about 1550 B.C. When we consider that the historical and archaeological evidence surrounding the Exodus suggests a date circa 1250 B.C. rather than 1450 B.C., it becomes clear that the two events cannot have been linked, for they were separated by at least 100 years and more likely nearly 400 years.

A similar suggestion linking the Exodus with the Egyptian expulsion of the Hyksos is also unlikely because of the time difference involved, unless the event was somehow preserved and incorporated into later folk memories. We know from archaeological and historical evidence that the Hyksos were expelled from Egypt in approximately 1570 B.C. This is at least a 100 years before even the Bible says the Exodus occurred. Moreover, if the Hebrews left Egypt and settled in Canaan by 1570 B.C., we would expect some literary mention of them during the three centuries between 1570 and 1207 B.C., when Israel is first mentioned on Merneptah's Israel Stele, and yet there are no such mentions, as we have seen.

It has also recently been suggested that the entire Exodus story, as told in the biblical account, did not occur, but rather is a much later creation. Here, I do not include the more far-fetched, minimalist claims that the story was fabricated during the Persian or Hellenistic periods. Instead, I am referring to the suggestions made by scholars such as Donald Redford, Israel Finkelstein, and Neil Asher Silberman that the story is a seventh-century B.C. creation by writers living and working during the time of Josiah in Judah and/or the 26th (Saite) Dynasty in Egypt. As an aside, I should note that, although many would label him a minimalist, Finkelstein refers to himself as a "centrist," somewhere in between the maximalists who believe the biblical account is infallible and the minimalists who dismiss most or all of it.

Finkelstein and Silberman point out, for instance, that "the most evocative and consistent geographical details of the Exodus story come from the seventh century B.C.E., during the great era of prosperity of the kingdom of Judah—six centuries after the events of the Exodus were supposed to have taken place." They state in particular that all of the major places that are mentioned in the Exodus story—including those visited by the Israelites during their 40 years of wandering—were inhabited in the seventh century B.C. and that some were inhabited *only* during the seventh century B.C. Such arguments are only just beginning to be fully discussed and debated in scholarly literature. It remains to be seen what impact these new suggestions made by Redford, Finkelstein, and Silberman will ultimately have.

Of course, numerous additional suggestions have been made, especially by enthusiastic amateurs, concerning everything from where the Red Sea was located and how it was parted to where Mount Sinai was located and where the manna came from that the wandering Hebrews ate. I will not take the time to document these here, since we would run long on space as well as on entries. I suspect that the great interest in the Exodus is owing to the fact that it has so many subtopics, and none that can be readily proved or disproved. I will simply say that none of the alternate suggestions by enthusiasts and nonprofessionals have been of sufficient interest to encourage mainstream professional archaeologists, ancient historians, and biblical scholars to adopt them into their thinking and hypotheses.

———————

OF ALL THE SUGGESTED historical contexts in which the Exodus might be placed, the reign of Ramses II in the 13th century B.C. seems the most likely, despite the noted lack of correlation with the biblical chronology. However, here, too, we have a problem, because Ramses II was one of the strongest Egyptian pharaohs ever to rule, and it is unlikely that he would have allowed a large group of slaves such as the Hebrews to simply leave Egypt (although the biblical account suggests that God intervened).

Of course, there is no mention of this event in any extra-biblical texts, including those of the Egyptians (where we would be most likely to find it), unless we somehow link the Exodus to the renegade groups of Habiru mentioned in Egyptian texts from the 14th and 13th centuries B.C. Then again, the lack of Egyptian texts specifically mentioning the Exodus may not be surprising at all, considering that the Egyptians hardly ever mentioned defeats in their inscriptions and, from the Egyptian point of view, that is exactly what the Exodus would have been considered to be.

In sum, if we suggest that the Exodus actually occurred and are looking to find a historical context that fits best with the known variables, there are two real choices. One is to suggest that the Exodus was a single event that most likely would have taken place during the reign of Ramses II. The other is to suggest that the Exodus was a process that took place gradually, in the form of small groups of families escaping one by one over the course of two or more centuries, from about 1450 B.C. until 1250 B.C. There are problems with both of these scenarios, but they are more likely than postulating that the Exodus took place during the time of Thutmose III in the 15th century B.C., as the biblical chronology suggests.

It is, of course, also possible that the Exodus did not take place as the Bible describes it, as some archaeologists, Egyptologists, and biblical scholars have recently argued. Again, I do not include the complete naysayers who have suggested the story was made up during the Persian or even the Hellenistic period, but rather the more credible centrist scholars who have presented archaeological and historical data that suggest the story could have been created during the seventh century B.C. for political, religious, and ideological reasons. If this were the case, then we would need to look at the situation in seventh century B.C. Judah and the time of King Josiah, but then we would be looking at quite a different historical context—one in which a story was fabricated for some reason, rather than one in which an actual event took place.

THE BIBLICAL ACCOUNT of the Exodus is filled with problems and questions similar to those concerning Abraham and the Patriarchs. How much of this biblical story can be believed, and how much can be corroborated by archaeology or other sources? In brief, we have the biblical narrative and precious little else. It may be a matter of faith to believe that the events of the Exodus took place as the Bible describes, but that has not stopped people from attempting to prove that it occurred.

In fact, we should note at the outset that of all the tales and mysteries in the Hebrew Bible, the Exodus story has been perhaps the most abused by amateurs and enthusiasts. There has been no shortage of attempts to find archaeological evidence and scientific explanations to account for all of the miracles and events that occurred. The sheer number of books and documentaries that have been produced to promote absolute nonsense, junk science, and bad historical theories is frankly overwhelming . . . and shows no sign of letting up.

Clearly it is impossible to solve the question of the Exodus to everyone's satisfaction, and certainly not for lack of trying. In essence, we can only shrug and say that there is a good reason why these things are still mysteries and were not resolved long ago. So, did the Exodus even occur? My own belief is that there is no clear answer. Whatever theory we choose to adhere to will depend upon our own belief system.

As an archaeologist, I again must point out that there is no archaeological evidence yet available to prove that the Exodus, as described in the Hebrew Bible, took place. As I stated in the National Geographic Channel television show *Exodus Revealed,* "We do not have a single shred of evidence to date. There is nothing [available] archaeologically to attest to anything from the biblical story. No plagues, no parting of the Red Sea, no manna from heaven, no wandering for 40 years." However, I should add that there is also no archaeological evidence that proves it did not take place. So at this point in time, the archaeological record can neither be used to confirm nor deny the existence of the Exodus.

As a historian of the ancient world, I find no particular reason to doubt that the Exodus happened; for me, the real questions are when, and to what degree? Of the various alternatives, following the biblical chronology and placing the Exodus in the 15th century B.C. seems the most unlikely, but some will want to do that anyway, based upon faith rather than reason. The suggestion that the Exodus was a process rather than an event creatively solves the dilemma of the timing, but it is compromised by the lack of textual or other evidence supporting the presence of Hebrews/Israelites in the land of Canaan before the year 1207 B.C. And if the Israelites were present in the land by 1410 B.C. or thereabouts, such textual evidence should exist, since there are plenty of Canaanite and Egyptian texts from the period of 1410 to 1210 B.C. that could have mentioned the Israelites if they had been in Canaan or even in the Sinai.

Assuming that the Exodus did occur as described in the Bible, I am most inclined to place it in or around 1250 B.C., in part because of the lack of existing textual evidence before that period and in part because there was a series of destructions in the land of Canaan during the late 13th and early 12th centuries B.C. that might be attributed to the invading Israelites, as we shall see in chapter 5. If the Exodus did not take place at all, however, as some have recently suggested, I would prefer to accept Redford, Finkelstein, and Silberman's suggestions that the story was made up in the seventh century B.C. for a variety of political and religious reasons (as opposed to thinking that it had been fabricated for no reason at all).

In the end, though, we must ask, What really matters? We have just looked at the story of the Exodus line by line, and have shown that there is much to be doubted about virtually every aspect of it, and that there is little that can be proven, whether by archaeology or history. The Bible was not primarily written to be a history book—all scholars agree on that point. Therefore, we cannot expect to be able to corroborate all of the historical events mentioned in it, or at least we should not be dismayed when we cannot.

Many explanations have been suggested for the Ten Plagues, including the plague of locusts, pictured in this woodcut from the Gutenberg Bible, but none have proved completely convincing.

Rather than it being a strictly historical account, the tale of the Exodus in the Hebrew Bible is interpreted by some as simply the story of an oppressed people, a theme that still resonates today as much as it did back in ancient Israel and Judah. Israel Finkelstein perhaps said it best in an interview with the Israeli newspaper *Ha'aretz,* which noted that he "sees no contradiction between holding a proper Pesach [Passover] seder and telling the story of the Exodus from Egypt, and the fact that, in his opinion, the Exodus never occurred." Finkelstein said, "I am a great believer in a total separation between tradition and research. I myself have a warm spot in my heart for the Bible and its splendid stories. During our Pesach seder, my two girls, who are 11 and 7, didn't hear a word about the fact that there was no Exodus from Egypt. When they are 25, we will tell them a different story. Belief, tradition and research are three parallel lines that can exist simultaneously. I don't see that as a gross contradiction."

Contradiction or not, it was only after Moses and most of his generation had died that the Hebrews, now renamed the Israelites, were finally allowed to enter the land of Canaan. Even then they had to take Canaan by force, with Joshua leading them into battle. And still the miracles continued, for as the Bible recounts, it is in this context that the capture of Jericho occurred, its walls tumbling down when the Israelites blew their horns. Or did they? This we will discuss in the next chapter.

JOSHUA AND THE
BATTLE OF JERICHO

How did Joshua capture Jericho?
Did he in fact do so?

In the Book of Joshua within the Hebrew Bible, we are told that Joshua and the Israelites captured the city of Jericho as part of their overall conquest of the land of Canaan. The most familiar version of the story is that Joshua and his men marched around the city with the Ark of the Covenant for seven days in a row; on the seventh day, they knocked down the city's walls by blowing their trumpets.

The Bible states that Joshua took over as the leader of the Israelites after Moses died on Mount Nebo, within sight of the Promised Land (Deuteronomy 34:1-9). Joshua's accession to the leadership marked a change in the fortunes of the Israelites, as they ended their 40 years of wandering through the wilderness and finally entered the land of "milk and honey" (Exodus 3:8). It also signified a change in strategy on the part of the Israelites, as they shifted from a fairly passive existence in the desert to an active military campaign designed to wrest the land from the Canaanites.

We do not need to repeat the entire story of Joshua's capture of Jericho, because it is most likely familiar to the readers of this book. Instead, we will focus on two of the most mysterious parts of the tale. These are of greatest interest to archaeologists and subject to the fiercest debates. The first episode we are specifically interested in comes at the beginning of the story, after Moses' death, when Joshua and his men enter the land of Canaan and begin their conquest. First, they needed to cross the Jordan River. Yet just as the Red Sea parted long enough for the Hebrews to escape from Egypt, so now the Jordan River miraculously ceases flowing long enough for the Israelites to cross into Canaan. Later in the chapter, we will examine this event using archaeological and geological evidence. But, before we do so, let us read the biblical account:

> When the people set out from their tents to cross over the Jordan, the priests bearing the ark of the covenant were in front of the people. Now the Jordan overflows all its banks throughout the time of harvest. So when those who bore the ark had come to the Jordan, and the feet of the priests bearing the ark were dipped in the edge of the water, the waters flowing from above stood still, rising up in a single heap far off at Adam, the city that is beside Zarethan, while those flowing towards the sea of the Arabah, the Dead Sea, were wholly cut off. Then the people crossed over opposite Jericho. While all Israel were crossing over on dry ground, the priests who bore the ark of the covenant of the Lord stood on dry ground in the middle of the Jordan, until the entire nation finished crossing over the Jordan. (Joshua 3:14-17)

Once they are safely on dry land, the 40,000 armed warriors who have crossed over with Joshua and are now encamped on the plains of Jericho (4:13) begin their preparations for the upcoming battle.

This now brings us to the second episode: the walls of Jericho. In the sixth chapter of Joshua, we are told that the Israelites have surrounded the city of Jericho and placed it under siege. God then gives Joshua further instructions:

> Now Jericho was shut up inside and out because of the Israelites; no one came out and no one went in. The Lord said to Joshua, "See, I have handed Jericho over to you, along with its king and soldiers. You shall march around the city, all the warriors circling the city once. Thus you shall do for six days, with seven priests bearing seven trumpets of rams'

Trumpets made of rams' horns were used in the ancient Near East.
The use of shofars in Judaism continues the tradition today.

horns before the ark. On the seventh day you shall march around the city seven times, the priests blowing the trumpets. When they make a long blast with the ram's horn, as soon as you hear the sound of the trumpet, then all the people shall shout with a great shout; and the wall of the city will fall down flat, and all the people shall charge straight ahead." So Joshua son of Nun summoned the priests and said to them, "Take up the ark of the covenant, and have seven priests carry seven trumpets of rams' horns in front of the ark of the Lord." To the people he said, "Go forward and march around the city; have the armed men pass on before the ark of the Lord." (Joshua 6:1-7)

The Bible tells us that it came to pass just as God had commanded. Joshua and his army marched around Jericho on six consecutive days, blowing their trumpets continuously. On the seventh day, after marching around the city seven times, they blew mightily on their trumpets, and Joshua said to the people, "Shout! For the Lord has given you the city" (6:8-16). The biblical account continues: "As soon as the people heard the sound of the trumpets, they raised a great shout, and the wall fell down flat; so the people charged straight ahead into the city and captured it" (6:20).

In this chapter, we will investigate the following questions: Did Joshua and his men really knock down the city walls with a blast of their trumpets? Or as some have suggested, did an earthquake help Joshua capture the city? Did he even capture the city at all? If he did capture Jericho, was it inhabited at the time?

These questions are still being fiercely debated by archaeologists, ancient historians, and biblical scholars. Unfortunately, before we can attempt to answer them, we need to ask an even bigger set of questions: Can we believe the biblical account of the Israelite conquest of Canaan? Did it really take place as we are told?

To BEGIN, WE SHOULD note that an earlier story with similar elements to the biblical account of Joshua and the battle of Jericho comes to us from the city of Ugarit, in northern Syria. In the *Legend of Keret,* probably dating to the 14th century B.C., we are told that King Keret marched his army to the city of Udum, ruled by King Pabel, and then waited six days. At dawn on the seventh day, King Keret attacked, accompanied by a tremendous noise. The walls of Udum did not fall down—and we are not told that the invaders specifically used any trumpets—but the city did surrender to King Keret. The legend states:

> Tarry a day and a second;
> A third, a fourth day;
> A fifth, a sixth day.
> Thine arrows shoot not into the city,
> [Nor] thy hand-stones flung headlong.
> And behold, at the sun on the seventh [day],
> King Pabel will sleep
> Till the noise of the neighing of his stallion,
> Till the sound of the braying of his he-ass,
> Until the lowing of the plow ox,
> [Until] the howling of the watchdog.

Numerous scholars have already commented on the similarities between the *Legend of Keret* and the story of Joshua's capture of Jericho. Moreover, other scholars have noted that stories in which actions are repeated for six days and then culminate on the seventh, as in Joshua's storming of Jericho, are a standard, and usually a religious or divine, motif in earlier Mesopotamian literature. Tales such as these are often repeated in Canaanite and Ugaritic literature and in the Hebrew Bible as well. Also, there are additional instances in the Hebrew Bible of military actions that took seven days. For instance, the biblical account states that when Ahab and the army of the northern kingdom of Israel fought against Ben-Hadad and the Arameans in the ninth century B.C., "They encamped opposite one another seven days. Then on the seventh day the battle began" (I Kings 20:29).

Moreover, there are numerous historical accounts of armies marching around cities, blowing their trumpets to signal an attack. The famous Israeli archaeologist Yigael Yadin noted in his 1963 book, *The Art of Warfare in Biblical Lands,* that Joshua's tactics at Jericho could be compared with later Roman tactics, because the Romans also marched repeatedly

*The oasis of Jericho has provided water, food, and shelter for
weary travelers since time immemorial.*

around besieged cities in order to lull and confuse the enemy, and then
blew their trumpets to sound the attack. We should note, however, that
Flavius Josephus, the Jewish general turned Roman historian who wrote
in the first century A.D., says absolutely nothing about the trumpets of
Joshua's army causing the walls of Jericho to fall. He says instead, "When
they [Joshua's troops] had gone round it [Jericho] seven times, and had
stood still a little, the wall fell down, while no instruments of war, nor
any other force, was applied to it by the Hebrews" (Josephus, *Antiquities
of the Jews* 5.1.6).

It seems very likely that we can cite the story of Joshua and the Battle
of Jericho either as one more possible example of an earlier Canaanite or
Mesopotamian story (or elements thereof) that was transmitted through
the centuries and incorporated into the later biblical account, or as an
example of a story that incorporates religious or divine elements and
ritual. In either event, we must keep in mind these comparable (and
in some cases, earlier) tales and understand that, as a result, many

scholars discount the apparent miracles or mysteries connected with Joshua's capture of Jericho.

FORTUNATELY, THERE IS a lot more archaeological data available in connection with this mystery than for the other biblical stories we have examined. But this data is also the subject of fierce debates, because there are major problems surrounding the archaeology connected to Joshua and his capture of Jericho. The dilemma revolves around when Jericho was inhabited, destroyed, and abandoned. Therefore, it is also connected to the question of when the Israelite conquest of Canaan actually took place—which in turn is related to the question of when the Exodus occurred.

British engineer Charles Warren first excavated the ancient site of Jericho, today known as Tell es-Sultan, in 1867 and 1868. Some 40 years later, an Austro-German team led by archaeologists Ernst Sellin and Carl Watzinger excavated at the site from 1907 to 1909 and again in 1911. John Garstang next excavated parts of Jericho from 1930 to 1936, followed by Dame Kathleen Kenyon from 1952 to 1958.

Sellin and Watzinger believed that Jericho had been destroyed about 1550 B.C. and was then uninhabited for the remainder of the Late Bronze Age, through 1200 B.C. British archaeologist John Garstang did not agree with their interpretation, however, and launched his own excavations at the site. Ultimately, he believed his data showed that the fourth city (City IV) in the tell (the artificial mound that was created by building city after city on the same location for hundreds or thousands of years) at Jericho had been destroyed about 1400 B.C., more than a century later than Sellin and Watzinger had claimed. He based this destruction date in part on an absence of imported Mycenaean pottery (from Greece) at the site, because such Mycenaean pottery is commonly found at Canaanite sites from the 14th and 13th centuries B.C. According to Garstang, the fact that there wasn't any Mycenaean pottery found at Jericho meant that the city must have been destroyed before this period—that is, by 1400 B.C.

Garstang also believed that the city wall had fallen as the result of an earthquake at that time and that the Israelites had simply taken advantage of the catastrophe and destroyed the city. The city was essentially uninhabited after that date, except for a large "palace or residency"–Garstang called it the "Middle Building"–that was constructed on the eastern side of the now-unfortified tell during the second half of the 14th century B.C. According to Garstang, the palace, along with a few small, related buildings, was abandoned after only a generation or so, by 1300 B.C. at the latest, leaving the site empty and completely uninhabited.

Not all scholars were swayed by his data and interpretations, so Garstang asked the young British archaeologist Kathleen Kenyon to reexamine his data and come to her own conclusions. She did so, to his ultimate chagrin, for she concluded that Garstang was incorrect about the date for the destruction of City IV and that Sellin and Watzinger had been correct after all. Some years later, she began her own excavations at the site, which yielded additional data confirming her suspicions that City IV at Jericho had been destroyed about 1550 B.C., perhaps by the Hyksos following their expulsion from Egypt in 1570 B.C., or by the Egyptians pursuing those fleeing Hyksos.

According to Kenyon, Jericho was essentially abandoned after the destruction of City IV, except for the small area that Garstang had shown was occupied by the Middle Building during the 14th century B.C., when the city was apparently unfortified. As for the city wall that Garstang had found, it may well have been destroyed by an earthquake, Kenyon said, but it did not belong to City IV. In fact, its destruction had taken place a thousand years earlier during the Early Bronze Age, at about 2400 B.C.– not 1400 B.C., as Garstang claimed.

Kenyon's excavations therefore implied that, if Joshua and the Israelites had invaded Canaan during the Middle or Late Bronze Age, between 1550 B.C. and 1200 B.C., they would have found Jericho almost totally, if not completely, deserted and without any of its vaunted fortifications still present. If Kenyon was correct, then the biblical account of Joshua and the Battle of Jericho cannot be believed. Moreover, we could even perhaps call into question the entire biblical account of the Israelite conquest of Canaan, because if the conquest and capture of the first significant city could be questioned, then why should we believe the rest of the account?

Kenyon's findings, of course, caused consternation in some parts of the archaeological and biblical communities, as had Sellin and Watzinger's. Since Kenyon's day, the debate has continued to rage, for archaeological evidence by its very nature is frequently open to interpretation. This renewed battle for Jericho has most recently been taken up in the pages of *Biblical Archaeology Review* magazine by Bryant G. Wood, director of the Associates for Biblical Research, and Piotr Bienkowski, former curator of Near Eastern and Egyptian antiquities at National Museums in Liverpool, England.

Their arguments are quite detailed and do not need to be repeated here. Suffice it to say, Wood argued on the basis of his restudy of the pottery found by both Kenyon and Garstang that the destruction of City IV at Jericho should indeed be dated to 1400 B.C., as Garstang believed, and that it therefore can be attributed to Joshua and the Israelites. His statement, of course, assumes that the Exodus occurred according to the biblical chronology, about 1450 B.C., and that Joshua's capture of Jericho would have occurred some 40 or more years later, in approximately 1400 B.C.

Bienkowski, however, stood firm with Kenyon, and with Sellin and Watzinger as well. He rejected each of the arguments Wood used to redate the destruction of City IV from 1550 to 1400 B.C., stating, "There is strong evidence to confirm Kathleen Kenyon's dating of City IV to the Middle Bronze Age." He concluded, "Wood's attempt to equate the destruction of City IV with the Israelite conquest of Jericho must therefore be rejected."

If Bienkowski (and Kenyon, Sellin, and Watzinger before him) is correct, then the destruction of City IV at Jericho could not be attributed to Joshua, because virtually no one is willing to date the Exodus to the 16th century B.C. If, however, Wood (and Garstang before him) is correct, then the destruction of City IV at Jericho could be attributed to Joshua and the Israelites, but only if the biblical chronology is followed, which would place the Exodus in about 1450 B.C. and Joshua's subsequent conquest of Jericho around 1400 B.C.

The scholarly arguments between Bryant Wood and Piotr Bienkowski perfectly encapsulate the debate over the date of the destruction of Jericho. So who is right? And, in the end, does any of this matter? Why should we care whether Jericho was destroyed in 1550 B.C. or in 1400 B.C.? And why should we care if there were a gap in occupation at the site between 1550 and 1400 B.C.? Furthermore, does it matter that the site was apparently unfortified when it was partially reoccupied during the 14th century B.C.? And what happens if the biblical chronology is not correct and the Exodus took place in 1250 B.C., rather than 1450 B.C.? Then all of the debate is moot, because if Joshua and the Israelites came rampaging through the area around 1210 B.C., they would have found Jericho completely unfortified, and probably not even inhabited.

As we shall see, Jericho might not be the only ancient site to fall into this category, because if the Exodus did take place in 1250 B.C., or if it were a process that took place over two or more centuries, then modern archaeology indicates that the biblical account is incorrect about the sites it says Joshua and his men destroyed. Specifically, archaeologists have shown that the sites that the Bible says were destroyed by the invading Israelites either were not destroyed or were not even inhabited at that time, while a number of other sites that were destroyed at that time are not even listed in the Bible.

IN THE EVENT that Garstang and Wood are correct that Joshua and the Israelites captured Jericho in about 1400 B.C., it is worth considering the most intriguing part of the biblical account—that the walls came tumbling down.

The only persistent scientific suggestion that attempts to explain the collapse of the walls of Jericho is one that states that it may have been caused by a fortuitous earthquake, since shouting and the blowing of

*Could an earthquake have blocked the Jordan River, as shown here,
and allowed the Israelites to cross over and attack Jericho?*

trumpets alone will not bring down a wall. It is frequently pointed out that Jericho is located in a zone that is still seismically active, since the Great Rift Valley where Jericho is situated straddles the boundary between two tectonic plates: the Arabian plate and the African-Sinai plate. As the two plates rub against each other, the resulting stress is released in the form of earthquakes, both today and in antiquity.

In addition, we should remember that just as the Red (Reed) Sea parted long enough for the Hebrews to escape from Egypt, so the Jordan River miraculously ceased to flow just long enough for the Israelites to cross over into Canaan, right before the battle at Jericho. The biblical account says, "The waters flowing from above stood still, rising up in a single heap far off at Adam, the city that is beside Zarethan, while those flowing towards the sea of the Arabah, the Dead Sea, were wholly cut off" (Joshua 3:14-17).

An earthquake at Jericho that occurred less than a century ago, in the early afternoon of July 11, 1927, is frequently cited to prove that an earthquake could have affected Jericho and caused the Jordan River to cease flowing. This quake measured 6.5 on the Richter scale; its epicenter was said to have been about 19 miles north of Jericho in the Jordan Valley, by the modern Damiya Bridge.

The quake created cracks and fissures in the ground and buildings of modern Jericho. More important, it reportedly caused a mudslide near the Damiya Bridge when the 150-foot-high embankment on the western side of the Jordan River collapsed, stopping the river's waters from flowing south until cleanup crews could remove the earth some 21 hours later. Moreover, Damiya is generally identified with ancient "Adam, the city that is beside Zarethan." In other words, the 1927 earthquake supposedly resulted in the exact same situation as that described in the Hebrew Bible. Similar earthquakes with similar results have been reported at least six times in the past thousand years: in 1906, 1834, 1546, 1534, 1267, and 1160.

If such an earthquake did take place some three millennia ago, and was sufficiently strong enough to dam up the Jordan River at Adam/Damiya, then it would also have affected the buildings and walls of the city of Jericho, just as the 1927 earthquake did. It is certainly possible that an earthquake may have leveled the massive fortification wall of Jericho, just as a similar earthquake may have hit the city of Troy in ancient Turkey. In fact, the earlier excavators at Jericho pointed to cracks in the walls and other evidence of what appeared to be earthquake damage at the site. It is not out of the question that an invader such as Joshua might have been able to take advantage of a catastrophe caused by Mother Nature (or God) and capture a city that he and his men would not otherwise have been able to take.

However, in 1993, a team of earthquake specialists, including Amos Nur, professor of geophysics at Stanford University and an expert on both modern and ancient earthquakes, published an article reestimating the epicenter of the 1927 Jericho earthquake, placing it about 12 miles south of Jericho, rather than 19 miles north. According to Nur and others, the epicenter of the quake was, then, somewhere in the northern end of the Dead Sea, opposite modern Kibbutz Mitspeh-Shalem, and not up by the Damiya Bridge.

In 2002, the team published a second article confirming its original findings. The team also cited both its own studies and those of other researchers who believe the story of the damming of the Jordan River can be traced back to a 1931 book published by John Garstang. The book is, as the article stated, "the only source reporting about the Jordan's damming at Damiya." The team of earthquake experts strongly suggests that Garstang's testimony is unreliable, especially since he was not even in the country at the time and since no other sources, including official police reports or press releases, mention a damming of the Jordan River. They speculate that Garstang's desire to prove that Damiya is the biblical "city of Adam" and his desire to show that the Jordan could have stopped flowing as a result of an earthquake affected his reporting.

If this team is correct, then the 1927 earthquake must be removed from consideration as a modern parallel for what happened at Jericho during the time of Joshua and the Israelites. Even so, there are other instances and photographs in which it appears that a modern collapse of the banks of the Jordan River caused a severe constriction, if not an outright damming, of the river. One such picture that is frequently shown depicts a 1957 landslide, which looks as if it almost completely cut off the flow of the river. So even if we remove the 1927 earthquake from consideration, we could still suggest that a seismic episode took place in antiquity that both caused the Jordan River to temporarily cease flowing and caused the "tumbling down" of the walls of Jericho.

Regardless, speculation that the walls collapsed as a result of an earthquake may be a completely moot point—or even a red herring—if the event occurred in 1550 B.C., during the Middle Bronze Age, as we have discussed. And, if Kenyon is correct that the earthquake damage dates even earlier, to 2400 B.C. (during the Early Bronze Age), then the walls would have collapsed at least a thousand years before the Israelites are said to have captured Jericho.

ACCORDING TO THE Hebrew Bible, Joshua's capture of Jericho was merely the first battle he and his men fought during their conquest of Canaan.

Did Joshua and the Israelites conquer the land of Canaan in a lightning campaign that annihilated the inhabitants, as depicted in this 19th-century painting by Gustave Doré?

Unfortunately, the Bible seems to present contradictory statements about the people and places Joshua and his men both did and did not conquer. In the Book of Joshua, we are told in great detail about the battles fought by Joshua and the Israelites in their capture of Canaan. These include the total destruction of Ai and the complete slaughter of all of its inhabitants (8:1-29); the battle at Gibeon, where the sun stood still and Joshua defeated a coalition of five kings and their armies, including Adoni-zedek, the king of Jerusalem (10:1-27); the capture of the cities of Makkedah, Libnah, Lachish, Eglon, Hebron, Debir, and the complete destruction of all their people (10:28-39); the great battle at the waters of Merom, where Joshua and the Israelites defeated a huge coalition army headed by King Jabin of Hazor (11:1-9); and finally the capture of the city of Hazor itself, the "head of all those kingdoms," and the Israelites' annihilation of its inhabitants, so that "there was no one left who breathed" (11:10-11).

The book also gives us a summary of Joshua's southern campaign, saying: "So Joshua defeated the whole land, the hill country and the Negeb and the lowland and the slopes, and all their kings; he left no one remaining, but utterly destroyed all that breathed, as the Lord God of Israel commanded. And Joshua defeated them from Kadesh-barnea to Gaza, and all the country of Goshen, as far as Gibeon. Joshua took all these kings and their land at one time, because the Lord God of Israel fought for Israel" (10:40-42).

This statement is later repeated almost verbatim as a summary of Joshua's northern campaign:

> So Joshua took all that land: the hill country and all the Negeb and all the land of Goshen and the lowland and the Arabah and the hill country of Israel and its lowland, from Mount Halak, which rises towards Seir, as far as Baal-gad in the valley of Lebanon below Mount Hermon. He took all their kings, struck them down, and put them to death. Joshua made war a long time with all those kings. There was not a town that made peace with the Israelites, except the Hivites, the inhabitants of Gibeon; all were taken in battle. For it was the Lord's doing to harden their hearts so that they would come against Israel in battle, in order that they might be utterly destroyed, and might receive no mercy, but be exterminated, just as the Lord had commanded Moses. (Joshua 11:16-20)

The Bible also gives us a list of 31 kings who were conquered by Joshua and the Israelites. These include the kings of Jericho, Ai, Bethel, Jerusalem, Hebron, Lachish, Gezer, Arad, Aphek, Hazor, Taanach, Megiddo, and a host of other well-known and well-excavated cities and sites (12:9-24). However, the Book of Joshua then goes on to state that, while the kings might have been conquered, the Canaanites within these cities were not defeated. This is strange, especially given the book's lengthy descriptions of Joshua's victories, and the insistence in each of the accounts that all of the Canaanites in a number of cities had been slaughtered so that no one was left alive. For instance, Joshua 15:63 says, "But the people of Judah could not drive out the Jebusites, the inhabitants of Jerusalem; so the Jebusites live with the people of Judah in Jerusalem to this day," while Joshua 16:10 says, "They did not, however, drive out the Canaanites who lived in Gezer: so the Canaanites have lived within Ephraim to this day but have been made to do forced labour." And Joshua 17:11-13 says, "Manasseh had . . . the inhabitants of Taanach and its villages, and the inhabitants of Megiddo and its villages. . . . Yet the Manassites could not take possession of those towns; but the Canaanites continued to live in that land."

Obviously, there are two tales within the biblical account: One in which Joshua and the Israelites were able to conquer the land of Canaan completely, and one in which they conquered the land but did not totally kill and suppress its inhabitants. The two tales do not actually contradict each other, though. In every case where the biblical account says that a city was besieged and that everyone in that city was killed, it does not later say that the inhabitants of that city could not be subdued.

Nevertheless, it is clear that the account in the Book of Joshua is guilty of hyperbole and that the Israelites did not actually succeed in conquering—and nearly exterminating—all of the Canaanites in the land. In fact, we are told at length in the Book of Judges just who survived, including the Jebusites in Jerusalem; the Canaanites in Beth-shean, Taanach, Dor, Ibleam, Megiddo, Gezer, Kitron, Nahalol, Acco, Sidon, Ahlab, Achzib, Helbah, Aphik, Rehob, Beth-shemesh, and Beth-anath; and the Amorites in Har-heres, Aijalon, and Shaalbim (Judges 1:21, 27-35).

If we can show there is exaggeration within the biblical account, we may well ask how much of the account can be trusted at all. Here is where we can try to correlate the biblical account with archaeology, since many of those sites identified in the Book of Joshua have felt the bite of the archaeologist's trowel over the course of the past century or more.

Let us concentrate, however, solely on the eight sites that the biblical account specifically states were either completely destroyed or burned, besieged and captured, or simply captured, by the invading Israelites (Joshua 8:18-28; 10:28-39; 11:10-11, 13), because if the account is true, we should be able to find archaeological evidence for the destruction and/ or capture of these sites. These are: Ai (completely destroyed); Hebron (besieged, captured, and utterly destroyed); Hazor (captured and burned); Lachish, Eglon, and Debir (besieged and captured); and Makkedah and Libnah (captured).

The ancient city of Ai has been identified with the site of et-Tell ever since the days of the early explorer Edward Robinson in 1838. The identification was supported by William F. Albright, among others, in part because both "Ai" and "et-Tell" can be translated into English as "the ruin." Unfortunately, although et-Tell was indeed a ruin, it was apparently ruined long before Joshua and his men invaded the area, as archaeology has now shown. A number of different expeditions have excavated at the site during the past century and have documented that it was an important city during much of the Early Bronze Age, during the third millennium B.C. But it was destroyed and abandoned by 2400 B.C., more than a thousand years before the Israelites could have possibly been in the region.

A new city did not rise upon the ruins at et-Tell until about 1200 B.C. This new city—which was both small and unfortified—may well have been founded by the Israelites, but it would not have taken a genocidal battle for them to capture the abandoned and uninhabited mound. Some scholars have suggested that the tale of the city's capture was made up at that time, or later by the biblical writers to explain the presence of the ruins.

Hazor, pictured above, was described as the leading Canaanite city in the land at the time of Joshua's conquests, and was later one of Solomon's royal cities and trading posts.

Yet this theory is not universally accepted. In fact, in an effort to attempt a better correlation between archaeology and the biblical account, some archaeologists and biblical scholars have suggested that et-Tell is not the site of biblical Ai after all. For instance, Bryant Wood has been conducting excavations since 1995 at the nearby site of Khirbet el Maqatir, just one mile from et-Tell. There, he claims to have found evidence of both occupation and destruction dating to the 15th century B.C., which he attributes to Joshua and the invading Israelites.

As for the other cities in the biblical account that were captured or destroyed by Joshua and his army? We have little luck with Hebron, Makkedah, Libnah, Eglon, and Debir. Most of these have either not been satisfactorily identified to date, or have not yet been extensively excavated, or both; the few that have yielded some evidence do not support the biblical account—for instance, Debir and Makkedah—for they either have no evidence of destruction that can be dated to the Late Bronze Age, or were not even occupied until the Early Iron Age, well after the arrival of the Israelites. Our best chances lie with Hazor, which the Bible describes as having been captured and burned by Joshua, and with Lachish, which the account describes as having been besieged and captured by Joshua.

Excavations were first conducted at Lachish between 1932 and 1938 by James L. Starkey, but were brought to an abrupt end when he was "murdered by Arab bandits while traveling from Lachish to Jerusalem for the dedication of the Palestine Archaeological Museum." Renewed excavations were conducted from 1973 to 1994 by David Ussishkin, emeritus professor of archaeology at Tel Aviv University. As Ussishkin notes, Starkey's excavations had identified the sixth stratum (Level VI) at the site as the last Canaanite city. Most archaeologists, including William F. Albright, had long believed that this city was destroyed in about 1230 B.C. and could therefore be used as evidence that archaeology and the biblical account could be corroborated.

Ussishkin's renewed excavations showed, however, that while Level VI is indeed the last Canaanite city at Lachish, and that it was indeed destroyed by a violent fire, it was not destroyed about 1230 B.C. During his excavations, Ussishkin found a bronze plaque that contained a cartouche of Ramses III, the Egyptian pharaoh who ruled from 1182 to 1151 B.C. With this plaque, it is now clear that the Canaanite city of Lachish was destroyed at least half a century later than anyone previously thought, at about 1150 B.C. Unless Joshua's conquests are dated later than most biblical scholars have suggested—around 1150 B.C., rather than 1210 B.C. or even 1410 B.C.—the destruction of Lachish is unlikely to be the result of a conquest by Joshua and his army of Israelites.

Intriguingly, Ussishkin's excavations also uncovered an earlier Canaanite city—Level VII—that Starkey had essentially missed. Judging from the pottery and other finds, this city was also destroyed violently, probably at the end of the 13th century B.C. This new discovery could potentially be used by archaeologists who believe that Joshua's conquests took place during the late 13th century B.C. (40 years after an Exodus that began around 1250 B.C.). But evidence shows that the site was reoccupied instantly, and the Canaanite city of Level VI quickly flourished, only to be destroyed about 1150 B.C. If the Israelites had caused the destruction of Level VII at Lachish, we would expect the city of Level VI to exhibit characteristics of an Israelite settlement, rather than a Canaanite settlement.

Thus, Ussishkin's renewed excavations at Lachish have broken what once seemed to be a firm link between archaeology and the biblical account of Joshua's conquest of the city. But what about Hazor? Yigael Yadin, professor of archaeology at the Hebrew University of Jerusalem and perhaps the best-known Israeli archaeologist, began excavating at Hazor in the 1950s. He quickly found what he thought was evidence for Joshua and the Israelites' destruction of the Canaanite city, which he dated to "not later than 1230 B.C." However, as eminent archaeologist Amnon Ben-Tor has noted, not everyone was convinced by Yadin's evidence, and it has been debated and disputed ever since.

Ben-Tor, Yigael Yadin's former student and now the Yigael Yadin Professor in the Archaeology of Eretz Israel at the Hebrew University of Jerusalem, has been in charge of the renewed excavations at Hazor since 1990 and has tremendously increased the amount of data available. Ben-Tor has shown that the destruction of the Canaanite city at Hazor can be dated roughly to the 14th or 13th century B.C., based on pottery found in the destruction debris. While Ben-Tor says that he is unable to confirm "Yadin's overly confident date of 1230 B.C." for the destruction of Hazor,

he is confident that the city was still flourishing about 1290 B.C., for the
Egyptian Pharaoh Seti I (who ruled from 1291 to 1278 B.C.) mentions
Hazor in the account of a campaign he led against various Canaanite cities
at that time.

Even so, it is difficult to identify who was actually responsible for the
destruction of Canaanite Hazor. It would be nice to be able to attribute it
to Joshua and the Israelites, since the Hebrew Bible says specifically that
the Israelites burned Hazor to the ground:

> Joshua turned back at that time, and took Hazor, and struck its king down
> with the sword. Before that time Hazor was the head of all those king-
> doms. And they put to the sword all who were in it, utterly destroying
> them; there was no one left who breathed, and he burned Hazor with
> fire. And all the towns of those kings, and all their kings, Joshua took,
> and struck them with the edge of the sword, utterly destroying them, as
> Moses the servant of the Lord had commanded. But Israel burned none
> of the towns that stood on mounds except Hazor, which Joshua did burn.
> (Joshua 11:10-13)

As Ben-Tor notes, though, there are several other possible culprits
besides the Israelites, including the Egyptians, rival Canaanites, and a
group of foreign invaders the Egyptians collectively referred to as the Sea
Peoples (whom we shall discuss further in a moment).

But Ben-Tor presents several persuasive arguments for why the destruction of Canaanite Hazor cannot be attributed to the Egyptians, including
the fact that he found defaced Egyptian statues among the debris, an act
of sacrilege that Egyptian soldiers would never have committed. He presents similar arguments for why the destruction cannot be attributed to
rival Canaanites, for he also found defaced Canaanite statues among the
debris, something Canaanite soldiers would not have done either. More
important, he notes that Hazor is described as the head of all the Canaanite
kingdoms; most likely, no other city would have been able to challenge
Hazor, let alone attack it.

His arguments against the Sea Peoples, and specifically the Philistines within this larger group, are less persuasive. He says only, "Hazor is located too far inland to be of any interest to those maritime traders," which is debatable, and that "among the hundreds of thousands of potsherds recovered at Hazor, not a single one can be attributed to the well-known repertory of the Sea Peoples." As we have noted, an absence of evidence does not necessarily mean evidence of absence— but at the same time, we do not have any evidence that the Sea Peoples destroyed Hazor.

Perhaps most important is that the succeeding city at the site—the one built upon the ruins of Canaanite Hazor—is an Israelite city. This does not necessarily mean that the Israelites destroyed the Canaanite city and then built their own city upon the still-smoldering ruins, but it is a good possibility. It is also possible that another group, such as the Sea Peoples, torched Hazor and that the Israelites came along afterward and reaped the benefits of this destruction by building their own city on top of the ruins. We shall come back to this point in a moment.

Thus, out of the eight sites mentioned in the biblical account as having been captured, burnt, and/or destroyed by Joshua and the invading Israelites, the current archaeological evidence suggests only one site, Hazor, that might demonstrate a destruction level that would correlate with the biblical account (if we date Joshua's conquest to the 13th century B.C.), and only one other city, Lachish (which has a destruction date of about the mid-12th century B.C.), that might correlate with a late destruction by the Israelites. In short, the data that we currently possess does not inspire confidence in the biblical account of the Israelite conquest of Canaan.

Our current situation is in stark contrast to the period from 1920 to 1970, when William F. Albright, the so-called father of biblical archaeology, dominated the field. A professor at the Johns Hopkins University, Albright confidently asserted through his "Conquest" model that the Israelite conquest of Canaan had taken place as told in the Hebrew Bible, and that archaeology had confirmed the biblical account. It was in this atmosphere that the German journalist Werner Keller wrote *The Bible as History*. Called "the ultimate Bar Mitzvah book of the 1950s," Keller's book euphorically discussed the archaeological discoveries that "proved" the Bible.

Yet even during this period, several alternate hypotheses were put forward by biblical scholars, ancient historians, and archaeologists who disagreed with Albright's interpretation. These hypotheses are known as the "Peaceful Infiltration" model and the "Revolting Peasants" model, whose names reflected their basic premise. And in recent years, an additional hypothesis was put forward: the so-called "Invisible Israelites" model, which suggests that the Israelites were a seminomadic subset of the Canaanites, who came into prominence after the collapse of Canaanite culture, which occurred when the Egyptians withdrew from the region in the 12th century B.C. In each of these alternate scenarios, biblical writers then made up the story of Joshua's invasion.

German scholar Albrecht Alt, followed by Martin Noth, first proposed the "Peaceful Infiltration" model in the 1920s. This hypothesis suggested that seminomadic Israelites had left Egypt in small groups, peacefully infiltrated unoccupied areas of the hill country in Canaan, gradually built settlements, and eventually became sedentary. Alt thought that the Israelites became tied to the land and only later displaced the Canaanites in the cities. He believed that the military encounters in which the Israelites fought against the Canaanites only took place after the Israelites began expanding out of these central highlands, long after they had first arrived peacefully in the region.

In the 1960s and 1970s, American scholars George Mendenhall and Norman Gottwald suggested that the Israelites were already present in Canaan and had been for quite some time (if not always). They speculated that the Israelites were an underclass of peasants who overthrew the Canaanite overlords as part of a revolutionary social movement. This hypothesis, affectionately referred to as the "Revolting Peasants" model by scholars, is essentially a Marxist approach to the problem of the Israelite conquest of Canaan. Working in this model's favor is the fact that no mass killing of the Canaanites is required, nor is any mass invasion from the outside.

The fourth possibility is the "Invisible Israelites" model proposed by Israel Finkelstein of Tel Aviv University. This model suggests that the Canaanites and the Israelites were one and the same people—that the Israelites were a seminomadic segment of the Canaanite population who had always been present. The theory posits that the Israelites did not take over via a formal revolution but rather through a general and gradual inheritance of the land. This took place, according to Finkelstein, when the political and economic networks in Canaan collapsed after Egyptian rule ended in the 12th century B.C. At that time, the big cities on the coast deteriorated and the smaller sites in the hill country and desert fringes began to multiply. In his book *The Bible Unearthed,* co-authored with Neil Asher Silberman, Finkelstein concludes: "The emergence of early Israel was an outcome of the collapse of the Canaanite culture, not its cause."

IN THE END, when discussing Joshua's capture of Jericho, we are left with more of a dilemma than a mystery. Did Joshua really capture Jericho, as the biblical account says? Did the walls really come tumbling down? Was the site fortified at the time Joshua came through? Was it even inhabited?

As far as whether City IV of Jericho was destroyed in 1550 B.C. or in 1400 B.C., I believe it is a moot point. Joshua and the Israelites did not cause the city's destruction, regardless of when it took place. I say this because, as I stated at the end of chapter 4, I am inclined to believe that the archaeological and textual evidence trump the biblical chronology, and they indicate that the Exodus did not take place until approximately 1250 B.C., if it happened at all.

The simple fact is that there is no mention of the Hebrews or Israelites in any texts from Canaan, Egypt, or elsewhere in the Near East before 1207 B.C. And yet there should be if the Exodus took place in 1450 B.C. and the Israelite conquest of Canaan took place in 1410 or 1400 B.C., because there are plenty of Canaanite and Egyptian texts that could have mentioned them if they were present. The biblical account of the capture and destruction of Jericho also seems rather unbelievable to me if no one was living in

*The Sea Peoples are depicted in great detail in this relief at Medinet Habu,
the mortuary temple of Pharaoh Ramses III, in Thebes, Egypt.*

Jericho during the second half of the thirteenth century B.C. (between 1250 and 1200 B.C.) and no walls were protecting the ruins at that time.

Of the major suggestions that have been made concerning the coming of the Israelites, I find it unlikely that they were "Revolting Peasants"—in part because I see no way they would have been able to effect an over-throw on their own. I also do not embrace the "Peaceful Infiltration" model that suggests the Israelites simply wandered in over time and eventually took over, again because there is no mention of them in the texts (unless the Israelites are the Habiru, an idea that scholars have slowly discounted over the past several decades). I am also not particularly fond of the suggestion that they were always there as "Invisible Israelites," and eventually took over the land from the others living there, because I don't think that theory sufficiently explains how they were physically able to do so. However, I do think that the "Invisible Israelites" model can be used in tandem with other suggestions.

The "Conquest" model still makes the most sense to me, but only if it is substantially altered, because I do not see how it possibly could have happened as the Bible tells us it did. If I were proposing my own model, I would add a missing piece of the puzzle that the Bible leaves out entirely and link the Israelite conquest of Canaan to an invasion of the Sea Peoples.

We know of the Sea Peoples from Egyptian inscriptions left to us by Pharaoh Merneptah in 1207 B.C. and Pharaoh Ramses III some 20 years later. These Sea Peoples, who probably originated in such lands as Sicily, Sardinia, and Italy, swept through the Aegean area and the Near East, reaching as far as Egypt. En route, they destroyed numerous cities and civilizations and brought the lively international world of the Late Bronze Age to a crashing halt all across the Aegean and Mediterranean regions.

I am not implying that the Israelites were among these Sea Peoples, because we know they most certainly were not. Rather, I am suggesting—using what I might call the "Piggyback" model—that the Israelites may have taken advantage of the havoc the Sea Peoples caused in Canaan and elsewhere in the Near East, and moved into areas they could not have taken over and occupied under their own power. Thus, the late 13th and early 12th century B.C. destructions at Hazor, Lachish, and perhaps even Megiddo in Canaan may not have been caused by the Israelites, as the Bible states. Instead, they might have been caused by the much more fierce and battle-proven Sea Peoples, who had already brought an end to the Mycenaeans in Greece, the Minoans in Crete, the Cypriots in Cyprus, and the Hittites in Anatolia.

Whether languishing in the Sinai for several decades, or already present in the land but "invisible," or toiling as an underclass, or infiltrating the land slowly over centuries, according to my model, the Israelites would have simply been the beneficiaries of these destructions. By "piggybacking" on the success of the Sea Peoples, they finally would have been able to take over all or most of Canaan in the first half of the 12th century B.C., including the still smoldering ruins of cities such as Hazor and Megiddo. This would provide the "how" that I believe is missing in most of the other hypotheses. How could the Israelites have possibly attacked and successfully captured the imposing Canaanite cities? The answer is they didn't; the Sea Peoples did. But once the Sea Peoples had brought the Canaanite culture to its knees, the Israelites may have been able to take over some of the lesser towns by themselves, thus completing the conquest of Canaan.

I do not see any other way to accommodate the archaeological and textual data currently available to us. How the biblical narrative then came to be, with its stories of the capture of towns that were not even inhabited at the time, is anyone's guess. Finkelstein and Silberman have suggested that it was created, embellished, or heavily edited in the seventh century B.C., and that may well have been what happened, just as Homer may have edited and embellished the tale of the Trojan War when writing about it five centuries later. At the very least, I would suggest that the later biblical writers gave complete credit for the capture and destruction of the Canaanite cities to the Israelites without even mentioning the role of the Sea Peoples, perhaps because they only knew of them as the biblical Philistines who caused such trouble for Saul and David.

The fact is that we have at least two different tales within the biblical account, particularly when comparing the details in the Book of Joshua and the Book of Judges about which towns and peoples Joshua captured. And this alone is a good indication that more than one story was being told about Joshua and his exploits, and that the biblical writers tried their best to weave these different stories into a coherent narrative that may or may not have reflected reality. The Book of Judges may give a slightly more accurate historical account of what actually happened than the Book of Joshua does, since it states that the Israelite conquest of Canaan was not completed easily as opposed to claiming that the land was conquered in a lightning series of campaigns.

Apart from Hazor, however, there is little archaeological evidence from any of the Canaan sites that can be used to support either of the biblical accounts of Joshua and the conquest of Canaan, regardless of whether we date Joshua's conquest to the 15th century B.C. (per the biblical chronology) or to the 13th and 12th centuries B.C. (as many modern scholars suggest). I agree completely with William G. Dever, emeritus professor of Near Eastern archaeology and anthropology at the University of Arizona, who recently wrote: "But what about the conquest and settlement of Canaan as depicted in the books of Joshua and Judges? As we have seen, there is little that we can salvage from Joshua's stories of the rapid, wholesale destruction of Canaanite cities and the annihilation of the local population. It simply did not happen; the archaeological evidence is indisputable. It is conceivable that there was a military chieftain and folk hero named Joshua, who won a few skirmishes here and there. But there was simply no Israelite conquest of most of Canaan."

Dever is not alone in this assessment; he is simply giving voice to what the vast majority of archaeologists now believe. And a majority of biblical scholars and ancient historians concur. Esteemed scholar Nadav Na'aman, professor of Jewish history at Tel Aviv University, wrote: "It is commonly accepted today that the majority of the conquest stories in the Book of Joshua are devoid of historical reality."

So there is no evidence that Joshua ever "fit the battle of Jericho" or that "the walls came a tumblin' down" from a blast from his men's trumpets, to quote the traditional African-American gospel song. In short, it would seem that the only mystery still remaining about the story of Joshua and the Battle of Jericho is how it came to be written in the first place.

We shall see if we have better luck with our next case, which involves the Ark of the Covenant, another mystery for the ages.

THE ARK OF THE COVENANT

Where is the Ark of the Covenant?

Speculating on the whereabouts of the lost Ark of the Covenant has been a time-honored parlor game for hundreds, if not thousands, of years. It is easy to trace the Ark of the Covenant through the Bible, from the time of its creation during the days of Moses until the time it was placed within the Holy of Holies in the Temple during the days of David and Solomon. But sometime between 970 B.C. and 586 B.C. the ark disappeared. What happened to it? Where did it go?

Suggestions for the present location of the ark have ranged from a hidden chamber deep within the Temple Mount in Jerusalem or a cave on Mount Nebo in modern Jordan to a church treasury in Ethiopia or a government warehouse in Washington, D.C. But does it even still exist? Might it have been melted down or otherwise destroyed thousands of years ago? Surely such a fearsome weapon—for that is how it is described in the Hebrew Bible—would have been put to use after it left Judean hands, so why does it disappear from history? Such questions have never been satisfactorily answered, despite numerous attempts to solve the riddles and to locate the missing ark.

The ark is mentioned numerous times in the Hebrew Bible. We first meet it at Mount Sinai. The story of how it is made is told to us several times, initially in a more extensive set of instructions in Exodus 25:10-22,

The Ark of the Covenant, depicted here in an 18th-century fresco by Luigi Ademollo, was extremely well-traveled before it was finally brought to Jerusalem by King David.

and then in an abbreviated description as it is actually being made by the craftsmen Bezalel and Oholiab in Exodus 37:1-9. For the sake of brevity, let us look at the latter version:

Bezalel made the ark of acacia wood; it was two and a half cubits long, a cubit and a half wide, and a cubit and a half high [about 4 feet 2 inches long by 2.5 feet wide by 2.5 feet high]. He overlaid it with pure gold inside and outside, and made a moulding of gold round it. He cast for it four rings of gold for its four feet, two rings on one side of it and two rings on its other side. He made poles of acacia wood, and overlaid them with gold, and put the poles into the rings on the sides of the ark, to carry the ark. He made a mercy-seat of pure gold; two cubits and a half was its length, and a cubit and a half its width. He made two cherubim of hammered gold; at the two ends of the mercy-seat he made them, one cherub at one end, and one cherub at the other end; of one piece with the mercy-seat he made the cherubim at its two ends. The cherubim spread out their wings above, overshadowing the mercy-seat with their wings. They faced one another; the faces of the cherubim were turned towards the mercy-seat. (Exodus 37:1-9)

In his final speech to the Israelites, Moses says that he had only placed in the ark the two tablets of stone containing the Ten Commandments (Deuteronomy 10:1-5). This is reiterated in II Chronicles 5:10 as well as I Kings 8:9: "There was nothing in the ark except the two tablets of stone that Moses had placed there at Horeb, where the Lord made a covenant with the Israelites, when they came out of the land of Egypt."

Of course, we know from the Bible that the tablets Moses placed in the ark were the second set he had been given, since he had smashed the original pair when he first came down the mountain and found the people worshipping a golden calf (Deuteronomy 9:10-17). Some later religious authorities believe that the smashed first set of tablets was placed in the ark along with the intact second set of tablets. Other later authorities suggest that additional items were placed in the ark, such as the staff of Aaron and a vessel containing manna, but these are all disputed.

The subsequent history of the ark can be easily traced throughout the books of the Hebrew Bible, although there are some scholarly disputes about the details. At first, the ark was based in Gilgal. From there, it was taken out as needed and carried in front of the Israelite army during

Joshua's campaigns against Jericho (Joshua 4:19–6:27) and the other cities of the land, including Ai, Gibeon, Makkedah, Libnah, Lachish, Eglon, Hebron, Debir, and Hazor (7:1-14:6). Following these conquests, Joshua then moved the ark to Shiloh, when the "whole congregation of the Israelites assembled . . . and set up the tent of meeting [the Tabernacle] there" (18:1).

The ark remained at Shiloh for an unspecified period, from the time of Joshua's death until the Old Testament prophet Samuel was a child. At one point during this period, the ark is said to have been in the city of Bethel, where "Phinehas son of Eleazar, son of Aaron, ministered before it in those days" (Judges 20:26-28), but this was either temporary or, more likely, reflects an alternate tradition woven into the otherwise seamless biblical account. When we meet the ark again, it is resting comfortably within the "tent of meeting" or the "temple of the Lord" at Shiloh, where it is tended by Eli and his two sons (I Samuel 1:3–3:3).

The Israelites' habit of taking the ark to war with them eventually turned out to be not such a good idea. Sometime during the 11th century B.C., in a battle against the Philistines in the region of Ebenezer and Aphek during the time of Samuel, the Israelites were defeated. The two sons of Eli, who had brought the ark to the battlefield, were killed, and the ark itself was captured by the Philistines (I Samuel 4:1-11).

The Philistines only kept the ark for seven months, moving it from Ashdod to Gath to Ekron, three of their five major cities, as the inhabitants of those cities were in turn afflicted by tumors (I Samuel 5:5–6:1). Eventually they had enough and sent the ark back to the Israelites in the city of Beth-shemesh (I Samuel 6:1-18), since Shiloh had apparently been destroyed in the interim (Psalms 78:59-67; Jeremiah 26:6-9). It was soon moved to the city of Kiriath-jearim, where it remained at the house of Abinadab for the next 20 years (I Samuel 7:1-2).

Then when Saul came to the throne as the first king of Israel, toward the end of the 11th century B.C., the ark apparently began to travel with the army again, because we are told, "At that time the ark of God went with the Israelites" (14:18). Eventually, it came back to rest in Kiriath-jearim;

when David decided to make Jerusalem his capital city and to move the ark there, his men went to the house of Abinadab in Kiriath-jearim in order to fetch it (II Samuel 6:1-3; I Chronicles 13:1-8).

The Bible reports, however, that while the ark was being transported to Jerusalem, God struck Uzzah, a son of Abinadab, dead on the spot "because he reached out his hand to the ark" (II Samuel 6:6-7; I Chronicles 13:9-10). Much has been made of this incident by modern enthusiasts, who have sought to provide a scientific explanation for what transpired; some have gone so far as to suggest that the ark was some sort of electric generator and that Uzzah was electrocuted. This suggestion is completely without merit or support, but it remains a favorite topic, as we shall see later.

David was disheartened by this incident and instead of bringing it immediately to the city of Jerusalem, he left the ark at the house of Obed-edom the Gittite. It remained at Obed-edom's house for three months (II Samuel 6:10-11; I Chronicles 13:13-14) until David finally brought it to the city amid much rejoicing, leaping, dancing, shouting, and blowing of trumpets (II Samuel 6:12-15; I Chronicles 15:1-28; II Chronicles 1:4). Once within the city limits, the ark was placed inside the tent that David had pitched for it (the Tabernacle; see II Samuel 6:17 and I Chronicles 16:1). Here it stayed until Solomon built his famous Temple and moved the ark to its final resting place in the Temple's Holy of Holies in about 970 B.C. (I Kings 6:19, 8:1-13; II Chronicles 5:2-10).

The ark is not mentioned again in the Hebrew Bible until it surfaces during the time of King Josiah in the seventh century B.C. It is therefore possible that the ark simply remained in Solomon's Temple for some 360 years, although this is a matter of some debate. In any event, we are told in II Chronicles 35:1-3: "Josiah . . . said to the Levites who taught all Israel and who were holy to the Lord, 'Put the holy ark in the house that Solomon son of David, king of Israel, built; you need no longer carry it on your shoulders. Now serve the Lord your God and his people Israel.'"

It is not completely clear why the ark had to be put back into Solomon's Temple during Josiah's time, or where it had been, if indeed it had been removed from the Temple even temporarily. One scholar has suggested that the Ark of the Covenant had possibly been removed during the rule of King Manasseh (698 to 644 B.C.), when he set up an Asherah image in the Temple, but this may not have anything to do with Josiah's statement.

In any event, it seems that the last time the ark was seen by anyone was during the reign of King Josiah, who ruled from 639 to 609 B.C. In addition to the Book of II Chronicles, the Book of Jeremiah also mentions the ark during Josiah's time:

> The Lord said to me in the days of King Josiah. . . . And when you have multiplied and increased in the land, in those days, says the Lord, they shall no longer say, "The ark of the covenant of the Lord." It shall not come to mind, or be remembered, or missed; nor shall another one be made. At that time Jerusalem shall be called the throne of the Lord, and all nations shall gather to it, to the presence of the Lord in Jerusalem, and they shall no longer stubbornly follow their own evil will. In those days the house of Judah shall join the house of Israel, and together they shall come from the land of the north to the land that I gave your ancestors for a heritage. (Jeremiah 3:6, 16-18)

Unfortunately, the context and meaning of this passage are unclear. Many scholars interpret the passage as a prophecy of a time the ark will no longer be needed; others view it as a statement about the ark having been seen in Josiah's or Jeremiah's time.

The ark is not mentioned again in the Hebrew Bible, except in the Psalms. In Psalm 132:8, the reference simply says, "Rise up, O Lord, and go to your resting-place, you and the ark of your might." However, Psalm 78:60-61 may contain an allusion to the capture of the ark by the Philistines: "He abandoned his dwelling at Shiloh, the tent where he dwelt among mortals, and delivered his power to captivity, his glory to the hand of the foe."

Most important, the Bible does not list the ark among the treasures and other items that Nebuchadnezzar and the Neo-Babylonians took from

Jerusalem during their attacks on the city in 598, 597, and 587-586 B.C. The only items the Hebrew Bible mentions that Nebuchadnezzar carried away are unspecified "vessels." For instance, we are told that in 598 B.C., "Nebuchadnezzar . . . carried some of the vessels of the house of the Lord to Babylon and put them in his palace in Babylon" (II Chronicles 36:7). In 597 B.C., "King Nebuchadnezzar sent . . . to Babylon . . . precious vessels of the house of the Lord . . ." (36:10). Finally, in 586 B.C., "All the vessels of the house of God, large and small, and the treasures of the house of the Lord, and the treasures of the king and of his officials, all these he brought to Babylon. They burned the house of God, broke down the wall of Jerusalem, burned all its palaces with fire, and destroyed all its precious vessels" (36:18-19). Here we must note again that neither the ark nor any of the objects usually associated with it is mentioned.

Additionally, the ark is not referenced among the objects that the Jewish exiles brought back to Jerusalem upon their return from Babylon in 538 B.C., either in the biblical account or in any of the extant inscriptions of Nebuchadnezzar or Cyrus the Great. For example, we are told in the Book of Ezra that:

> King Cyrus himself brought out the vessels of the house of the Lord that Nebuchadnezzar had carried away from Jerusalem and placed in the house of his gods. King Cyrus of Persia had them released into the charge of Mithredath the treasurer, who counted them out to Sheshbazzar the prince of Judah. And this was the inventory: gold basins, thirty; silver basins, one thousand; knives, twenty-nine; gold bowls, thirty; other silver bowls, four hundred and ten; other vessels, one thousand; the total of the gold and silver vessels was five thousand four hundred. All these Sheshbazzar brought up, when the exiles were brought up from Babylonia to Jerusalem. (Ezra 1:7-11)

Again, we must note that despite the list's minute detailing of the treasures, neither the ark nor any of its associated items is mentioned.

Thus, the last time the ark was definitely seen by anyone was when Solomon placed it within the Holy of Holies inside the Temple in Jerusalem during the tenth century B.C. If the mentions of the ark in II Chronicles and Jeremiah are considered to be true contemporary references to the ark during the time of Josiah, then we can say that it apparently sat in the Temple for some 360 years and was still there during the time of Josiah at the end of the seventh century B.C. However, if the mentions of the ark in II Chronicles and Jeremiah are discounted, as many scholars suggest, then the ark simply disappeared some time after the reign of Solomon. As Bezalel Porten, professor of Jewish history at the Hebrew University of Jerusalem says, "The mystery of the Ark stems from the silence of the Bible after we are told that it was placed in the Holy of Holies of Solomon's Temple (I Kings 8:6). Nowhere in the Bible, neither in the account of the Babylonian destruction of the Temple in 587/6 B.C.E. (II Kings 2:5), nor anywhere else, is there an indication of the fate of the ark. Over the years, its curious disappearance has given rise to a great deal of speculation."

There are, however, two additional mentions of the ark that are of great interest, if we can trust them. These are found in the Apocrypha— books that are not always included in our modern version of the Bible. In the Book of II Esdras, we are told that the Ark of the Covenant was "plundered" when Jerusalem was destroyed by the Neo-Babylonians in 586 B.C.:

> . . . the sorrow of Jerusalem. For you see how our sanctuary has been laid waste, our altar thrown down, our temple destroyed; our harp has been laid low, our song has been silenced, and our rejoicing has been ended; the light of our lampstand has been put out, the ark of our covenant has been plundered, our holy things have been polluted, and the name by which we are called has been almost profaned; our children have suffered abuse, our priests have been burned to death, our Levites have gone into captivity, our virgins have been defiled, and our wives have been ravished; our righteous men have been carried off, our little ones have been cast out, our young men have been enslaved and our strong men made powerless. (II Esdras 10:20-22)

The Neo-Babylonian attacks on Jerusalem eventually left the city in ruins and the Temple of Solomon completely destroyed, as depicted in this 19th-century painting by Eduard Bandemann.

In the Book of II Maccabees, however, we are told that the prophet Jeremiah secretly hid the Ark of the Covenant, along with other objects: "The prophet, having received an oracle, ordered that the tent and the ark should follow with him, and . . . he went out to the mountain where Moses had gone up and had seen the inheritance of God. Jeremiah came and found a cave-dwelling, and he brought there the tent and the ark and the altar of incense; then he sealed up the entrance" (II Maccabees 2:4-5). This would have occurred sometime after Josiah's death in 609 B.C. but before Jeremiah was taken off to Egypt following the destruction of Jerusalem and the Temple in 586 B.C.

This brief mention in II Maccabees has given rise to all sorts of speculation as to which mountain this was. This is probably a moot point, however, since most scholars interpret it as Mount Nebo, based on the description in Deuteronomy 34:1-4: "Then Moses went up from the plains of Moab to Mount Nebo, to the top of Pisgah, which is opposite Jericho, and the Lord showed him the whole land: Gilead as far as Dan, all Naphtali, the land of Ephraim and Manasseh, all the land of Judah as far as the Western Sea, the Negeb, and the Plain—that is, the valley of Jericho, the city of palm trees—as far as Zoar. The Lord said to him, 'This is the land of which I swore to Abraham, to Isaac, and to Jacob, saying, "I will give it to your descendants"; I have let you see it with your eyes, but you shall not cross over there.'" This, too, we shall soon discuss at greater length.

IN OUR REVIEW of the textual evidence, we may first note that the Ark of the Covenant is not mentioned in any contemporary extra-biblical references. Not one of the many enemies (or friends) of ancient Israel from the time of Moses through Solomon, or of ancient Judah from the time of Rehoboam through Josiah, ever mentions the ark, even in passing. Nor is it mentioned in the Hebrew Bible during the four centuries between Solomon and Nebuchadnezzar in connection with the many kings of Judah who were either threatened by enemies or had to dip into the Temple's coffers to pay off an enemy.

This is extremely surprising, because the biblical account tells us that the treasures kept in Solomon's Temple were plundered at least eight times between 970 and 586 B.C. According to the Bible, the Temple was (1) either looted by Shishak or used by Rehoboam to bribe Shishak in 925 B.C.; (2) used by Asa of Judah to bribe Ben-Hadad of Aram-Damascus in 875 B.C.; (3) either looted by Hazael of Aram-Damascus or used by Jehoash of Judah to bribe Hazael in 800 B.C.; (4) looted by Jehoash of Israel in 785 B.C.; (5) used by Ahaz of Judah to bribe Tiglath-pileser III of Assyria in 734 B.C.; (6) either looted by Sennacherib of Assyria or used by Hezekiah of Judah to bribe Sennacherib in 701 B.C.; (7) looted by Nebuchadnezzar of Babylonia in 598/597 B.C.; and (8) looted again by Nebuchadnezzar in 587/586 B.C.

If either Shishak, Hazael, Jehoash, or Sennacherib succeeded in looting the Temple, rather than agreeing to be paid off via a bribe, then the ark could have disappeared in either 925, 800, 785, or 701 B.C., rather than in the more commonly suggested years of 597 or 586 B.C. at the hands of Nebuchadnezzar. In fact, several of these possibilities have been investigated, or at least suggested by enthusiasts—with Shishak being a particular favorite. But if Shishak had taken the ark, we would expect to find a mention of it in Egyptian inscriptions, which we have not.

In fact, the ark is only mentioned in a few extra-biblical sources, the most important of which are an Ethiopian legend and three rabbinical accounts, all written centuries after its disappearance. Two of these rabbinical accounts are in the Talmud—the rabbinic discussions pertaining to Jewish law, ethics, customs, and history, compiled between the first and fifth centuries A.D.—when the rabbinical authorities were musing over its disappearance. The third is found in the Mishneh Torah, the code of Jewish law written by the famous Rabbi Maimonides about 800 years ago (during the late 12th century A.D.), which is followed by many Orthodox Jews today, particularly the Chabad Hasim.

The first reference in the Talmud is essentially a footnote to a statement made about a priest who was in the Temple's Sanctuary and "noticed that one of the paving-stones on one place appeared different from the others. He went out to tell others of it; but he had not yet finished speaking, when he gave up the ghost; thereby it was known to a certainty that the ark of the covenant was hidden there." A note after the words "ark of the covenant" explains:

> The ark was hidden during the existence of the first Temple in order to save it from the Babylonians, after all hope had been abandoned, and its hiding-place was underground. The priests who subsequently took charge probably noticed some sign made by the former generation when the ark was hidden, and this particular priest died as a consequence of his attempt to reveal the secret. (*Shekalim* 6:1-2)

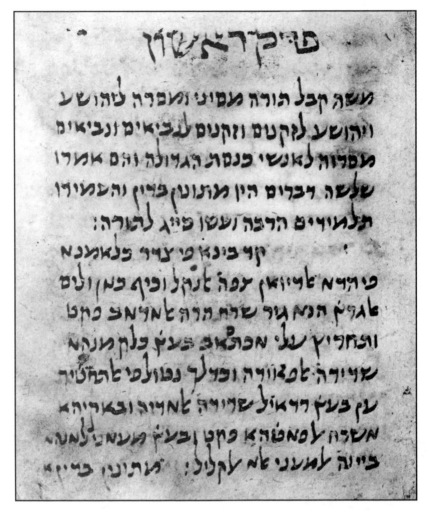

The whereabouts of the Ark of the Covenant have been a source of discussion for more than 2,000 years, including by Maimonides, whose Mishnah Torah manuscript is pictured here.

The second reference in the Talmud is found in a lengthy discussion concerning the location of the ark (*Yoma* 53b–54a). Here, the rabbis note that several different opinions had been expressed as to its location: Some argued that it had been carried off to Babylon by Nebuchadnezzar; others argued that it had been hidden by Josiah; still others argued that it was concealed within or underneath the Temple itself. In the end, despite the lengthy discussion, the rabbis were unable to reach a consensus or conclusion.

As for the reference found in Maimonides's Mishneh Torah, we are told: "When King Solomon built the Holy Temple, knowing that it was destined to be destroyed, he built a place in which to hide the Ark, [at the end of] hidden, deep, winding passageways. It was there that King Josiah placed the Ark twenty-two years before the Temple's destruction, as related in the Book of Chronicles" (Mishneh Torah, *Laws of the Holy Temple* 4:1). We do not know where Maimonides got his information, particularly the idea that Josiah placed the ark in a hidden location within the Temple or Temple Mount "twenty-two years before the Temple's destruction."

We must be careful when evaluating such declarations, particularly because counting back 22 years before the Temple's destruction in 586 B.C. brings us to 608 B.C. And Josiah could not have hidden the ark in 608 B.C., because he was killed in a battle at Megiddo one year earlier, in 609 B.C. So at the very least we must correct Maimonides's chronology—unless we suggest that Maimonides was counting backward from the beginning of the siege of Jerusalem in 587 B.C., rather than the end in 586 B.C. If so, then 22 years earlier would have been precisely 609 B.C., and we could argue that Josiah hid the ark before he met the Egyptians at Megiddo and was killed in battle.

It is precisely because of these late declarations in the Talmud and the Mishneh Torah—especially one reference during the discussion in the Talmud to I Kings 8:8 where it says, "The poles were so long that the ends of the poles were seen from the holy place in front of the inner sanctuary; but they could not be seen from outside; *they are there to this day*" (emphasis added)—that many Orthodox Jews and others believe that the ark is hidden in a subterranean chamber or vault under the Temple Mount. On the other hand, as we shall see, a minority of people believe it was carried off to Babylon by Nebuchadnezzar.

In addition, there is a discussion concerning the whereabouts of the ark in the Ethiopian *Kebra Nagast (Book of the Glory of Kings),* now well known to all ark seekers because of Graham Hancock's best-selling book, *The Sign and the Seal.* The *Kebra Nagast* has given rise to the belief that the ark is in Aksum, Ethiopia. It contains a description of how Solomon and the Queen of Sheba met; it also claims that the ark was brought back to Ethiopia by Prince Menelik I (a son born of the amorous union between King Solomon and the Queen of Sheba) after his journey to visit Solomon. We will discuss this possibility further as well.

––––––––––

So far we have looked extensively at the biblical account of the ark's history, from its creation to its ultimate disappearance sometime between the time of Solomon in 970 B.C. and Nebuchadnezzar in 586 B.C. We have also briefly discussed the available extra-biblical literary data. But is there any archaeological evidence to help trace the journey of the Ark of the Covenant, to confirm its time in Solomon's Temple, or to help determine where it is now?

We will discuss the various suggestions made by enthusiasts searching for the ark, as well as the claims of those who believe they have already found it, some of which involve archaeology. But in terms of tracing the path of the ark before it came to rest in Jerusalem, the short answer is that we have no real archaeological evidence. This is not surprising, for we are almost never told where in the various cities the ark was kept. Even in those few instances when we are given a specific location, such as the house of Abinadab in the city of Kiriath-jearim, where the ark remained for 20 years, we have not been able to find and excavate the specific location, despite occasional claims to the contrary.

In terms of confirming the length of its stay in Solomon's Temple, however, we may be able to use some archaeology. Even here, though, we are at a tremendous disadvantage, since no authorized excavations have been conducted on the Temple Mount by professional archaeologists in recent decades. The closest that we get to such excavations are the amateur explorations by British, French, and American explorers during the 1800s, the Israeli excavations around and nearby the Temple Mount during the past 50 years (including the excavations by Benjamin Mazar and now Eilat Mazar, as well as the tourist tunnel running along the Western Wall), and the illegal digging conducted by the Islamic Waqf in the late 20th century, during the construction of the new Marwani mosque.

From the early amateur explorations by people such as Frederick Catherwood, James Barclay, Charles Wilson, and Charles Warren, we have records of the "vast network of reservoirs" that lie beneath the Temple Mount, including the spot below where the First and Second Temples once stood and where the modern Dome of the Rock now stands. These have not been entered, at least officially, for decades, but they do lend support to the possibility that the ark could have been hidden below the Temple in antiquity.

Neither the excavations nor the illegal digging have helped us ascertain whether the ark was on the Temple Mount, but they do provide circumstantial evidence that Solomon's Temple was located there. For example, during the sifting of the dumped debris from the Temple Mount, the team led by Israeli archaeologists Gabriel Barkai and Tzachi Zweig found "a First Temple period bulla, or seal impression, containing ancient Hebrew writing, which may have belonged to a well-known family of priests mentioned in the Book of Jeremiah." Such findings also help discount the political statements by Yasser Arafat and other Islamic leaders that Solomon's Temple was not located in Jerusalem—claims that can be dismissed outright, as several scholars (including myself) have shown.

Moreover, in his recent book, *The Quest: Revealing the Temple Mount in Jerusalem,* Leen Ritmeyer, an architect who has participated in excavations in Jerusalem for more than 30 years (and who wrote his Ph.D. thesis on "The Architectural Development of the Temple Mount in Jerusalem" at the University of Manchester), speculates on the Ark of the Covenant's original location on the Temple Mount. He identifies a rectangular depression cut into the actual rock (inside the Dome of the Rock) as the place the ark could have stood within the Holy of Holies in Solomon's Temple, and suggests that the flat area would have stopped the ark from wobbling "in an undignified manner." Of course, there is no way to know whether Ritmeyer is correct, but it is an interesting speculation nevertheless.

Finally, in reviewing the archaeological evidence, we should discuss the ark's very nature. The ark was specifically built as a container to hold the tablets that Moses brought down from Mount Sinai. In this regard, it closely resembles other such containers found in the ancient Near East. Some of these, such as one well-known wooden chest found in the tomb of Tutankhamun in Egypt, were even equipped with long poles to carry them, just as the ark was.

In short, the ark, and its use as a container, is certainly not out of place in the ancient Near East, especially in a culture like the Israelites', who had supposedly just emigrated from Egypt. Outlandish suggestions—such as the claim that the ark was a transmitter Moses used to talk to God (which comes to us courtesy of Erich von Däniken and his book *Chariots of the Gods*), or that it was a fearsome weapon that could be used to kill enemies on a battlefield (as seen in *Raiders of the Lost Ark*), or that it was an electric generator or transformer of some kind (which would provide a scientific explanation for why Uzzah, son of Abinadab, was killed instantly when he reached out to steady the ark)—all must be dismissed outright, because there is no evidence whatsoever for such claims.

———————

WHILE THERE ISN'T any direct archaeological evidence that can help us answer where the Ark of the Covenant is today or what happened to it, there is no shortage of suggestions made by enthusiasts. In fact, even though there is absolutely no solid evidence that the Ark of the Covenant still exists today, more theories have been suggested concerning the ark than for any of the other mysteries we have discussed.

So far, it has been claimed that the ark was hidden under the Temple Mount by either Solomon or Josiah; hidden on Mount Nebo or elsewhere in Jerusalem by Jeremiah; hidden in a Dead Sea cave at Qumran; carried off to Egypt by Shishak; carried off to Ethiopia by Menelik; carried off to Babylon or destroyed by Nebuchadnezzar; removed by Manasseh; buried

The Temple Mount in Jerusalem has a large number of reservoirs and chambers underneath where the Temple of Solomon stood. Could the ark be buried here?

buried underneath a Hamas training camp in the West Bank; or crated in a government warehouse in Washington, D.C. Are any of these based on fact or are they sheer speculation? Let us briefly go through each of these suggestions and see if any of them stand up to scrutiny.

Under the Temple Mount—One of the most popular hypotheses today is the one stating that the ark is presently in a secret chamber deep within the Temple Mount, underneath the present-day Dome of the Rock. Basing this claim on the references in II Chronicles, Jeremiah, II Maccabees, the Talmud, and the Mishneh Torah, devotees of the various versions of this theory believe that the ark was hidden either by Solomon immediately after moving it into the Temple in the tenth century B.C., by Josiah sometime during his reign toward the end of the seventh century B.C., or by Jeremiah immediately before the Neo-Babylonian destruction of the Temple in 586 B.C.

For example, the Temple Institute, an ultra-Orthodox Jewish group based in Jerusalem that is dedicated to rebuilding the Temple, says Josiah hid the ark in a special place prepared by Solomon within the bowels of the Temple Mount. They say further, "This location is recorded in our sources, and today, there are those who know exactly where this chamber is. And we know that the ark is still there, undisturbed, and waiting for the day when it will be revealed."

There are several stories circulating that claim digs have been conducted under the Temple Mount in search of the ark, and that the ark has been found there. The most famous story claims that during the excavations of the present Western Wall tunnel in the early 1980s, two rabbis noticed water seeping from a wall. Moving a stone, they found a vaulted chamber, and then a second, lower, chamber in which they either saw or expected to see the Ark of the Covenant, along with the Table of Shewbread and the seven-branched candelabra. Before they could remove the objects or even record their existence, however, the Islamic authorities sealed up the entrance to the chambers.

Of course, the story has never been fully documented or confirmed by official authorities. The closest that we can get to a semiofficial statement is along the lines of a mention that Leen Ritmeyer made in his book *The Quest*. Ritmeyer says, "In 1981 workers of the Religious Affairs Ministry carried out a dig under the Temple Mount in search of the Ark. However, when this caused disturbances among the Arab population, the project was aborted." In his book *Searching for the Ark of the Covenant*, however, Randall Price provides details of an unofficial investigation that he conducted in the early 1990s, including interviews with several of the rabbis who were reportedly involved. Price's interviews document that the rabbis differ in the details of their stories and also diverge on whether they did or did not actually see the ark during their excavations.

There is no problem with this theory in and of itself, as it is based on an interpretation of the textual sources. The problem lies with the fact that nobody has been able to verify the claims that have been made about the existence of the objects in a chamber deep below the Temple Mount. We shall have to wait until permission is granted for archaeologists to investigate further, and that permission is unlikely to come anytime soon.

*Within the Western Wall tunnel, visitors can walk alongside masonry
dating to the time of Herod the Great.*

Elsewhere in Jerusalem—Another theory is that the ark was hidden in Jerusalem by Josiah, Jeremiah, or someone else, but not underneath the Temple Mount. Ron Wyatt, whom we have met in previous chapters, used the references in II Maccabees and other more dubious literary sources, including a late source called *The Paralipomena of Jeremiah*, to suggest that the Ark of the Covenant was hidden just before the destruction of the Temple in 586 B.C.

According to Wyatt's wife, he had never intended to search for the ark. As she writes on the Wyatt Archaeological Research Web site, "While waiting for his return flight to the United States [in 1978], Ron was walking along an ancient stone quarry, known to some as 'the Calvary Escarpment.' As he was walking, he began conversing with a local authority about Roman antiquities. At one point, they stopped walking, and Ron's left hand pointed to a site being used as a trash dump and he stated, 'That's Jeremiah's Grotto and the Ark of the Covenant is in there.' Even though these words had come from his own mouth and his own hand had pointed, he had not consciously done or said these things. In fact, it was the first time he had ever thought about excavating for the Ark."

According to the Wyatt Archaeological Research Web site, after researching the biblical accounts, Ron Wyatt began excavating for the Ark of the Covenant the very next year, in January 1979, within a cave system located north of the Damascus Gate in Jerusalem. After three and a half years of work, Wyatt claimed to have found the ark in a subterranean cave, along with the Table of Shewbread, the Golden Altar of Incense, the Golden Censer, the seven-branched candelabra, a very large sword, an ephod, a miter with an ivory pomegranate on the tip, a brass shekel weight, numerous oil lamps, and a brass ring. The site also reports: "On the back of the Ark is a small open cubicle which still contains the 'Book of the Law' and is presumably the one Moses, himself, wrote. Ron found the Scrolls, written on animal skins, to be in perfect condition."

Wyatt himself was reportedly never able to retrace his steps, and few scholars, if any, have accepted Wyatt's claims. A preface posted on his Web site in a section about Wyatt's search for the Ark of the Covenant sums up the problems involved with his claims. Written by Richard Rives, president of Wyatt Archaeological Research, it states: "Ron's account of his discovery of the Ark of the Covenant cannot be confirmed and . . . recent exploration reveals unexplained discrepancies in that account. . . . Ron had no second witness and provided no conclusive evidence as to the location of the Ark of the Covenant; therefore, his account . . . makes perfect sense from a Biblical standpoint but it is not yet a proven fact." As of this moment, it remains to be seen whether Wyatt's claims will ever be proven.

Removed by Manasseh—In 1963, Menahem Haran, a respected biblical scholar at the Hebrew University of Jerusalem, suggested that Manasseh, King of Judah during the early seventh century B.C., may have removed the ark when he set up a statue of Asherah and pagan altars in the Temple (II Kings 21:4-7; II Chronicles 33:4-7).

The problem with this theory is that it makes little sense even if the biblical account is followed in total. First and foremost, the ark itself is never mentioned in the biblical passages connected with Manasseh. The Bible says only that Manasseh set up both an idol and pagan altars in the Temple. It says nothing about him removing the ark; that he might have done so is simply a hypothesis formulated by Haran.

The Book of II Kings 21:4-7 states: "He built altars in the house of the Lord. . . . He built altars for all the host of heaven in the two courts of the house of the Lord. . . . The carved image of Asherah that he had made he set in the house of which the Lord said to David and to his son Solomon, 'In this house, and in Jerusalem, which I have chosen out of all the tribes of Israel, I will put my name for ever.'" (See also II Chronicles 33:4-7.) However, after Manasseh had been carried off to Babylon by the Assyrians and subsequently returned to Jerusalem, the biblical account simply says, "He took away the foreign gods and the idol from the house of the Lord, and all the altars that he had built on the mountain of the house of the Lord and in Jerusalem, and he threw them out of the city" (II Chronicles 33:15).

The ark is, once again, not mentioned in these passages, and yet surely it would have been had Manasseh moved the ark out in the first place and

According to Ethiopian lore, the ark was brought from Jerusalem by Menelik I to Ethiopia, where it is alleged to reside at this Coptic church, Our Lady Mary of Zion, in Aksum.

then brought it back in once he removed the idol and the altars. Either way, this is a quintessential example of an "argument from silence," which is always a dangerous type of argument to base a hypothesis on.

Ethiopia—One of the most popular theories today suggests that the ark is in Aksum, Ethiopia. The tradition originates in a story—really, a legend—related in the Ethiopian *Kebra Nagast (Book of the Glory of Kings)*. The book's origins are unclear; many scholars believe it was written in the 14th century A.D., but some say it could have been written as early as the 6th century A.D.

According to this tale, Solomon and Sheba had a son named David (but later more commonly referred to as Menelik I). David, or Menelik I, visited his father in Jerusalem, and upon departing for Ethiopia, took the ark with him to Aksum. There are numerous versions of this tale, each concerned with a different place the ark stopped before completing its journey to Aksum. It is now reportedly kept in a treasury near the Church of Our Lady Mary of Zion, but its actual presence there cannot be confirmed, for only the head priest of the church is allowed inside to see it.

The idea that the ark is in Aksum, Ethiopia, was resuscitated in 1992 by Graham Hancock, a former journalist who used to write for the London *Economist.* In his book *The Sign and the Seal: The Quest for the Lost Ark of the Covenant,* Hancock combines Haran's suggestion that the ark was removed from the Temple during the reign of Manasseh with the Ethiopian legend recorded in the *Kebra Nagast.* Hancock suggests that Menelik and his party did not take the ark from Jerusalem; instead it was removed from the Temple during the reign of King Manasseh, subsequently taken to Egypt, where it made its way to Elephantine Island, and eventually ended up in a church in Aksum, Ethiopia.

Hancock's theory was not universally well received by scholars, but it received much media attention and airplay on cable television. One proponent, however, was Bob Cornuke, the private investigator turned biblical investigator whom we have met in previous chapters. Cornuke essentially retraced Hancock's steps to see whether he agreed with the theory, but Cornuke's book is more of a first-person adventure story and makes Hancock's volume seem almost scholarly by comparison.

There are a number of problems with these hypotheses that state that somehow the ark was moved from Jerusalem to Aksum, Ethiopia. Nevertheless, these problems pale in comparison to the fact that there is no way to test Hancock's (and Cornuke's) ultimate conclusion, since no one in recent years has been able to enter the building in Ethiopia that supposedly houses the Ark of the Covenant.

When Hancock's book was first published, however, an article in the *Los Angeles Times* quoted Edward Ullendorff, a retired professor of Ethiopian Studies at the University of London as saying: "I've seen it. There was no problem getting access when I saw it in 1941. . . . They have a wooden box, but it's empty. . . . Middle to late medieval construction, when these were fabricated ad hoc." Ullendorff's statement seems enough to quash the speculation generated by Hancock's and Cornuke's expeditions, but the final word debunking their Ethiopian hypothesis was published posthumously in 2005 by noted Ethiopian scholar Stuart Munro-Hay in his book entitled *The Quest for the Ark of the Covenant: The True History of the Tablets of Moses,* in which Munro-Hay systematically addressed each of the points raised by Hancock and ultimately concluded that it was not the original Ark of the Covenant that lay within the building at Aksum.

Mount Nebo—In 1981, Tom Crotser, founder of the Institute for Restoring Ancient History, led an expedition to find the ark just months after the movie *Raiders of the Lost Ark* had been released. He followed the reference in II Maccabees 2:1-5 that claims Jeremiah hid the Ark of the Covenant on Mount Nebo in Jordan. In his search, Crotser also relied upon the notes and drawings of an earlier American explorer, Antonia F. Futterer, who had searched for the ark in that area in 1927. On October 30, 1981, Crotser and his team announced that they had found the ark, which they described as a gold-covered rectangular box, in a cave on Mount Pisgah (Mount Nebo), and that they had taken numerous photographs.

The story was picked up by UPI and was published in newspapers across the United States. Many scholars were skeptical because Crotser and his group had previously claimed to have found Noah's ark, the Tower of Babel, the city of Adam, and the great stone of Abel. *Biblical Archaeology Review* magazine asked the eminent archaeologist Siegfried H. Horn, a professor at Andrews University, to investigate Crotser's claims, and then published a story about Crotser and his findings.

Horn reported that, of all Crotser's pictures, only two showed anything; the rest were blank. Of the two pictures, *Biblical Archaeology Review* said, one "is fuzzy but does depict a chamber with a yellow box in the center. The other slide is quite good, according to Horn, and gives a clear front view of the box." Horn also noted, however, that there was a nail with a modern looking head in the upper right corner of the face of the box and that the metal of the box appeared to be machine-worked. In his opinion, whatever it was that Crotser had found was not an ancient artifact, and was therefore not the Ark of the Covenant.

Dead Sea Region—Vendyl Jones, a longtime enthusiast of biblical archaeology from Texas and founder of the Vendyl Jones Research Institute (VJRI), linked together three sources to formulate the hypothesis that the ark was hidden, not on Mount Nebo, but on the other side of the Dead Sea in the caves at Qumran, which also held the famous Dead Sea Scrolls. Jones linked the reference in II Maccabees, which states that Jeremiah hid the Ark of the Covenant, with the famous Copper Scroll that was discovered in Dead Sea Scroll Cave 3 and a previously unknown rabbinical text called *Emek Ha Melek (Valley of the Kings),* which was supposedly first published in 1648 by Rabbi Naftali Ben Ya'acov Elchanon. Using these sources, Jones claimed the ark was hidden in a "Cave with Two Columns, near the River of the Dome" and began a series of explorations and excavations in the region near Qumran.

At Qumran in April 1988, Jones and his team claimed they had found the Shemen Afarshimon—the holy anointing oil—from the Temple. In 1992, Jones also claimed to find 600 pounds of reddish organic material that he said was a compound of eleven ingredients found in the holy incense from the Temple. In both cases, scholars met his claims primarily with skepticism. Then, in 2005, he was quoted as saying that the Ark of the Covenant would be discovered by August 14 of that year (on Tisha B'Av, a day of mourning in the Jewish tradition). He did not discover it by that date. Later, a correction was posted on his Web site, stating that he had been misquoted and that he had actually said "it would be very appropriate *if* he could discover the Ark by Tisha B'Av."

Egypt (Valley of the Kings)—Using the same three sources as Vendyl Jones, Andis Kaulins, a German lawyer with a law degree from Stanford University, claims that Jeremiah hid the ark and that now it lies in the Valley of the Kings in Egypt, specifically in the tomb of King Tutankhamun. In fact, he claims that the portable chest with accompanying poles found in King Tut's tomb, which we mentioned earlier, is not only similar to the ark, it *is* the Ark of the Covenant.

Kaulins's claims, as far as I can tell, can only be found on the Internet. He is apparently the owner and operator of four Web sites and nearly fifty Internet blogs that feature topics ranging from archaeology to law, golf, and museums. Kaulins's own Web site states that he is "the best in the world—ever—at what I do, which is decipherment work." However, he never addresses the most important question of all: How did the ark get all the way to Egypt and into the tomb of King Tut, in light of the fact that Tut died toward the end of the 14th century B.C., more than 700 years before the time of Jeremiah?

Carried off by Shishak—There is a reference in I Kings 14:25-26 that reads: "In the fifth year of King Rehoboam, King Shishak of Egypt came up against Jerusalem; he took away the treasures of the house of the Lord and the treasures of the king's house; he took everything." (See also II Chronicles 12:2-9.) This looting would have taken place about 925 B.C. and is probably the same invasion that is recorded by the Pharaoh Shoshenq on the wall of the Temple of Amon at Karnak in Egypt.

It is quite possible that Shishak carried off the Ark of the Covenant at this point, since it was the first time after Solomon's rule that the city of Jerusalem had come under attack. Moreover, it would explain why the ark was never mentioned again in the biblical account, for the event occurred within a few years of Solomon's death.

This is known as the "Indiana Jones" theory, since the hypothesis that Shishak had taken the ark back to Egypt, and specifically to the site of Tanis, was the underlying premise of the 1981 film *Raiders of the Lost Ark,* created by Steven Spielberg and George Lucas. Few scholars seriously believe that Shishak actually carried off the ark, however, and not just because the biblical account fails to mention such an event. There is also no mention of the ark in any of Shoshenq's own inscriptions or in any traditions in Egypt dating to that period. Moreover, the primary Egyptian inscription written by Pharaoh Shoshenq detailing his campaign in Canaan—the account carved into the wall of the Temple of Amon at Karnak—does not seem to mention Jerusalem. There are also no other

*Pharaoh Shoshenq left an inscription recording his campaign in the lands
of Israel and Judah after the death of Solomon.*

extra-biblical inscriptions to corroborate the biblical account that Shishak
even attacked Jerusalem, let alone captured it.

Nevertheless, Michael S. Sanders, the self-taught "Biblical Scholar
of Archaeology, Egyptology and Assyriology" we met earlier, says that
Shishak carried off the ark, but that "its secret burial site could be at a
terrorist stronghold on the West Bank." Once again enlisting the use of
NASA satellite images, as he did in his quests to find the Garden of Eden,
Noah's ark, and Sodom and Gomorrah, as well as documents in the British
Museum and elsewhere, Sanders suggests that the ark is buried near a vil-
lage called Djahiriya in the Judean hills, in an area reportedly known as a
Hamas training ground.

Sanders says, "It is in very dangerous territory, but it must be worth the
risk. We believe that we may have found the configuration of an Egyptian
temple and it is under there that we will dig for the Ark. There will be
archaeologists with us, but the search for the Ark is bound to be more

of a treasure hunt than a classical archaeological dig." That statement is enough to send shivers up a professional archaeologist's spine, regardless of where the site is located or what modern facilities might be built above it today. Fortunately, Sanders hasn't "yet received permission to start an excavation." If and when he does, let us hope that it is less like a treasure hunt and more like a typical archaeological dig, just in case anything important is actually found.

We should also remember that in addition to Shishak's raid, there are at least three other instances in which the Temple might have been looted between the time of Solomon and Nebuchadnezzar. As we noted earlier, if either Hazael, Jehoash, or Sennacherib succeeded in looting the Temple (rather than being bought off via a bribe), then the ark could have disappeared in either 800, 785, or 701 B.C., rather than in the more commonly suggested years of 597 or 586 B.C. at the hands of Nebuchadnezzar. However, as Herbert G. May, professor of Old Testament language and literature at the Oberlin Graduate School of Theology (and a participant in the University of Chicago's excavations at Megiddo), wrote in 1936:

> That the Jerusalem ark still existed at the time of Josiah is hardly to be doubted. The fact that it is not mentioned in the account of the sack of the Temple in 586 B.C. is insufficient reason for assuming that it must have disappeared earlier at the time when Shishak sacked the Temple of its treasures in the reign of Rehoboam, or when the wealth of the Temple was seized at the time of Asa and Ben-Hadad, or Amaziah and Jehoahaz, or Ahaz and Tiglath Pileser. If the ark did disappear before 586, it would seem to have done so between 621 and 586.

Destroyed by Nebuchadnezzar—Among the most likely hypotheses—but one that is not followed by most enthusiasts because it would mean the ark is lost forever—is that Nebuchadnezzar and the Neo-Babylonians destroyed the Ark of the Covenant during their destruction of the Temple in 586 B.C. The apocryphal Book of II Esdras 10:20-22 implies that the ark was either destroyed or looted by the Neo-Babylonians ("Our sanctuary has been laid waste, our altar thrown down, our temple destroyed . . . the ark of our covenant has been plundered"), and the rabbinical authorities in the Talmud (*Yoma* 53b–54a) further debate this possibility.

The fact that there is no mention of the ark either among the objects carried off by Nebuchadnezzar or subsequently returned by Cyrus the Great (see II Chronicles 36:7, 10, 18-19 and Ezra 1:7-11) strongly suggests that the Neo-Babylonians are more likely to have destroyed it than carried it off. Of course, we could also argue using some of the sources we mentioned earlier that the ark was no longer in the Temple by the time the Neo-Babylonians destroyed the building, so even this suggestion is hypothetical, but it is also entirely possible.

THE ARK OF THE COVENANT can be framed within the context of the entire history of the Israelites and the Judeans, from the time of Moses in the 13th century B.C. (or the 15th century B.C., as we have mentioned) through the capture of Jerusalem, the destruction of the Temple, and the Babylonian Exile in 586 B.C. How much of this grand sweep of history we include in our study depends upon when we believe the ark disappeared. At the very least, we should include the last part of the journey from Egypt (that is, the final stages of the Exodus, after Moses received the Ten Commandments); the entire period of the Israelite conquest of Canaan; the entire period of the Judges and the United Monarchy of David and Solomon; and part, if not all, of the era of the Divided Kingdoms of Israel and Judah. In short, we could write a book on the entire history of ancient Israel and Judah, as told from the point of view of the Ark of the Covenant.

As a result, it is out of the question to discuss its complete historical context, as we have done with previous mysteries (and will do with the Ten Lost Tribes in chapter 7). What we can do, however, is point out that the creation of the ark is integrally connected to the story of the Exodus, and its early history is tied to the Israelite conquest of Canaan, whose historical context we discussed in chapters 4 and 5. And the final part of its history, up to the point where we essentially lose sight of it in the Temple, is directly linked to the reigns of David and Solomon.

Thus, we should mention here that David and Solomon themselves, and their territorial expansions, have been severely called into question over the past decade or more. The biblical minimalists such as Niels Peter Lemche, Thomas L. Thompson, Philip R. Davies, and Keith W. Whitelam, all now either at the University of Copenhagen or the University of Sheffield, were especially vocal early on, with some even suggesting that David (and perhaps Solomon as well) never even existed and were simply figments of later writers' imaginations.

Such extreme suggestions were silenced when fragments of an inscription mentioning the "House of David" (*Beit David* in Hebrew) were discovered at the site of Tel Dan in northern Israel in 1993 and 1994. The debate continues today, however, as to the extent of David's and Solomon's kingdoms: Did they in fact rule over a huge empire that stretched from the Euphrates to Egypt, as the biblical account suggests (I Kings 4:21), or were they simple tribal chieftains whose exploits were exaggerated by the later biblical writers?

We will not deal with this debate here, because it is still evolving and will ultimately be decided by additional archaeological excavations and further interpretations of new data being found at sites from Jerusalem to Megiddo and beyond. But we can suggest that any future discussions of the Ark of the Covenant may need to take into account the new positions reached by archaeologists, ancient historians, and biblical scholars concerning the reigns of David and Solomon, because it is clear that just as the early days of the ark are intertwined with the lives of Moses and Joshua, so are its middle days intertwined with the lives of David and Solomon.

———

To MY KNOWLEDGE, not a single professional archaeologist has ever gone in search of the Ark of the Covenant. To their credit, however, amateur enthusiasts have been exhaustively searching for the ark everywhere that ancient literary sources suggest it might be: underneath the Temple

Mount, on Mount Nebo, near Qumran, in Ethiopia, in Egypt, in the West Bank, or simply somewhere else in Jerusalem. There is not a single possibility that they have not investigated or speculated about, though all to no avail.

The problem does not usually reside in the locations for the ark that the enthusiasts suggest, because almost all of them are faithfully following at least one literary source. The rabbis looking beneath the Western Wall in Jerusalem followed the Babylonian Talmud and the Mishneh Torah. Tom Crotser followed II Maccabees, as did Ron Wyatt, although Wyatt also used other late and dubious sources as well, such as the *Paralipomena of Jeremiah.* Vendyl Jones followed II Maccabees, plus his interpretation of the Copper Scroll and the mysterious rabbinical text *Emek Ha Melek,* supposedly published in 1648. Andis Kaulins used the same three sources that Jones did. Graham Hancock and Bob Cornuke followed the Ethiopian story told in the *Kebra Nagast,* combined with an interpretation of the biblical accounts concerning Manasseh, first suggested by scholar Menahem Haran. And Michael Sanders followed the account in I Kings.

Where most of them have gone wrong, however, is in overstating their claims and conclusions, especially if they claim to have found the ark. In almost every single instance, their claims are not backed up by proof, or by any indisputable evidence for that matter. Kaulins's theory has chronological problems. Crotser's pictures are blurry and apparently show a modern nail in his ark. Nobody, including Ron Wyatt himself, has been able to retrace his steps to locate the ark again. Nobody has recently been able to get into the building in Ethiopia to see if Hancock and Cornuke are right. Nobody has been able to get under the Temple Mount to confirm the rabbis' story. Nobody has received permission to dig at the West Bank site to verify Sanders' theory. And no scholars were surprised when Vendyl Jones failed to find the ark by August 14, 2005.

Since no one has seen the ark since at least Josiah's time, I would venture to say that it is no longer in existence. In fact, if I had to really guess, I would argue that it was melted down or otherwise destroyed, certainly by the time of Nebuchadnezzar, if not long before. The only other conceivable possibility I see is that the ark is hidden or buried somewhere underneath the Temple Mount, but I think it is more likely that it was destroyed by Nebuchadnezzar's army in 586 B.C.

At a recent family reunion, a cousin I hadn't seen in 25 years came up to me and earnestly asked, "Is the Ark of the Covenant located underneath the Temple Mount, as the Talmud says?" When I told him that it probably was not, his face fell. I hastily amended my statement and said that while it probably wasn't there, there was no way to really tell until archaeologists could do further digging and exploration, which wouldn't happen in the foreseeable future. That seemed to make him happier, and we proceded to talk about other topics.

It is now time for us to move on and try to locate the Ten Lost Tribes of Israel. It might be easier to find them than the Ark of the Covenant . . . but then again, it might not.

THE TEN LOST TRIBES OF ISRAEL

Where are the Ten Lost Tribes of Israel?

Speculating on the whereabouts of the Ten Lost Tribes of Israel has been another longstanding tradition, popular for longer than the search for the Ark of the Covenant and the Holy Grail. Suggestions for where the tribes ended up have ranged from America and Britain to India and Africa—and virtually everywhere in between.

In order to investigate this mystery properly, we will need to explore the chain of events that led to the destruction of the northern kingdom of Israel at the hands of the Neo-Assyrians in 720 B.C. We shall also need to look at the Neo-Assyrian practice of deporting captured peoples to the far corners of their empire, paying particular attention to what happened in northern Israel during the period of Neo-Assyrian aggression from 733 to 720 B.C. Then, and only then, will we be in a position to answer the age-old questions concerning the Ten Lost Tribes of Israel: Where did they go and where are they now?

Before we begin, I should also note that in many ways, especially from an ancient historian's point of view, this is the most interesting and technical mystery we will explore. It offers us a chance to study some extra-biblical accounts written by contemporary Neo-Assyrian kings—the very ones the Bible accuses of having attacked the northern kingdom of Israel and created what we now call the missing Ten Lost Tribes—and wrestle with some of the

Neo-Assyrian kings came into contact with the northern kingdom of Israel from the mid-ninth century B.C. onward. This image appears on a fresco in the palace of Tiglath-pileser III.

problems that emerge when these sources are compared with the biblical account. We have not always had the chance to do this with previous mysteries, so it is a pleasure to be on firmer ground, because by this point the biblical account seems actually to reflect history as we know it from other independent sources (even if the Bible and these sources aren't always in complete agreement). From this vantage point, we can investigate the Ten Lost Tribes from a variety of angles and finally be able to utilize three separate and independent sources: the biblical account, the Neo-Assyrian inscriptions, and the archaeological remains.

If we begin by examining the account in the Hebrew Bible, it is clear that the end was in sight when the Neo-Assyrian King Tiglath-pileser III (who ruled from 744 to 727 B.C.) turned his attention to the northern kingdom of Israel and its capital city, Samaria. The first time the fighting occurred was during the reign of Menahem, probably in 738 B.C. According to the biblical account, Menahem paid Tiglath-pileser—whom the Bible calls "Pul" (probably his real name, as opposed to the adopted throne name Tiglath-pileser)—a large and perhaps exaggerated sum of money, most likely to help him secure his place on the throne. The Bible says, "King Pul [Tiglath-pileser III] of Assyria came against the land; Menahem gave Pul a thousand talents of silver, so that he might help him confirm his hold on the royal power. Menahem exacted the money from Israel, that is, from all the wealthy, fifty shekels of silver from each one, to give to the king of Assyria. So the king of Assyria turned back, and did not stay there in the land" (II Kings 15:17-20).

Just a few years later, Tiglath-pileser III attacked Israel during the reign of Pekah, around 733 B.C. This time Tiglath-pileser instigated the first known deportation from the northern kingdom of Israel, when the first members of the Ten Lost Tribes were carried off into exile. We are told in the Book of II Kings: "In the days of King Pekah of Israel, King Tiglath-pileser of Assyria came and captured Ijon, Abel-beth-maacah, Janoah, Kedesh, Hazor, Gilead, and Galilee, all the land of Naphtali; and he carried the people captive to Assyria" (15:27-29).

The account in I Chronicles provides more information: "So the God of Israel stirred up the spirit of King Pul of Assyria, the spirit of King Tiglath-pileser of Assyria, and he carried them away, namely, the Reubenites, the Gadites, and the half-tribe of Manasseh, and brought them to Halah, Habor, Hara, and the river Gozan, to this day" (5:26). We even learn the name of an Israelite chieftain who was carried off: "Beerah . . . whom King Tiglath-pileser of Assyria carried away into exile; he was a chieftain of the Reubenites" (5:6).

Then came Shalmaneser V, the successor to Tiglath-pileser III, who ruled Assyria from 727 to 722 B.C. He apparently attacked the northern kingdom of Israel twice during his reign. The first time, King Hoshea of Israel gave in right away and became Shalmaneser's vassal. But almost immediately, and for reasons that are unclear (but probably involve a revolt on Hoshea's part), Shalmaneser imprisoned Hoshea. The biblical account states:

> In the twelfth year of King Ahaz of Judah, Hoshea son of Elah began to reign in Samaria over Israel; he reigned for nine years. He did what was evil in the sight of the Lord, yet not like the kings of Israel who were before him. King Shalmaneser of Assyria came up against him; Hoshea became his vassal, and paid him tribute. But the king of Assyria found treachery in Hoshea; for he had sent messengers to King So of Egypt, and offered no tribute to the king of Assyria, as he had done year by year; therefore the king of Assyria confined him and imprisoned him. (II Kings 17:1-4)

We are then told that Shalmaneser returned to Israel and besieged the capital city of Samaria for three years before finally capturing it. At this point, he carried off numerous people into exile, where they most likely joined those who had been taken away by Tiglath-pileser III. The Hebrew Bible states:

> Then the king of Assyria invaded all the land and came to Samaria; for three years he besieged it. In the ninth year of Hoshea, the king of Assyria captured Samaria; he carried the Israelites away to Assyria. He placed them in Halah, on the Habor, the river of Gozan, and in the cities of the Medes. (II Kings 17:5-6)

These details are repeated soon after in the Book of II Kings (although this time in relation to the reign of Hezekiah of Judah):

> In the fourth year of King Hezekiah, which was the seventh year of King Hoshea son of Elah of Israel, King Shalmaneser of Assyria came up against Samaria, besieged it, and at the end of three years took it. In the sixth year

of Hezekiah, which was the ninth year of King Hoshea of Israel, Samaria was taken. The king of Assyria carried the Israelites away to Assyria, settled them in Halah, on the Habor, the river of Gozan, and in the cities of the Medes. (18:9-11)

To replace the deportees, we are told, "The king of Assyria brought people from Babylon, Cuthah, Avva, Hamath, and Sepharvaim, and placed them in the cities of Samaria in place of the people of Israel; they took possession of Samaria, and settled in its cities" (II Kings 17:24). Thus, the land was instantly repopulated by people from other areas controlled by the Neo-Assyrians (modern Syria and Iraq, as well as the Syro-Arabian desert). Those Israelites who were not deported reportedly intermarried with the new arrivals. They became the Samaritans, mentioned in both the Hebrew Bible and the New Testament.

In sum, according to the biblical account, Shalmaneser V attacked Samaria and the northern kingdom of Israel twice. The first time, he imprisoned King Hoshea. The second time, he besieged the city of Samaria for three years and eventually captured it. At that point, he "carried the Israelites away to Assyria . . . He placed them in Halah, on the Habor, the river of Gozan, and in the cities of the Medes" (II Kings 17:5-6).

We are not told, however, how many Israelites were deported. Moreover, the places in Assyria where Shalmaneser V deported the Israelites are nearly the same ones listed in I Chronicles 5:26, but in that case Tiglath-pileser III is given credit for sending the exiles to those places. Most important, the Bible does not really announce the end of the kingdom of Israel; it just seems to have simply happened, with little mention.

Is this really what took place? Was it really Shalmaneser V who destroyed the northern kingdom of Israel and sent the Ten Lost Tribes into oblivion? Or was someone (or something) else involved? Could the biblical writers have been pointing their fingers at the wrong party? And how many people were actually taken off into exile? Did all of the ten tribes get exiled, and did they really end up where Shalmaneser says they did? If so, are they still in those places today?

Clearly, before we can investigate the Ten Lost Tribes further, we must look at the extra-biblical textual sources and the archaeological data that is available.

WE CAN START our discussion of the extra-biblical material on a positive note: Tiglath-pileser III's own inscriptions confirm the biblical account of the separate interactions between Tiglath-pileser III and the two kings of Israel, Menahem and Pekah. One of these inscriptions says, "I received tribute from . . . Menahem of Samaria." Another says:

> As for Menahem I overwhelmed him like a snowstorm and he . . . fled like a bird, alone, and bowed to my feet. I returned him to his place and imposed tribute on him, to wit: gold, silver, linen garments with multicolored trimmings . . . I received from him. Israel . . . all its inhabitants and their possessions I led to Assyria. They overthrew their king Pehak and I placed Hoshea as king over them. I received from them 10 talents of gold, 1,000 talents of silver as their tribute and brought them to Assyria.

In additional inscriptions from his annals, Tiglath-pileser claimed that he spared only the city of Samaria, and captured and annexed the rest of the northern kingdom of Israel. We are finally also given the specific number of captives that he carried off into exile in Assyria: 13,520. And we can probably date his attack on Israel and Samaria to the year 733 B.C., according to the most recent scholarly discussions on the topic.

Thus, we can feel confident that we are in an era where the biblical account can be tested against historical inscriptions from other civilizations that interacted with the kingdoms of Israel and Judah during the early first millennium B.C. Unfortunately, we begin running into problems almost immediately. For example, in his inscriptions, Tiglath-pileser III does not state the specific locations in Assyria to which he carried off the Israelites; he only says "to Assyria." But what about the passage from the Book of

I Chronicles, which does list specific locations? As we have just noted, the exile locations listed in I Chronicles are virtually the same as those given in II Kings, including Halah, Habor, and Gozan. While it is possible that each set of deportations took the exiles off to the same destinations, biblical scholars consider it more likely that the passage in I Chronicles is a late addition to the Bible and that "the mention of the exile locations may be anachronistic or a confusion in transmission." As a result, the references in I Chronicles are usually ignored by most scholars, or relegated to a footnote, and we are left to wonder where in Assyria Tiglath-pileser III actually deposited his Israelite captives.

Comparing extra-biblical inscriptions of Shalmaneser V, successor to Tiglath-pileser III, to the biblical account has also given rise to some debate among biblical scholars, archaeologists, and ancient historians. The problem here is that, for some unknown reason, we have been left with no inscriptions of Shalmaneser V, and therefore have no confirmation by his own sources that he actually captured Samaria and deported some of the inhabitants of Israel's northern kingdom, as the biblical account states.

Fortunately, we do have the Babylonian Chronicles, a contemporary record kept by the Neo-Babylonian priests describing the chief events of each year for much of this period. These state: "On the twenty-fifth of the month Tebet [in 726 B.C.:] Shalmaneser ascended the throne in Assyria. . . . He ravaged [or ruined] Samaria." This would seem to provide confirmation of the biblical account, but some scholars see it only as a reference to his first attack, when he imprisoned Hoshea; they see no mention here, or any confirmation, of his second attack and besieging of Samaria. The same Babylonian Chronicles then tell us: "The fifth year [722]: Shalmaneser died in the month Tebet. For five years Shalmaneser ruled Akkad [Babylonia] and Assyria. On the twelfth day of the month Tebet, Sargon [II] ascended the throne in Assyria."

This is surprising, for the name Sargon II is nowhere to be found in the biblical account. He simply seems to be missing from the Hebrew Bible, though we know him well from other, extra-biblical inscriptions. He was indeed Shalmaneser V's successor, and he ruled Assyria from 722 to 705 B.C. Moreover, in the extra-biblical inscriptions it is Sargon II who claims credit for capturing the city of Samaria and deporting the inhabitants of the northern kingdom of Israel. Did he usurp the deeds of his predecessor or is something else going on? Who was responsible for the destruction of the northern kingdom and the deportation of its inhabitants, the Ten Lost Tribes of Israel?

At Sargon's palace in Khorsabad, Assyria, there are inscriptions recording his attack on Samaria and the exile of its inhabitants to Assyria. In addition, a wall relief in Room 5 of the palace may depict the city of Samaria and its defeated defenders. All of Sargon's inscriptions dealing with Israel's northern kingdom are linked to his campaign of 720 B.C. Three of the more relevant inscriptions read as follows:

I besieged and conquered Samaria . . . led away as booty 27,290 inhabitants of it. I formed from among them a contingent of 50 chariots and made remaining [inhabitants] assume their [social] positions. I installed over them an officer of mine and imposed upon them the tribute of the former king.

[The Sa]marians with a king [hostile to] me consorted not to do service and not to bring tribute and they did battle. In the strength of the great gods, my lords I clashed with them, [2]7,280 people with their chariots and the gods they trust, as spoil I counted, 200 chariots (as) my royal muster I mustered from among them. The rest of them I caused to take their dwelling in the midst of Assyria. The city of Samaria I restored, and greater than before I caused it to become. People of lands conquered by my two hands I brought within it; my officer as prefect over them I placed, and together with the people of Assyria I counted them.

The tribes of Tamud, Ibadid, Marsimanu and Haiapa, distant Arabs, who inhabit the desert, who know neither high nor low officials, and who had not brought their tribute to any king—with the weapon of the god Assur, my lord, I struck them down [in 716 B.C.], the remnant of them I deported and settled them in Samaria.

Israelites carried off into exile by the Neo-Assyrians may well have ended up in major cities such as Nineveh, where these statues stood at the gates of King Sargon II's palace.

These tell us all we need to know. In eight separate inscriptions, Sargon II claims that he besieged and conquered Samaria. Furthermore, he states that he carried off a total of 27,280 people into exile in Assyria. This probably represents the total number of deportees from both Samaria and the entire northern kingdom (the first number given, 27,290, is corrected in the other inscriptions). Later, he repopulated Samaria with "distant Arabs" he had conquered elsewhere, rebuilt Samaria and its surrounding area, and made it into an Assyrian province, known as Samerina, complete with an appointed governor.

THERE IS NO QUESTION that the Neo-Assyrians destroyed the northern kingdom of Israel and deported its inhabitants into exile, but we are still left with the question of who did it. The Bible never mentions Sargon II, instead giving credit (or blame) to Shalmaneser V. Was it Shalmaneser V, as per the biblical account, or was it Sargon II, as per his own extra-biblical inscriptions? Did Sargon II claim credit for something his immediate predecessor did, or did the Bible get its facts mixed up?

After decades of scholarly debate, many possible suggestions have been put forward, but the problem has never been resolved. Of these suggestions, three hypotheses seem the most probable. The first suggests that while the biblical account does leave out Sargon II, the final capture of Samaria, and the downfall of Israel's northern kingdom, it is correct in what it says about Shalmaneser V—that he, too, captured Samaria and exiled some of its inhabitants. If this is the case, then Samaria was besieged and captured twice (probably in 722 B.C. and 720 B.C.) and there were two separate deportations within a span of just a few years. But here, the biblical account would be guilty of omitting key events—completely leaving out Sargon II, the second capture of the city in 720 B.C., and the final ending to the northern kingdom of Israel.

Eminent scholars Mordechai Cogan and Hayim Tadmor have put forth an alternative version of this first hypothesis in the most recent scholarly translation and commentary on the Book of II Kings. They argue that the account does not stop short, but rather that a later editor was guilty of "telescoping" the events and combining the two sieges into one. Thus, they say, "[The text] reads as if the same king of Assyria besieged Samaria . . . took it . . . and exiled Israel to Assyria. Historically, however, this construing of the text cannot stand. Two kings of Assyria oversaw the events referred to in v. 6; Shalmaneser V captured Samaria; Sargon II exiled Israel. . . . The present telescoping of events might be as early as the Deuteronomic editing of Kings [that is, in the sixth century B.C.]." They continue, "The Assyrian account . . . makes it clear that the biblical account . . . has telescoped two events: the fall of Samaria to Shalmaneser in 722, after the three-year siege; and the captivity of Samaria two years later in 720 by Sargon."

The second hypothesis tries to meld the biblical and extra-biblical accounts into a coherent whole by suggesting that there was only one siege but two Neo-Assyrian kings who were involved. It posits that Shalmaneser V began the siege, as the biblical account states, but then died (of natural causes) before he could conclude it. Sargon II then continued the siege, ended it by capturing the city and deporting the inhabitants in 720 B.C., and claimed credit for the entire episode, as recorded in his inscriptions.

The third hypothesis gives the Bible the most credit. Set out most recently by Nadav Na'aman, professor of Jewish history at Tel Aviv University, this suggestion contains three major points: Sargon II is indeed mentioned in the Bible, but not by name; Samaria was only besieged once, by Sargon II; and Shalmaneser V did not carry off any of the Israelites into exile—it was all Sargon II's doing.

How does Na'aman explain this? He simply suggests, like Cogan and Tadmor above, that the biblical account that mentions Shalmaneser in II Kings 17:1-6 is actually an account of two campaigns—that of Shalmaneser V (II Kings 17:1-4) and Sargon II (II Kings 17:5-6). However, according to Na'aman, rather than telescoping the two campaigns, the later editor kept them separate but simply didn't mention Sargon by name: He just referred to Sargon as "the king of Assyria." If Na'aman is correct, we only have to insert the words "Sargon II" and two commas into the biblical account in order for it to make sense and to give us the full story:

In the twelfth year of King Ahaz of Judah, Hoshea son of Elah began to reign in Samaria over Israel; he reigned for nine years. He did what was evil in the sight of the Lord, yet not like the kings of Israel who were before

Other Israelites carried off into exile by the Neo-Assyrians may well have ended up in the Zagros Mountains.

him. King Shalmaneser of Assyria came up against him; Hoshea became his vassal, and paid him tribute. But the king of Assyria found treachery in Hoshea; for he had sent messengers to King So of Egypt, and offered no tribute to the king of Assyria, as he had done year by year; therefore the king of Assyria confined him and imprisoned him. Then [Sargon II,] the king of Assyria[,] invaded all the land and came to Samaria; for three years he besieged it. In the ninth year of Hoshea, the king of Assyria captured Samaria; he carried the Israelites away to Assyria. He placed them in Halah, on the Habor, the river of Gozan, and in the cities of the Medes. (II Kings 17:1-6)

Na'aman concludes, "Sargon II is the king who conquered Samaria, annexed it to the Assyrian territory, deported its people and brought in others to take their place." If Na'aman is right, Shalmaneser V did interact with Israel and take Hoshea prisoner, but he did not besiege the city of Samaria for three years or carry off any inhabitants. More important, in this scenario, the Bible does not omit Sargon II; it simply doesn't name him, just as it never names the pharaoh of the Exodus. And it also has not left out the ending of the story. It is Sargon II who besieges Samaria, carries off the Ten Lost Tribes, and brings an end to the northern kingdom of Israel.

While I find Na'aman's suggestion to be an elegant solution to a complex problem, not all scholars support his interpretation. So the argument continues and will likely only be resolved by the discovery of additional textual inscriptions (Shalmaneser V's in particular would be most helpful).

What about the Ten Lost Tribes? Taking into account both the biblical and the extra-biblical evidence, we know that between the efforts of Tiglath-pileser III, Shalmaneser V, and Sargon II, more than 40,000 people were carried off from 733 to 720 B.C. (13,520 people in the first conquest and 27,280 in the second). Moreover, we know that these captives were exiled to Assyria, with a few specific locations given in the biblical account.

As we have mentioned, the Bible says the deported members of the Ten Tribes were sent off into exile "in Halah, on the Habor, the river of Gozan, and in the cities of the Medes." Although there has been much speculation about where these areas are, scholars are confident that they were all in Mesopotamia, within the core of the Assyrian Empire proper. For instance, Halah was "a district north of Nineveh" (modern Iraq); Gozan was "situated on one of the branches of the Habor river in northern Mesopotamia" (modern Syria) and is probably identified with Tell Halaf; and the cities of the Medes "were located in the Zagros mountains" (modern Iraq).

If the biblical account in I Chronicles is considered accurate, then Tiglath-pileser III carried off the captives to the same locations in Assyria that Sargon II did (or Shalmaneser V, if we don't agree with Na'aman's suggestion). However, if we consider the account in I Chronicles to be a later, anachronistic addition to the biblical text, as many biblical scholars do, then we are simply left with one specific set of locations that Sargon II/Shalmaneser V carried the deportees off to, and a more general designation from II Kings of "Assyria" for Tiglath-pileser III's earlier captives. It is of interest to note, though, that these specific locations are only ever named in the Bible; the Neo-Assyrian inscriptions only say "to Assyria."

But were all members of the Ten Tribes really carried off into oblivion or did some remain behind? Is there any truth to the mystery of the Ten Lost Tribes? And when and where do we first hear about these Ten Lost Tribes, meaning at what point in history is the story first told?

This last question is probably the easiest to answer. Although they are not specifically called the "Ten Lost Tribes," references to the scattered peoples of Israel are found in the biblical books of the Latter Prophets: Isaiah, Jeremiah, and Ezekiel. The prophet Isaiah was active just after the northern kingdom of Israel had been destroyed by the Neo-Assyrians, while the Books of Jeremiah and Ezekiel were compiled soon after the destruction of Jerusalem and the Temple in 586 B.C. In fact, the Book of Isaiah contains an apparent reference to both the exiled Israelites (deported between 733 and 720 B.C.) and the exiled Judeans (deported in 701 B.C. and between 598 and 582 B.C.). It says, "On that day the Lord will extend his hand yet a second time to recover the remnant that is left of his people, from Assyria, from Egypt, from Pathros [Upper Egypt], from Ethiopia, from Elam [southwestern Iran], from Shinar [Babylonia], from Hamath [Syria], and from the coastlands of the sea [Greece and the Aegean]. He will raise a signal for the nations, and will assemble the outcasts of Israel, and gather the dispersed of Judah from the four corners of the earth" (Isaiah 11:11-12).

These biblical allusions by the prophets are most likely references to the Ten Lost Tribes. For more information about their whereabouts, however, we might also turn to a slightly later biblical source—though one we may not trust as much. Within the Apocrypha, there are two mentions of the deportations, both giving the credit to Shalmaneser V. One of these is found in the Book of Tobit, which is a fairly late source, written somewhere between 225 and 175 B.C.:

This book tells the story of Tobit . . . who in the days of King Shalmaneser of the Assyrians was taken into captivity from Thisbe, which is to the south of Kedesh Naphtali in Upper Galilee, above Asher toward the west, and north of Phogor. I, Tobit, walked in the ways of truth and righteousness all the days of my life. I performed many acts of charity for my kindred and my people who had gone with me in exile to Nineveh in the land of the Assyrians. (Tobit 1:1-9)

If we can trust this source, noting that the author attributes the exile to Shalmaneser V rather than to Sargon II, then we can add the city of Nineveh to the list of places in Assyria that at least some of the deportees were taken. Interestingly, this would fit well with the suggestion by some scholars who think they may have identified some of the deported Samarians in Neo-Assyrian records at Nineveh, among other places, and that at least some of these exiles, particularly the charioteers, had been incorporated into the Neo-Assyrian army. Others rose even higher; one exiled Israelite from Samaria, a professional soldier by the name of Sama', apparently came to be a close friend and advisor to Sargon in his court at Nineveh. It is quite possible, therefore, that this fragment from the Book of Tobit contains at least a kernel of truth.

The other passage within the Apocrypha is found in II Esdras 13. Here, the text is even more relevant to the beginning of the mystery of the Ten Lost Tribes, because it actually names them as such. We should note, however, that II Esdras was also composed quite late, probably near the end of the first century A.D. The passage reads:

These are the nine [ten] tribes that were taken away from their own land into exile in the days of King Hoshea, whom Shalmaneser, king of the Assyrians, made captives; he took them across the river [the Euphrates], and they were taken into another land. But they formed this plan for themselves, that they would leave the multitude of the nations and go to a more distant region, where no human beings had ever lived, so that there at least they might keep their statutes that they had not kept in their own land.

And they went in by the narrow passages of the Euphrates river. For at that time the Most High performed signs for them, and stopped the channels of the river until they had crossed over. Through that region there was a long way to go, a journey of a year and a half; and that country is called Arzareth. (II Esdras 13:40-45)

The author of II Esdras believed that the deportees, the Ten Lost Tribes, crossed the Euphrates and traveled for a year and a half, eventually settling in a country called Arzareth. Since II Esdras was composed so late, however, we cannot tell if the author is relating an accurate piece of information or is simply guessing where the Ten Lost Tribes ended up. As we shall see, it is this passage that enthusiasts have seized upon in trying to locate the Ten Lost Tribes. But first, we must evaluate the relevant archaeological evidence that is available.

THE ARCHAEOLOGICAL DATA that is relevant to the Ten Lost Tribes of Israel falls into two broad categories. In the first category is the excavated data that might confirm the Neo-Assyrian attacks upon, and annexation of, the northern kingdom during the years 733 to 720 B.C. In other words, we should be able to look at the results from the excavation of sites such as Samaria to see if there are any destruction levels that would correspond to the reported Neo-Assyrian siege(s) and capture of the city. In the second category is the data collected during recent archaeological surveys conducted in the regions of what were once the northern kingdom of Israel and the southern kingdom of Judah; from these surveys, archaeologists have been able to accurately estimate the Israelite and Judean populations during and immediately after the Neo-Assyrian attacks.

If we turn to the first set of data, we immediately run into a stumbling block, because the excavations at the site of Samaria itself have yielded findings that are open to interpretation. This is due in large part to the manner in which the digging—and subsequent publications—was carried out. The original excavations were conducted by Harvard University and then by

The site of Megiddo, photographed here from above, contains more than twenty cities built one upon another over the course of nearly 3,000 years.

a British team that included archaeologist Dame Kathleen Kenyon, who also dug at Jericho and Jerusalem, whom we have met. She was convinced that she had found clear evidence for the Assyrian destruction of Samaria, which she dated to 722 B.C. However, the digging, recording, and storage methods followed by the British team left much to be desired, according to Ron Tappy, professor of Bible and archaeology at Pittsburgh Theological Seminary, who conducted a complete reexamination of their excavation results. This has recently called many of their conclusions into question.

Even though there is clear evidence of Neo-Assyrian occupation at the site, including a fragment of an inscription attributable to Sargon II, as well as pieces of cuneiform tablets and significant quantities of "Assyrian palace ware," Tappy suggests that "the destruction debris found by Kenyon . . . does not date to the time of the Assyrian destruction" and believes that it was a "nondestructive Assyrian takeover." Such a suggestion certainly flies in the face of the Neo-Assyrian and biblical textual accounts, because a three-year siege (or two different sieges, if we separate Shalmaneser V's actions from those of Sargon II's) surely would have resulted in some sort of destruction. As a result of his findings, Tappy has called for renewed excavations at the site. Samaria is located in the West Bank, though, and given the conflict embroiling that region, it may be a while before excavations can be resumed.

But what about Megiddo and other major sites that were occupied by the Neo-Assyrians after they took over the area from the northern kingdom of Israel? Here we are in better shape. As Magen Broshi, former curator of the Shrine of the Book at the Israel Museum in Jerusalem, and Israel Finkelstein, professor of archaeology at Tel Aviv University, have written: "Signs of destruction are discernible in almost every site excavated in the area of the former Kingdom of Israel: Some, such as Beth Shean, 'Ein Gev, and Khirbet Marjameh, were deserted following their conquest. At other sites there is clear evidence of decline: Hazor Stratum IV; Shechem; Dothan; and Tell el-Far'a (N). Gezer and Dor also show evidence of decline, in spite of their having been Assyrian administrative centers. As for Megiddo and Samaria, the evidence is by no means unequivocal. Both cities underwent considerable change, but it is not clear whether there was a decline in the number of their inhabitants."

Whether there was a decline in the number of inhabitants or not, the city of Megiddo IVA, as it was called by the University of Chicago team that excavated it, suffered a destruction that was readily observable by the archaeologists excavating various buildings at the site. The destruction can most likely be attributed to the Neo-Assyrians, and therefore dates sometime between 733 and 720 B.C. (from Tiglath-pileser III to Sargon II), because the subsequent city built directly upon the ruins has a completely new layout that is Neo-Assyrian in character. It is as if a city near the Euphrates River, such as Assur for instance, had been picked up, moved several hundred miles, and dropped on top of the mound at Megiddo. Neo-Assyrian palaces, houses, pottery, and other artifacts are all part of Stratum III at Megiddo. It was a grand city, in keeping with the extra-biblical texts that record that it became the capital city of the Neo-Assyrian province known as Magidu, and was home to at least one Neo-Assyrian governor (Itti-Adad-aninu, who was governor in the year 679 B.C.).

Other scholars have noted that sites such as Hazor, Dor, and Kinnereth also boast new Assyrian-style palaces in the cities built or rebuilt following the Neo-Assyrian takeover. Thus, from the data retrieved at Megiddo as well as Samaria (however disputed) and from other sites in what was once northern Israel, we have evidence that confirms the Neo-Assyrians destroyed some cities, resettled others, and in general took over the area and incorporated it into their empire during the years 733 to 720 B.C. and beyond.

However, if we turn now to the second category of evidence, which comes from recent surveys of the regions once inhabited by Israel's northern kingdom, it becomes clear that Israel was not decimated by the Neo-Assyrians since only about 40,000 of its people were carried off during the years of deportations. Archaeologists say that at least five times and perhaps nearly ten times that many people were living in the region during that time.

The most recent comprehensive archaeological data, published in 1992 by Broshi and Finkelstein, suggest that the population of the northern kingdom of Israel was at least 222,500 and perhaps closer to 350,000 at the time of the Neo-Assyrian invasions. If the Neo-Assyrian sources say that 40,000 Israelites were carried off (13,500 by Tiglath-pileser III and 27,280 by Sargon II), and if there were 222,500 inhabitants at that time, then the Neo-Assyrians would have deported some 20 percent of the kingdom's population. If the population were as high as 350,000 inhabitants, then the Neo-Assyrians would have deported only a little more than 10 percent of the kingdom's population. Either way, 80 to 90 percent of the Ten Tribes of Israel would have been left to either stay on the land or flee to Judah (or elsewhere). Therefore, there is no possibility that the Neo-Assyrians carried off the entire membership of the Ten Tribes of northern Israel, regardless of what contemporary or later sources may have thought.

Moreover, in this second category of data are the excavations that have been carried out in the city of Jerusalem itself and the surveys that have been conducted in the hinterland of Judah, especially those done since the Six Day War in 1967. These excavations and surveys, along with subsequent studies published by archaeologists such as Magen Broshi, Jane Cahill, Hillel Geva, Ann Killebrew, Roni Reich, Eli Shukron, Israel Finkelstein, and Dan Bahat provide evidence for a tremendous explosion of growth not only in the city of Jerusalem but in all of Judah during the last decades of the eighth century B.C., just after the fall of Israel's northern kingdom. According to these studies, the population of Jerusalem suddenly increased "as much as fifteen times, from about one thousand to fifteen thousand inhabitants," while the population of Judah "which had long hovered at a few tens of thousands, now grew to around 120,000." Most archaeologists suspect that this sudden expansion is closely related to the collapse of Israel and the sudden influx of large numbers of refugees into Judah.

So although perhaps as many as 20 percent of the inhabitants were carried off into exile, the vast majority of the so-called Ten Lost Tribes went either nowhere or south to Judah. In brief, the Ten Lost Tribes were never lost; we know exactly where they went.

AS WE HAVE MENTIONED, biblical scholars, archaeologists, and ancient historians are reasonably confident that they know where the deported inhabitants were taken, as well as where those who were not deported went. As a result, few professional archaeologists, biblical scholars, or ancient historians, with the welcome exception of Rivka Gonen—who has a Ph.D. in archaeology from the Hebrew University of Jerusalem and is currently senior curator of Jewish Ethnography at the Israel Museum in Jerusalem—have bothered to write anything on the possible whereabouts of the Ten Lost Tribes, unless they are reviewing a book or commenting on a television program created by an enthusiast or documentary producer.

However, there is a wide divergence of opinion among these amateur enthusiasts and documentary producers, most of whom haven't read the scholarly literature or haven't deigned to follow it, on how to interpret the specific locations in which the biblical account places the exiled members of the Ten Tribes. Thus, suggestions for where these members of the Ten Lost Tribes ended up have ranged from America and Britain to India and Africa, and virtually every place in between.

Surprisingly, most of these enthusiasts do not follow the description in the Book of II Kings that says that the deportees were placed "in Halah, on the Habor, the river of Gozan, and in the cities of the Medes." Rather, they gravitate to the apocryphal Book of II Esdras, which mentions that at some point, the deportees traveled beyond the Euphrates for a year and a half, eventually settling in a country called Arzareth: "They went in by the narrow passages of the Euphrates river. For at that time the Most High performed signs for them, and stopped the channels of the river until they had crossed over. Through that region there was a long way to go, a journey of a year and a half; and that country is called Arzareth" (II Esdras 13:43-45).

As we have noted, II Esdras was probably composed near the end of the first century A.D. This was also approximately the time when Flavius Josephus, the Jewish general turned Roman historian, was writing his histories of the Jewish War and of the Jewish people. Josephus is also one of the first authors to mention these Ten Tribes specifically by that name. He says, "There are but two tribes in Asia and Europe subject to the Romans, while the ten tribes are beyond the Euphrates until now, and are an immense multitude, and not to be estimated by numbers" (Josephus, *Antiquities of the Jews* 11.5.2). Clearly, by the first century A.D. (if not long before), the myth of the Ten Lost Tribes had already begun. The tradition continued thereafter, as seen in rabbinical musings in the Talmud, compiled between the first and fifth centuries A.D.

Enthusiastic efforts to identify where Arzareth was located, and where the Ten Lost Tribes might have ended up, have led to some fairly wild speculations over the years. Just recently, books have been published suggesting that the descendants of the Ten Tribes can be found in the Native Americans of North America, the Falasha of Ethiopia, the Lemba of South Africa, and the B'nai Menashe of India, as well as in Japan, Central Asia, and England, among other places. Some of these books have even reached the best-seller lists. We do not have the space here to discuss the pros and cons of each of these theories. There is really no need to do so, however, for Rivka Gonen, in one of the best—and most serious—books that has been published on the Ten Lost Tribes, points out that Arzareth is not an actual placename, but is instead a corruption of two Hebrew words, *Eretz Aheret,* and simply means "another land."

THE BIBLICAL ACCOUNT of the last days of the northern kingdom of Israel seems fairly straightforward, but as we have seen, there are some problems correlating the specific details with the extra-biblical evidence. As we have also mentioned, there was more to the story than the Bible indicates.

We know that after the death of Solomon in about 930 B.C., the United Monarchy established by David and Solomon split in half. The northern part became the kingdom of Israel, with its capital at Samaria; the southern part became the kingdom of Judah, with its capital at Jerusalem. Within a few decades, by the middle of the ninth century B.C., Israel found itself dealing with the rising and belligerent power of Neo-Assyria, a growing empire located north of Babylon, now modern Iraq. The Neo-Assyrians were the dominant power not only in this region but also in most of the ancient Near East before the rise of Nebuchadnezzar and the Neo-Babylonians. While the Neo-Babylonians ruled in the Middle East during the late seventh century and early sixth centuries B.C., the Neo-Assyrians were dominant earlier, in the ninth, eighth, and most of the seventh centuries B.C.

Fortunately, we have plentiful extra-biblical literary materials that allow us to supplement and perhaps confirm the biblical account, since the Neo-Assyrians kept good records and were prone to boasting about their accomplishments, as we have seen. Thus, we know that in 853 B.C., Ahab, king of Israel, sent troops and chariots to a coalition of small kingdoms facing Shalmaneser III and the Neo-Assyrian Empire. In the ensuing Battle of Qarqar, the coalition was defeated, as Shalmaneser reports in his Monolithic Inscription:

I . . . approached Qarqar. I destroyed, devastated, and burned with fire Qarqar, his royal city. 1,200 chariots, 1,200 cavalry, and 20,000 soldiers of Adad-iri of the land of Imerisu [Aram-Damascus]; 700 chariots, 700 cavalry, and 10,000 soldiers of Irhulenu the Hamathite; 2,000 chariots and 10,000 soldiers of Ahab the Israelite. . . . Like Adad, I rained destruction upon them.

A few years later, Shalmaneser III forced the new king of Israel, Jehu, to pay him tribute. The Neo-Assyrian Black Obelisk, dated to 838 B.C., shows Jehu bowing before Shalmaneser, with the accompanying text reading: "Tribute of Iaua [Jehu], son of Omri. Silver, gold, a golden bowl, a golden beaker, golden goblets, pitchers of gold, lead, staves [staffs] for the hand of the king, javelins, I received from him."

As we can see, it was really just a matter of time before the Neo-Assyrians expanded their empire enough to incorporate Israel into their boundaries (which finally occurred near the end of the eighth century B.C.). By the time Tiglath-pileser III, Shalmaneser V, and Sargon II were through with the area, Israel's northern kingdom had been attacked several times, dismembered, and destroyed, all within a period of less than 20 years. By 720 B.C., it had literally ceased to exist. At least a portion of the population—primarily the upper class, the artisans and craftsmen, and members of the army—was deported to Assyria.

This deportation and repopulation, known in politically correct terms as "population exchange," was a standard and very deliberate practice of the Neo-Assyrians. As Israel Finkelstein and Neil Silberman said in their book *The Bible Unearthed:*

> This policy had many objectives, which all served the goals of continuing imperial development. From a military point of view, the capture and removal of native villages had the effect of terrorizing and demoralizing the population and splitting them up to prevent further organized resistance. . . . The forced resettlement of artisans in the centers of the Assyrian heartland boosted the trained human resources at the disposal of the Assyrian

In a rare scene, the Israelite king Jehu bows before the Neo-Assyrian ruler
Shalmaneser III on the so-called Black Obelisk.

economy. And finally, the systemic resettling of new populations in empty
or recently conquered territory was intended to expand the overall agricultural output of the empire.

The Neo-Assyrians had long been rearranging the populations of the
lands they conquered, moving people around as soon as they could. They
believed that conquered peoples were less likely to rebel if moved far from
their native soil. This policy, harsh as it may seem, was effective.

In fact, Nadav Na'aman suggests that during the period between 733
and 701 B.C., there were several different variations of deportation and
repopulation tactics being practiced by the Neo-Assyrians in both Israel
and Judah. He notes that Tiglath-pileser III implemented a "one-way"
deportation in order "to weaken the national spirit and reduce the possibility of rebellion against the Assyrian government." Sargon II, on the other
hand, instituted a "two-way" deportation "aimed at integrating Palestine

into the Assyrian empire." And Sennacherib (later, in 701 B.C.) initiated a massive "one-way" deportation from the kingdom of Judah in order "to create a balance of power among the small weak kingdoms situated near his border with Egypt."

The Neo-Assyrians have a well-deserved reputation for cruelty, but in this case their policy of deportation and repopulation may have kept the number of revolts against their empire to a minimum. It probably also kept the number of deaths—and outright genocide—of conquered peoples down as well.

IT IS WITHIN THE historical context of these Neo-Assyrian policies that we must understand the deportations of the Israelites and their replacement by numerous peoples from elsewhere in the Neo-Assyrian Empire. After 720 B.C., or perhaps even earlier, the rolling hills and fertile valleys of what had been the northern kingdom of Israel had become several Neo-Assyrian provinces (such as Samerina and Magidu).

So what happened to the so-called Ten Lost Tribes of Israel? The answer is simple: They are not lost and never were. Yes, the northern kingdom of Israel itself officially ended by 720 B.C., when it was incorporated into the Neo-Assyrian Empire. And yes, inhabitants of Samaria and Israel were indeed deported from 733 to 720 B.C. As the Bible says, at least some of these were exiled "in Halah, on the Habor, the river of Gozan, and in the cities of the Medes"—all places in the Neo-Assyrian Empire. However, only 20 percent of the inhabitants of the northern kingdom of Israel, at most, were sent into exile. A substantial portion of the rest fled as refugees to the southern kingdom of Judah, but the others remained on the land, intermarrying with the new immigrants brought in by Neo-Assyrian overlords as part of their policy of deportation and repopulation. Those who remained and intermarried are said to have become the Samaritans, whose descendants may still live in Israel today.

To summarize, it is clear that at least 40,000 members of the Ten Lost Tribes were indeed sent into exile by the Neo-Assyrians, according to both the biblical account and Neo-Assyrian records, specifically those of Sargon II, who says he carried them off "to Assyria" and replaced them in Samaria with "distant Arabs." He does not say where exactly in Assyria he carried them off to, but the Bible (which, as we have seen, may or may not give credit to Sargon for doing so) says that the exiled Israelites were sent to "Halah, on the Habor, the river of Gozan, and in the cities of the Medes." These are all areas in Mesopotamia and within the Assyrian Empire, which fits well with scholars' suggestions that some of the deported Samarians are mentioned in Neo-Assyrian records, such as charioteers who had been incorporated into the Neo-Assyrian army.

While Israel's northern kingdom was indeed destroyed and a portion of its peoples were carried off by Tiglath-pileser III and Shalmaneser V/ Sargon II, these 40,000 Israelites represented only a fraction of the population, 10 to 20 percent at most, since recent archaeological surveys indicate that Israel's population was between 222,500 and 350,000 inhabitants at that time.

Meanwhile, the archaeological evidence from recent surveys and excavations done in the southern kingdom of Judah indicates that after 720 B.C., the population of Jerusalem increased 15 times over, from 1,000 to 15,000 inhabitants, and the overall population of Judah tripled or quadrupled, from approximately 30,000 or 40,000 people to about 120,000 people. The evidence also indicates a dramatic increase in production and large buildings, which also point toward a population surge. It is unlikely that this surge was caused by anything other than the incorporation of thousands of refugees from the northern kingdom of Israel, who were fleeing the Neo-Assyrians. Since the population of Judah suddenly increased from approximately 40,000 to 120,000 people, there may have been as many as 80,000 such refugees—which also helps to explain why Judah suddenly came out of the backwater and entered the mainstream of the world's stage at the end of the eighth century B.C.

Moreover, the archaeological evidence from recent surveys and excavations done in the northern kingdom of Israel further indicates that a large percentage of its inhabitants were not exiled or driven to flee as refugees. Instead, they simply stayed put and lived alongside the newcomers imported into the region by their new Neo-Assyrian overlords. Even if 40,000 people were taken into exile and 80,000 fled south to Judah, at least 100,000 more—and perhaps as many as 230,000 people—would have remained in what was once Israel's northern kingdom.

Thus, I believe the archaeological and textual evidence indicates that Israel's northern population was divided into three parts after 720 B.C.: 40,000 people were carried off into exile in Assyria; perhaps as many as 80,000 fled as refugees to Judah; and between 100,000 and 230,000 simply stayed put, intermarrying with the newcomers and becoming the group known as the Samaritans.

If this is the case, then the fate that befell the inhabitants of Samaria and the northern kingdom of Israel mirrors exactly the fate that would befall the people of Jerusalem and Judah a little more than a century later, when they suffered at the hands of the Neo-Babylonians from 598 to 586 B.C. It is well documented that they too ended up being split into three groups—those who were carried off into exile in Babylon, those who fled to Egypt as refugees, and those who remained on the land.

We may therefore have another "Myth of the Empty Land" in the north, just as there was later in the south. That is, contrary to what most ancient sources believed (not to mention many modern scholars until recently), in neither case was the land left empty by invaders. While both groups—the northern Israelites in 720 B.C. and the southern Judeans in 586 B.C.—had their capital city besieged and their country captured and annexed, in each case only a portion of the population was exiled, with as much as 70 or 80 percent of the population left behind.

Finally, even if 40,000 people were carried off by the Neo-Assyrians from 733 to 720 B.C., this number pales in comparison with the number of people reportedly deported from Judah in 701 B.C. and exiled to an unknown location by the Neo-Assyrian King Sennacherib, successor to Sargon II. While campaigning in Judah, Sennacherib says that he deported 200,150 people from its cities and villages:

Sennacherib claimed to have led more than 200,000 Judeans into exile in 701 B.C., but this number may be an exaggeration.

As for Hezekiah, the Judaean, he did not submit to my yoke. I laid siege to 46 of his strong fortified cities, and countless small villages in their vicinity, and conquered them by means of well-stamped earth ramps, and battering rams brought thus near to the walls combined with the attack by foot soldiers, using mines, breeches, as well as sapper work. I brought out of them [the cities and villages] 200,150 people, young and old, male and female, horses, mules, donkeys, camels, big and small cattle beyond number, and counted them booty.

As some scholars have suggested, this figure of 200,150 people is probably a gross exaggeration, especially since, as we have noted, the entire population of Judah was probably no more than about 120,000 people at the time. Nevertheless, it is ironic that some of the refugees who fled south in 720 B.C. may have been subsequently exiled by Sennacherib when he attacked Lachish, Ashkelon, Jerusalem, and more than 40 other cities in Judah in 701 B.C. If so, when they reached Assyria, these new exiles may have greeted old friends and neighbors, or children of old friends and neighbors, who had been carried off approximately 20 years earlier.

Of course, some of them may have eventually come back, while others may have stayed where they were and assimilated, much as some Judeans later chose not to return from Babylon in 538 B.C. when they were allowed to do so by Cyrus the Great. Did any of those who were exiled in 701 B.C. eventually make their way to India or to Ethiopia or elsewhere in the world? Is this really when the Jewish Diaspora first began—not after the Roman destructions of Jerusalem in A.D. 70 and A.D. 135, but after the Neo-Assyrian deportations of 733 to 701 B.C.? It is possible, but it cannot be documented archaeologically, for the most part.

And so, like the Ark of the Covenant and Noah's ark, it is going to be difficult—if not impossible—to ever find the Ten Lost Tribes of Israel. In this case, however, it is not for lack of evidence but simply because the vast majority of these people were never lost. And yet the quest to locate them continues today, as numerous books are published each decade that claim to have found the Lost Tribes or suggest that the author knows where to look. Why that trend continues is one of the most interesting mysteries of all.

EPILOGUE

"When you set out on your journey to Ithaca,
then pray that the road is long,
full of adventure, full of knowledge."
—Constantine P. Cavafy (1911)

In trying to unravel the various mysteries of the Bible, we have literally gone from Eden to exile—from looking for the Garden of Eden to looking for members of the Ten Lost Tribes of Israel who were sent off into exile by the Neo-Assyrians. While we may not have located Noah's ark, I believe that we have successfully documented that the Ten Lost Tribes weren't lost after all, that the Ark of the Covenant was most likely destroyed during the obliteration of Solomon's Temple by Nebuchadnezzar and the Neo-Babylonians, that Jericho was probably not destroyed by Joshua and the Israelites, that we can neither confirm nor deny the biblical account of the Exodus, that Sodom and Gomorrah are still missing, and that the Garden of Eden is most likely to have been located in Mesopotamia.

Although we have had mixed success in solving these mysteries, it is my sincere hope some interesting things have been revealed along the way, as we have reviewed the available data and looked at each topic from a variety of angles, evaluated the various suggestions, and then, whenever possible, considered what I believe to be the most likely solution at this time. Of course, my suggestions will be immediately added to the pile of previous hypotheses to be considered and evaluated by other scholars, and may be overturned at any moment by future archaeological discoveries.

There are also a number of other mysteries in the Hebrew Bible, both major and minor, that are still out there waiting to be discussed and possibly solved. One that immediately comes to mind is the mysterious plague that the biblical account tells us killed 185,000 Neo-Assyrians in Sennacherib's army in a single night, right before they were to attack Hezekiah and the city of Jerusalem in 701 B.C. (II Kings 19:32-36; II Chronicles 32:20-21). How can we explain that? Was it the wrath of God? Or is the alternate version, that Hezekiah bribed Sennacherib to go away—which is duly noted not only in the biblical account (II Kings 18:14-16) but also in Sennacherib's own inscriptions—more believable? Then of course, if we move into the New Testament period, we will find a whole additional set of mysteries that we could discuss. But those are best left for another book.

Some readers will be disappointed that we have not solved all of the mysteries here. To that, I would say that it is acceptable not to have a definitive answer at the end of each chapter, especially if we are trying not to abuse the data presently available. Moreover, in some cases it is the journey that matters more than the destination, as the modern Greek poet Constantine Cavafy says in his poem "Ithaca":

> Always keep Ithaca fixed in your mind.
> To arrive there is your ultimate goal.
> But do not hurry the voyage at all.
> It is better to let it last for long years;
> and even to anchor at the isle when you are old,
> rich with all that you have gained on the way,
> not expecting that Ithaca will offer you riches.

We may have come up empty-handed in some instances, but now we are also more certain about what we do and do not know, and how we can better evaluate the claims that have been made. Moreover, if archaeologists do not yet have an answer, they can simply keep digging and retrieve more information, and any new piece of data can radically change or confirm hypotheses in an instant. For example, the discovery of the fragmentary House of David (*Beit David*) inscription found at Tel Dan in the early 1990s finally provided extra-biblical confirmation that King David really lived. As Hershel Shanks, the editor and publisher of *Biblical Archaeology Review* once said about archaeological evidence, it "is subject to change tomorrow."

One thing that remains intriguing is what these topics tell us about ourselves. Is it simply human nature that we still wonder about these mysteries? At the end of chapter 2, I asked why it was that so many people are still looking for Noah's ark, when not a single person is looking for Utnapishtim's ark or Atrahasis's ark or Ziusudra's ark. And at the end of chapter 7, I admitted that I am puzzled as to why people are still looking for the Ten Lost Tribes when it is clear they were never lost in the first place. But I think I can explain some of the continued intrigue.

People need stories, not just data, to make sense of their lives. As a friend of mine likes to say, human beings are stories made flesh and blood. We make sense of our lives and of our history with narratives, and the Bible is one of the greatest stories ever told. People read the Bible to find themselves in it, and many people don't just read the story, they live it. They don't just watch history unfold on a stage, they see themselves as actors under the lights. As such, even if the Bible cannot always be taken as literal history, its words can still speak a certain truth—and can transform people's lives in the process. And the biblical story says nothing about Ziusudra and everything about Noah. Hence the search continues today for Noah, but not for the other heroes of the Flood.

There are undoubtedly other more mundane factors involved as well. Robert Eisenman, professor of biblical archaeology at California State University in Long Beach, once said, "These adventure stories appeal to the imagination of the gullible. Yet there is the remote possibility that they are true and that's what makes them so interesting."

Yes, there is certainly the remote possibility that they are true, because each of these mysteries contains a historical context that must be considered. As we have seen, Sodom and Gomorrah must be considered within the context of Abraham and the Patriarchs: Did these men exist, and if so, when? The Exodus must be considered within the framework of Egyptian and Canaanite history. Joshua and Jericho must be considered in light of the Israelite conquest of Canaan. The Ark of the Covenant must be considered within the question of David and Solomon's existence and empire (not to mention the entire history of Jerusalem up until the Neo-Babylonian destruction of the city in 586 B.C.). And the Ten Lost Tribes of Israel must be considered within the context of the Neo-Assyrian deportations that took place during the late eighth century B.C. This is, however, rarely stated by any of the enthusiasts or on any of the television shows.

In this age of the Internet and vanity publishing, anyone can claim anything, and gullible people everywhere will send their money to fund dubious "archaeological" expeditions. In fact, based upon what we have seen in the preceding pages, it would be prudent to be wary of anyone with a Web site or multiple publications who claims to have been able to "solve" more than one of these mysteries or locate more than one of these objects or places. It is frequently said in archaeology, "If something seems to be too good to be true, it probably is."

It is not likely, or logical, that a single person can solve more than one, if any, of these mysteries in their lifetime, so for an amateur enthusiast to claim that he or she has found not only the whereabouts of the Garden of Eden, but also the location of Sodom and Gomorrah, the Ark of the Covenant, and Noah's ark defies both logic and common sense. So why do the major television and cable networks keep producing shows on these topics and featuring such people, reducing the real experts to nattering nabobs of negativism? "Because it makes good television" or "because it is entertaining" are not valid enough reasons—the general public is more intelligent and deserves better treatment than that.

What we really should be promoting is a shared methodology that can be used by everyone, even if it turns out that we cannot reach a consensus on the final results. In fact, such a methodology already exists. It was suggested several years ago by Randall Younker, director of the Institute of Archaeology and professor of Old Testament and biblical archaeology at Andrews University in Berrien Springs, Michigan. Andrews University is a Seventh-day Adventist institution, and the archaeologists who work and teach there sometimes discover that their archaeological findings affect their own belief systems. In a candid article, Younker said that the "Andrews Way" of doing archaeology, as he phrased it, is as follows:

1. Be forthright with findings. Do not minimize problems or stretch interpretations of data to explain things away.
2. Do not make claims beyond what the data can support.
3. Be quick and complete in publishing results.
4. Engage and work within mainstream scholarship.
5. Include a diversity of people and specialists.
6. Take the history of the Bible seriously, but do not place upon archaeology the burden of "proving" the Bible.

I would like to think that most professional archaeologists and ancient historians already follow Younker's six points and that the "Andrews Way" is actually an excellent blueprint for how to conduct biblical (or Syro-Palestinian) archaeology. And three of his points (1, 2, and 6) seem eminently appropriate for enthusiasts, pseudoscientists, documentary filmmakers, and even the most fervent evangelical biblical maximalists and minimalists to adhere to as well.

Rather than practicing junk science, if we are instead forthright with our findings and do not minimize problems or stretch interpretations of data, if we do not make claims beyond what the data can support, and if we take the history of the Bible seriously but do not place upon archaeology the burden of proving it (as so many presently do), then I believe that both the general public and academia will be much better served in future publications and television presentations. This would be true not only for those books and television shows concerned with specific biblical mysteries, but also with those exploring the ancient world of the Bible in general.

Virtually everything that I have stated in these pages has been said before by numerous other archaeologists, ancient historians, or biblical scholars. Strange or even heretical as some of my statements and conclusions may seem, almost nothing is particularly novel, almost nothing is totally new. I have simply been looking at the available evidence from an archaeological and historical point of view—gathering the facts, subjecting them to analysis, and then presenting my thinking and interpretation of the data. Some people may agree with my interpretations; others will almost certainly disagree.

In fact, I am quite sure that the data and opinions I have presented here will not end the debates. I do hope, however, that they will serve to jumpstart new discussions in classrooms, study groups, and homes. What I have tried to do in this book is introduce an ancient historian's and archaeologist's point of view, along with genuine archaeological and historical data and considerations—information that is all too frequently lacking in the publications and television specials written and produced by nonspecialists. Still, I harbor some small hope that future discussions will be based more upon facts and less upon flights of fantasy. We owe it to the ancient world, and to the people of the Hebrew Bible, to do nothing less.

FURTHER READING

There are many, many books and articles that have been written about the topics touched on in this book. Some are good, some are bad, some are fascinating, some have interesting insight—and some are just plain wrong. Here, I have listed some of the ones that I have found useful:

GENERAL BOOKS ON MYSTERIES OF THE BIBLE
Archaeology Magazine, eds. *Secrets of the Bible*. New York: Hatherleigh Press, 2004.
Meinhardt, Molly Dewsnap, ed. *Mysteries of the Bible: From the Garden of Eden to the Shroud of Turin*. Washington, D.C.: Biblical Archaeology Society, 2004.

GENERAL BOOKS ON THE RELATIONSHIP BETWEEN ARCHAEOLOGY, ANCIENT ISRAEL, AND THE BIBLE
Dever, William G. *What Did the Biblical Writers Know and When Did They Know It?: What Archaeology Can Tell Us about the Reality of Ancient Israel*. Grand Rapids, Mich.: William B. Eerdmans Publishing Company, 2001.
Feiler, Bruce S. *Walking the Bible: A Journey by Land Through the Five Books of Moses*. New York: William Morrow, 2001.
Finkelstein, Israel, and Neil A. Silberman. *The Bible Unearthed: Archaeology's New Vision of Ancient Israel and the Origin of Its Sacred Texts*. New York: Free Press, 2001.

Kitchen, Kenneth A. *On the Reliability of the Old Testament.* Grand Rapids, Mich.: William B. Eerdmans Publishing Company, 2003.

Marcus, Amy D. *The View from Nebo: How Archaeology Is Rewriting the Bible and Reshaping the Middle East.* Boston: Little, Brown and Company, 2000.

Maxwell, Miller J. and John H. Hayes. *A History of Ancient Israel and Judah,* 2nd ed. Louisville, Ky.: Westminster John Knox Press, 2006.

Provan, Iaian, V. Philips Long, and Tremper Longman III. *A Biblical History of Israel.* Louisville, Ky.: Westminster John Knox Press, 2003.

Shanks, Hershel, ed. *Ancient Israel: From Abraham to the Roman Destruction of the Temple,* 2nd ed. (rev.) New York: Prentice-Hall, 1999.

The Garden of Eden

Hamblin, Dora Jane. "Sleuthing the Garden of Eden," *Smithsonian* 18, no. 2 (1987): 127-135.

Hess, Richard S. "Eden: A Well-Watered Place," *Bible Review* 7, no. 6 (1991): 28-33.

Sauer, James. "A Lost River of Eden: Rediscovering the Pishon." In *Mysteries of the Bible: From the Garden of Eden to the Shroud of Turin,* ed. Molly Dewsnap Meinhardt. Washington, D.C.: Biblical Archaeology Society, 2004.

Scafi, Alessandro. *Mapping Paradise: A History of Heaven on Earth.* Chicago: University of Chicago Press, 2006.

Noah's Ark

Ryan, William B., and Walter C. Pitman. *Noah's Flood: The New Scientific Discoveries about the Event That Changed History.* New York: Simon and Schuster, 1998.

Stiebing, William H., Jr. *Ancient Astronauts, Cosmic Collisions, and Other Popular Theories about Man's Past.* Buffalo, N.Y.: Prometheus Books, 1984.

Abraham and the Patriarchs

Feiler, Bruce S. *Abraham: A Journey to the Heart of Three Faiths.* New York: William Morrow, 2002.

Hendel, Ronald S. *Remembering Abraham: Culture, Memory, and History in the Hebrew Bible.* New York: Oxford University Press, 2005.

Van Seters, John. *Abraham in History and Tradition.* New Haven: Yale University, 1975.

Sodom and Gomorrah

Rast, Walter E. "Bab edh-Dhr'a and the Origin of the Sodom Saga." In *Archaeology and Biblical Interpretation: Essays in Memory of D. Glenn Rose*, ed. Leo D. Perdue, Lawrence E. Toombs, and Gary L. Johnson. Atlanta: John Knox Press, 1987.

Rast, Walter E. "Bronze Age Cities along the Dead Sea," *Archaeology* 40, no. 1 (1987): 42-49.

van Hattem, Willem C. "Once Again: Sodom and Gomorrah," *Biblical Archaeologist* 44 (1981): 87-92.

The Exodus

Bimson, John J. *Redating the Exodus and Conquest*, 2nd ed. Sheffield, U.K.: Almond Press, 1981.

Halpern, Baruch. "The Exodus from Egypt: Myth or Reality?" In *The Rise of Ancient Israel*, ed. Hershel Shanks. Washington, D.C.: Biblical Archaeology Society, 1992.

Hoffmeier, James K. *Israel in Egypt: The Evidence for the Authenticity of the Exodus Tradition*. Oxford: Oxford University Press, 1997.

Hoffmeier, James K. *Ancient Israel in Sinai: The Evidence for the Authenticity of the Wilderness Tradition*. Oxford: Oxford University Press, 2005.

Redford, Donald B. *Egypt, Canaan, and Israel in Ancient Times*. Princeton, N.J.: Princeton University Press, 1992.

Joshua and the Battle of Jericho

Bartlett, John R. *Jericho*. Grand Rapids, Mich.: William B. Eerdmans Publishing Company, 1982.

Bienkowski, Piotr. *Jericho in the Late Bronze Age*. Warminster, U.K.: Aris and Phillips, 1986.

Garstang, John, and J. B. E. Garstang. *The Story of Jericho*, rev. ed. London: Marshall, Morgan and Scott, 1948.

Kenyon, Kathleen. *Digging Up Jericho*. London: Ernest Benn, 1957.

The Israelite Conquest of Canaan

Ben-Tor, Amnon, and Maria T. Rubiato. "Excavating Hazor, Part Two: Did the

Israelites Destroy the Canaanite City?" *Biblical Archaeology Review* 25, no. 3 (1999): 22-39.

Dever, William G. *Who Were the Early Israelites and Where Did They Come From?* Grand Rapids, Mich.: William B. Eerdmans Publishing Company, 2003.

Silberman, Neil A. "Who Were the Israelites?" *Archaeology* 45, no. 2 (1992): 22-30.

THE ARK OF THE COVENANT

Hancock, Graham. *The Sign and the Seal: A Quest for the Lost Ark of the Covenant.* New York: Crown Publishers, 1992.

Munro-Hay, Stuart. *The Quest for the Ark of the Covenant: The True History of the Tablets of Moses.* London: I. B. Tauris, 2005.

Munro-Hay, Stuart, and Roderick Grierson. *The Ark of the Covenant: The True Story of the Greatest Relic of Antiquity.* London: Weidenfeld and Nicolson, 1999.

Price, Randall. *Searching for the Ark of the Covenant: Latest Discoveries and Research.* Eugene, Ore.: Harvest House Publishers, 2005.

DAVID AND SOLOMON

Finkelstein, Israel, and Neil A. Silberman. *David and Solomon: In Search of the Bible's Sacred Kings and the Roots of the Western Tradition.* New York: Free Press, 2006.

Halpern, Baruch. *David's Secret Demons: Messiah, Murderer, Traitor, King.* Grand Rapids, Mich.: William B. Eerdmans Publishing, 2001.

Kirsch, Jonathan. *King David: The Real Life of the Man Who Ruled Israel.* New York: Ballantine Books, 2001.

McKenzie, Steven L. *King David: A Biography.* New York: Oxford University Press, 2000.

TEN LOST TRIBES OF ISRAEL

Becking, Bob. *The Fall of Samaria: A Historical and Archaeological Study.* Leiden, Netherlands: E. J. Brill, 1992.

Gonen, Rivka. *To the Ends of the Earth: The Quest for the Ten Lost Tribes of Israel.* North Bergen, N.J.: Book-Mart Press, 2002.

Parfitt, Tudor. *The Lost Tribes of Israel: The History of a Myth.* London: Weidenfeld and Nicolson, 2002.

ACKNOWLEDGMENTS

I would like to thank Eleanor Grant and French Horwitz, the executive producer and senior series producer of the National Geographic television series *Science of the Bible,* for approaching the book division of the National Geographic Society on my behalf and pitching this project to them. I am particularly grateful to my editor, Garrett Brown, who championed this project from the beginning, provided advice and encouragement throughout, and kept me firmly on schedule right to the end, despite my vehement protests on occasion.

I would also like to thank: Steve Feldman, Eleanor Grant, Rachel Hallote, Tremper Longman III, Alan Mairson, Tammi Schneider, and Elizabeth Snodgrass, who all read and commented on the entire manuscript; Rebecca Kennedy, who read and commented on rough drafts of several of the chapters; Justine Benanty, who assisted in some of the initial research for the various chapters; Matthew Chwastyk, for his thorough and insightful comments on the maps; copy editor Betsy Holt, for making my academic prose more lucid; the administration of the George Washington University for granting me a sabbatical that allowed me to finish this book in a timely manner; and Shmuel Ben-Gad and the rest of the staff of the Gelman Library at the George Washington University for their help in procuring books and articles so quickly.

Last, but certainly not least, I would especially like to thank my wife, Diane, and children, Hannah and Joshua, for putting up with me while I was writing this book. I know that it wasn't easy, but I hope that it was worth it.

ILLUSTRATION CREDITS

NOTES

INTRODUCTION

ix *The greatest challenge*   Molly Dewsnap Meinhardt, ed., *Mysteries of the Bible: From the Garden of Eden to the Shroud of Turin* (Washington, D.C.: Biblical Archaeology Society, 2004), vii.

x   *the work of such enthusiasts frequently meets the criteria*   Elizabeth H. Gierlowski-Kordesch, review of *Discovered: Sodom and Gomorrah! A Video,* by Ron Wyatt, *Biblical Archaeology Review* 24, no. 5 (1998): 60-62; Ron W. Pritchett, "Recognizing Junk Science," *Professional Geologist* 34, no. 13 (1997): 5-7.

x   *former Vice President Spiro Agnew and William Safire in a new context*   Former Vice President Spiro Agnew used the phrases "nattering nabobs of negativism" and "an effete corps of impudent snobs who characterize themselves as intellectuals" to describe members of the media; http://www.bartleby.com/59/12/agnewspiro.html, http://www.bartleby.com/73/1876.html, and http://www.bartleby.com/63/8/408.html, accessed on February 5, 2007. For more information, see http://www.bartleby.com/73/1553.html, accessed on February 5, 2007, which states with further references that Agnew first used the phrase "nattering nabobs of negativism" in his address to the California Republican State Convention in San Diego, California, on September 11, 1970, and that William Safire, then a speechwriter for President Nixon, was the author of the phrase. It seems particularly relevant in this context to redirect the phrases toward the scholars who appear as "talking heads" on these shows and who are frequently forced to assume the roles of naysayers.

xii   *their ostensible ancestors the invading Israelites?*   Eric H. Cline, *Jerusalem Besieged: From Ancient Canaan to Modern Israel* (Ann Arbor: University of Michigan Press, 2004), 33-35.

xii   *more like a sibling rivalry or a family reunion gone bad*   I would like to thank Alan Mairson at the National Geographic Society for suggesting this and other cogent points.

xiii   *the standard "historical method" followed by most historians*   See for instance, Jacques Barzun and Henry F. Graff, *The Modern Researcher* (Boston: Houghton Mifflin, 1992); Martha C. Howell and Walter Prevenier, *From Reliable Sources: An Introduction to Historical Methods* (Ithaca, N.Y.: Cornell University Press, 2001); John Lewis Gaddis, *The Landscape of History: How Historians Map the Past* (New York: Oxford University Press, 2002). I should note that asking for three independent sources is sometimes wishful thinking in a field where scholars are often lucky just to find two sources—or even a single source—in their efforts to reconstruct the periods in the ancient Near East before the first millennium B.C.

CHAPTER I

1   *the Lord God*   This and all other additional citations from the Bible follow the New Revised Standard Version. See Bruce M. Metzger and Roland E. Murphy, eds., *New Oxford Annotated Bible, with the Apocryphal/Deuterocanonical Books* (New York: Oxford University Press, 1991).

2   *two of the four rivers*   See commentary by the editors of the *New Oxford Annotated Bible*, page 4OT. See also Ephraim A. Speiser, *Genesis: Introduction, Translation, and Notes,* the Anchor Bible (New York: Doubleday and Company, 1964), 16-17, 19-20; Ephraim A. Speiser, "The Rivers of Paradise," *Festschrift Johannes Friedrich zum 65. Geburtstag am 27. August 1958,* ed. R. von Kienle, A. Moortgat, H. Otten, E. von Schuler, and W. Zaumseil (Heidelberg: Carl Winter, 1959), 475-478; Alessandro Scafi, *Mapping Paradise: A History of Heaven on Earth* (Chicago: University of Chicago Press, 2006), 35.

4   *the Bible seems to connect it with Mesopotamia*   On Cush in Mesopotamia, see Speiser, "The Rivers of Paradise," 475-476. For the quote from Scafi, see Scafi, *Mapping Paradise,* 13; see also pages 32-43 for a discussion of the biblical account of the Garden of Eden and some of the problems of interpretation that have been addressed over the centuries.

4   *according to Joseph Smith, Jr.*   See Joseph Fielding Smith, Jr., *Doctrines of Salvation,* vol. 3 (Salt Lake City, UT: Bookcraft, 1954-1956), 74-75; Bruce R. McConkie, *Mormon Doctrine,* 2nd ed. (Salt Lake City, UT: Bookcraft, 1966). McConkie says, "The early brethren of this dispensation taught that the Garden of Eden was located in what is

known to us as the land of Zion, an area for which Jackson County, Missouri, is the center place" (p. 20). For a discussion of other suggested locations, see Scafi, *Mapping Paradise,* 342-364.

4   *can provide us with an exact parallel*   For a discussion of the word "Eden" and its origins and suggested translation, see Richard S. Hess, "Eden: A Well-watered Place," *Bible Review* 7, no. 6 (1991): 28-33; Speiser, *Genesis: Introduction, Translation, and Notes,* 16; Dora Jane Hamblin, "Sleuthing the Garden of Eden," *Smithsonian* 18, no. 2 (1987): 127-135; Scafi, *Mapping Paradise,* 34-36. See also the discussions that suggest that the biblical description of Eden essentially reflects the nature of the Temple in Jerusalem, by Lawrence E. Stager, "Jerusalem as Eden," *Biblical Archaeology Review* 26, no. 3 (2000): 36-37, 66; Lawrence E. Stager, "Jerusalem and the Garden of Eden," *Eretz-Israel* 26 [Frank M. Cross Festschrift] (1999): 183*-194*.

5   *The land Dilmun is pure*   Translation follows James B. Pritchard, ed., *Ancient Near Eastern Texts Relating to the Old Testament,* 3rd ed. (Princeton: Princeton University Press, 1969), 38-39.

5   *There are also Creation stories from this area*   See David Toshio Tsumura, "Genesis and Ancient Near Eastern Stories of Creation and Flood: An Introduction," *I Studied Inscriptions from Before the Flood: Ancient Near Eastern, Literary and Linguistic Approaches to Genesis 1-11,* eds. Richard S. Hess and David Toshio Tsumura (Winona Lake, IL: Eisenbrauns, 1994), 27-57.

5   *When on high*   Translation follows Pritchard, *Ancient Near Eastern Texts,* 60-61.

5   *the "Babylonian Genesis"*   See the famous book on *Enuma Elish* by Alexander Heidel, *The Babylonian Genesis,* 2nd ed. (Chicago: University of Chicago Press, 1963). See also the brief discussion by Peter Enns, *Inspiration and Incarnation: Evangelicals and the Problem of the Old Testament* (Grand Rapids, Mich.: Baker Academic, 2005), 25-27.

5   *Scholars generally agree*   On the date for the writing of the Hebrew Bible, see various discussions in Richard E. Friedman, *Who Wrote the Bible?* (San Francisco: HarperSanFrancisco, 1987); William G. Dever, *What Did the Biblical Writers Know and When Did They Know It?* (Grand Rapids, Mich.: William B. Eerdmans Publishing Company, 2001); William M. Schniedewind, *How the Bible Became a Book: The Textualization of Ancient Israel* (Cambridge: Cambridge University Press, 2004); Israel Finkelstein and Neil Asher Silberman, *The Bible Unearthed: Archaeology's New Vision of Ancient Israel and the Origin of its Sacred Texts* (New York: Simon and Schuster, 2001).

7   *domesticated some 10,000 to 12,000 years ago*   See Graeme Barker, *The Agricultural Revolution in Prehistory: Why Did Foragers Become Farmers?* (Oxford: Oxford University Press, 2006);

Daniel C. Snell, *Life in the Ancient Near East, 3100-332 B.C.E.* (New Haven: Yale University Press, 1998). For a general overview, further references, and bibliography on both the origins of agriculture and the invention of irrigation in this region, see Susan Pollock, *Ancient Mesopotamia* (Cambridge: Cambridge University Press, 1999).

8   *based on a variety of environmental, geological, and archaeological data, Juris Zarins*   On Zarins's suggestion for the location of the Garden of Eden (he has not published his own theory), see Hamblin, "Sleuthing the Garden of Eden," 127-135; T. Krausz, "Paradise Found," *Jerusalem Report*, February 1, 1999. Much of Zarins's related scholarly research may be found in his review article entitled "The Early Settlement of Southern Mesopotamia: A Review of Recent Historical, Geological and Archaeological Research," *Journal of the American Oriental Society* 112, no. 1 (1992): 55-77.

9   *In a brief article entitled "The Rivers of Paradise"*   See Speiser, "The Rivers of Paradise," 473-485.

9   *A second possibility*   See James Sauer, "A Lost River of Eden: Rediscovering the Pishon," in *Mysteries of the Bible: From the Garden of Eden to the Shroud of Turin,* Molly Dewsnap Meinhardt, ed. (Washington, D.C.: Biblical Archaeology Society, 2004), 3-11.

10   *More recently, British archaeologist David Rohl*   See David Rohl, *Legend: The Genesis of Civilisation* (London: Century, 1998), 46-68. For articles written about his hypothesis, see Peter Martin, "The Secret Garden," *Sunday Times,* October 11, 1998; Krausz, "Paradise Found," 38-43. See also now the discussion of Rohl's hypothesis in Scafi, *Mapping Paradise,* 12-14, 369-370, and figures 0.4-0.5. Rohl's earlier work regarding his "New Chronology" for redating the ancient world is probably best known through his *Pharaohs and Kings: A Biblical Quest* (New York: Crown, 1996), which was made into a three-part television documentary program. As a whole, Rohl's "New Chronology" has not been particularly well received by the academic community; it is seen as falling into the same general category as Immanuel Velikovsky's *Ages in Chaos: A Reconstruction of Ancient History from the Exodus to King Akhnaton* (New York: Doubleday, 1952) and Peter James's *Centuries of Darkness: A Challenge to the Chronology of Old World Archaeology* (London: Jonathan Cape, 1991), each of which also suggest alternate chronologies to those generally accepted by the scholarly world.

10   *Two years after Rohl's hypothesis was first published, Gary Greenberg*   See Gary Greenberg, *101 Myths of the Bible: How Ancient Scribes Invented Biblical History* (Naperville, IL: Sourcebooks, 2000), 59-61. See also http://ggreenberg.tripod.com (accessed on January 5, 2007).

11   *originated in Africa and migrated outward from there*   See the most recent, interesting books on ancestry and genetics by Spencer Wells, *Deep Ancestry: Inside the Genographic Project*

(Washington, D.C.: National Geographic, 2006); Spencer Wells, *The Journey of Man: A Genetic Odyssey* (Princeton: Princeton University Press, 2002). See also Luigi Luca Cavalli-Sforza, *Genes, Peoples, and Languages*, trans. Mark Seielstad (New York: North Point Press, 2000); Luigi Luca Cavalli-Sforza and Francesco Cavalli-Sforza, *The Great Human Diasporas: The History of Diversity and Evolution*, trans. Sarah Thorne (Reading, MA: Addison-Wesley Publishing Company, Inc., 1995).

12   *In 2001, Michael S. Sanders*   On Sanders's claim to have located the Garden of Eden, see Peter Goodspeed, "Garden of Eden in Turkey, Says Bible Scholar," Canadian *National Post,* January 11, 2001; Peter Goodspeed, "Garden of Eden Said to Be in Turkey," *Chicago Sun-Times,* January 12, 2001; Matthew Kalman, "Has a Satellite Spotted the Original Garden of Eden in Eastern Turkey?" *Daily Mail,* January 17, 2001. See also Carol McGraw, "Thou Shalt Search Archaeology: Irvine Scholar Says He May Know Where the Tablets of the Ten Commandments Lie," *Orange County Register,* March 3, 2001; Sanders's own Web site: http://www.biblemysteries.com, with his mission/message statement and numerous linked pages (accessed on January 5, 2007).

13   *the Primeval History*   See Robert Alter, *The Five Books of Moses: A Translation with Commentary* (New York: W. W. Norton and Company, 2004), 12-14; Speiser, *Genesis: Introduction, Translation, and Notes,* 20. See also Pope John Paul II, *Man and Woman He Created Them: A Theology of the Body,* trans. Michael Waldstein (Boston: Pauline Books and Media, 2006), 137-138, 157. The pope refers to this portion of Genesis as "manifesting . . . [an] early mythical character" and elaborates, "The term 'myth' does not refer to fictitious-fabulous content, but simply to an archaic way of expressing a deeper content."

13   *the Garden of Eden was obviously a geographic reality*   See Speiser, "The Rivers of Paradise," 473.

14   *a battered sign standing at the site of Querna in Iraq*   See Scafi, *Mapping Paradise,* 370-371 and figure 12.1.

15   *As Victor Hurowitz*   As quoted by Krausz, "Paradise Found," 38-43.

CHAPTER 2

19   *consists of two different stories that have been woven together*   For a concise and readable explanation of the two sources woven together in Genesis, called J and P by biblical scholars, and explicit comparisons of the details from the two stories about Noah and his ark, see Richard E. Friedman, *Who Wrote the Bible?* (San Francisco: HarperSanFrancisco, 1997), 54-60; Ephraim A. Speiser, *Genesis: Introduction, Translation, and Notes,* the Anchor Bible (New York: Doubleday and Company, 1964), xx-xliii, 54-56; Robert Alter, *Genesis:*

Translation and Commentary (New York: W. W. Norton and Company, 1996), 30; Robert Alter, *The Five Books of Moses: A Translation with Commentary* (New York: W. W. Norton and Company, 2004), 10-12, 42. See also William H. Stiebing, Jr., *Ancient Astronauts, Cosmic Collisions, and Other Popular Theories about Man's Past* (Buffalo, N.Y.: Prometheus Books, 1984), 9-16; William H. Stiebing, Jr., "A Futile Quest: The Search for Noah's Ark" in *Mysteries of the Bible: From the Garden of Eden to the Shroud of Turin*, ed. Molly Dewsnap Meinhardt (Washington, D.C.: Biblical Archaeology Society, 2004), 25-26.

20   *In 1872, George Smith*   See William H. Stiebing, Jr., *Ancient Astronauts, Cosmic Collisions, and Other Popular Theories about Man's Past* (Buffalo, N.Y.: Prometheus Books, 1984), 9-11; William H. Stiebing, Jr., *Uncovering the Past* (New York: Oxford University Press, 1993), 110-111; Stiebing, "A Futile Quest," 17-18. See also the interesting and useful article by Tikva Frymer-Kensky, "What the Babylonian Flood Stories Can and Cannot Teach Us about the Genesis Flood," *Biblical Archaeology Review* 4, no. 4 (1978): 32-41.

22   *All the destructive winds*   Translation originally published in Joan Aruz, ed., *Art of the First Cities: The Third Millennium B.C. from the Mediterranean to the Indus* (New York: Metropolitan Museum of Art, 2003), 478.

23   *I will reveal to you a mystery*   Translation following Nancy K. Sandars, *The Epic of Gilgamesh* (Harmondsworth, England: Penguin Books, 1972), 107. For the date of the historical Gilgamesh and the evolution of the *Epic of Gilgamesh*, see Jeffrey H. Tigay, *The Evolution of the Gilgamesh Epic* (Philadelphia: University of Pennsylvania Press, 1982). See also the discussion by Peter Enns, *Inspiration and Incarnation: Evangelicals and the Problem of the Old Testament* (Grand Rapids, Mich.: Baker Academic, 2005), 27-29, 39-41, 49-51.

24   *These are the measurements*   Translation following Sandars, *The Epic of Gilgamesh*, 108-109. See also the discussion in Ralph K. Pederson's "Was Noah's Ark a Sewn Boat?" *Biblical Archaeology Review* 31, no. 3 (2005): 18-23, 55-56.

25   *You know the city Shurrupak*   Translation following Sandars, *The Epic of Gilgamesh*, 108.

25   *the Flood is sent for a moral reason*   For a deeper discussion of the reasons why the Flood was sent in the Genesis story, see Frymer-Kensky, "What the Babylonian Flood Stories," 32-41.

26   *Ea . . . warned me in a dream*   Translation following Sandars, *The Epic of Gilgamesh*, 108.

27   *some sort of Flood legend*   See the brief discussion in Stiebing, *Ancient Astronauts*, 17-22.

27   *made the front page of newspapers around the world that year*   See Molly Dewsnap, "The Ur-Flood? Uncovering the Deluge," *Biblical Archaeology Review* 22, no. 4 (1996): 56; Susan Pollock, "Ur," in *The Oxford Encyclopedia of Archaeology in the Near East*, vol. 5, ed. Eric M. Meyers (New York: Oxford University Press, 1997), 288-291; P. R. S. Moorey, *Ur of*

the Chaldees: A Revised and Updated Edition of Sir Leonard Woolley's Excavations at Ur (Ithaca, N.Y.: Cornell University Press, 1982). See also Stiebing, *Ancient Astronauts,* 19; Stiebing, "A Futile Quest," 19-20. See the discussion by Max Mallowan (longtime assistant to Sir Leonard Woolley and an important archaeologist in his own right, as well as the husband of Agatha Christie), "Noah's Flood Reconsidered," *Iraq* 26 (1964): 62-82.

28   *A much more relevant discovery*   See William B. Ryan and Walter C. Pitman, *Noah's Flood: The New Scientific Discoveries about the Event That Changed History* (New York: Simon and Schuster, 1998). See also Ian Wilson, *Before the Flood: The Biblical Flood as a Real Event and How It Changed the Course of Civilization* (New York: St. Martin's Press, 2002).

28   *that a freshwater lake was inundated by the Black Sea some 7,500 years ago*   See some of the results and a discussion of Ballard's expedition posted on the National Geographic Web site: http://www.nationalgeographic.com/blacksea/ax/frame.html (accessed on January 25, 2007).

29   *Most expeditions going in search*   For a brief discussion of the ancient sources, see Stiebing, *Ancient Astronauts,* 22-23 and figure 1; Stiebing, "A Futile Quest," 20-21.

30   *William Stiebing*   For the list of modern expeditions that have gone in search of the ark, see Stiebing, *Ancient Astronauts,* 22-27; see also the update in Stiebing, "A Futile Quest," 21-24 (also see footnote 5 on page 20 for a list of books published by "Arkeologists," as such people are frequently called).

30   *Another infamous set of claims came from Fernand Navarra, who in 1955*   See Stiebing, "A Futile Quest," 23-24; Stiebing, *Ancient Astronauts,* 25-27.

30   *Perhaps the most infamous set of claims*   For these claims about Noah's ark and for more about Ron Wyatt himself, see the official Web site of Wyatt Archaeological Research, especially https://safeco3.net/wyattmuseum/donations2.htm and http://wyattmuseum. com/noahs-ark.htm (and linked pages). An informal position statement for Wyatt Archaeological Research can be found at http://wyattmuseum.com/meetings.htm (all pages accessed on January 5, 2007). On his being held hostage by Kurdish separatist rebels, see the brief mention on the above Web site and, among other articles, Maria Puente, "Ark Hunters Abducted: 3 from USA among 5 Seized in Turkey," *USA Today,* September 3, 1991.

31   *a former police investigator and SWAT team member*   Bob Cornuke is the founder and president of the BASE Institute; see http://www.baseinstitute.org and especially http://www. baseinstitute.org/bob.html. For the BASE Institute's mission statement, see http://www. baseinstitute.org/explore.html (all pages accessed on January 5, 2007). See also Mark I. Pinsky, "A Bible-based Indiana Jones," *Orlando Sentinel,* January 13, 2007, for Cornuke's

recent statement, "The word of God is never wrong. Archaeology can only reveal truths that are already existing in the Bible."

31   *Media reports announced that Cornuke's 2006 expedition* For the details, claims, and reactions to Cornuke's recent expedition, see Kate Ravilious, "Noah's Ark Discovered in Iran?" *National Geographic News,* July 5, 2006, http://news.nationalgeographic.com/news/2006/07/060705-noahs-ark.html. See also Robert Cornuke and David Halbrook, *In Search of the Lost Mountains of Noah: The Discovery of the Real Mts. of Ararat* (Nashville, Tenn.: Broadman and Holman Publishers, 2001), and Robert Cornuke, *Ark Fever* (Wheaton, IL: Tyndale House Publishers, 2005).

33   *could be reflected in the actual archaeological record* See Speiser, *Genesis,* 75-76.

33   *The original story* See commentary by Bruce M. Metzger and Roland E. Murphy, eds., *New Oxford Annotated Bible, with the Apocryphal/Deuterocanonical Books* (New York: Oxford University Press, 1991), 14-15OT.

34   *Hanging Gardens of Babylon* Irving L. Finkel, "The Hanging Gardens of Babylon," in *The Seven Wonders of the Ancient World,* eds. Peter A. Clayton and Martin J. Price (London: Routledge, 1998), 38-58.

34   *linking the Tower of Babel* Placing the Tower of Babel in the city of Babylon is entirely more plausible, from an archaeological and historical point of view, than the recent suggestion by Michael S. Sanders, the self-taught "Biblical Scholar of Archaeology, Egyptology and Assyriology," who announced in 1999 that he had located the Tower of Babel "in the Pontus region of the Black Sea coast of Turkey" by using "satellite photographs from NASA, the American space agency." On Sanders's theory for the location of the Tower of Babel, see Jack Grimston, "Tower of Babel Is 'Found' Near the Black Sea," *Sunday Times,* April 4, 1999.

35   *Deucalian and the Flood* On the transmission of the Flood stories around the world, see Stiebing, *Ancient Astronauts,* 3-4, 17-19. On the influence of the Near East on Greek mythology and literature, see Walter Burkert, *The Orientalizing Revolution: Near Eastern Influence on Greek Culture in the Early Archaic Age* (Cambridge, MA: Harvard University Press, 1998).

CHAPTER 3

41   *the land of Shinar* See J. Maxwell Miller and John H. Hayes, *A History of Ancient Israel and Judah,* 2nd ed. (Louisville, Ky.: Westminster John Knox Press, 2006), 62.

42   *Most archaeologists and biblical scholars think* See the discussion in David M. Howard, Jr., "Sodom and Gomorrah Revisited," *Journal of the Evangelical Theological Society* 27 (1984):

387-388. See also J. Penrose Harland, "Sodom and Gomorrah. Part I. The Location of the Cities of the Plain," *Biblical Archaeologist* 5, no. 2 (1942): 17-32; J. Penrose Harland, "Sodom and Gomorrah. Part II. The Destruction of the Cities of the Plain," *Biblical Archaeologist* 6, no. 3 (1943): 41-54.

43   *The text* In fact, the editors of the *New Oxford Annotated Bible* simply say "the Dead Sea" rather than the "Salt Sea." See Bruce M. Metzger and Roland E. Murphy, eds., *New Oxford Annotated Bible, with the Apocryphal/Deuterocanonical Books* (New York: Oxford University Press, 1991), 17OT.

43   *the Valley of Shaveh* See commentary by the editors of the *New Oxford Annotated Bible*, 18OT.

43   *The only other tidbit of biblical information* See Howard, "Sodom and Gomorrah Revisited," 392.

43   *The other texts* See Harland, "Sodom and Gomorrah. Part I," 22-23, and "Sodom and Gomorrah. Part II," 44-47.

44   *a flurry of excitement took place* See Paolo Matthiae, *Ebla: An Empire Rediscovered* (London: Hodder and Stoughton, 1977); Giovanni Pettinato, *The Archives of Ebla: An Empire Inscribed in Clay* (Garden City, N.Y.: Doubleday, 1981).

45   *were soon shown to be faulty* See Alan Millard, "Ebla and the Bible: What's Left (if Anything)?" *Bible Review* 8, no. 2 (1992): 18-31, 60, 62; Hershel Shanks, "Ebla Evidence Evaporates," *Biblical Archaeology Review* 5, no. 6 (1979): 52-53; Alfonso Archi, "Are 'The Cities of the Plain' Mentioned in the Ebla Tablets?" *Biblical Archaeology Review* 7, no. 6 (1981): 54-55. See also Hershel Shanks, "BAR Interviews Giovanni Pettinato," *Biblical Archaeology Review* 6, no. 5 (1980): 46-52, in which Pettinato stands by his original identifications.

45   *as Rast and Schaub have noted, Bab edh-Dhra* For the data concerning the excavations at Bab edh-Dhra and Numeira, see the report by Walter Rast and Thomas Schaub, "Expedition to the Southeastern Dead Sea Plain, Jordan, 1979," *ASOR Newsletter*, June 1980, 12-17, especially the subsection entitled "Are These Sites Sodom and Gomorrah?" 16-17. See also the discussions by Hershel Shanks, "Have Sodom and Gomorrah Been Found?" *Biblical Archaeology Review* 6, no. 5 (1980): 26-36; Willem C. van Hattem, "Once Again: Sodom and Gomorrah," *Biblical Archaeologist* 44 (1981): 87-92; Bryant G. Wood, "The Discovery of the Sin Cities of Sodom and Gomorrah," *Bible and Spade* 12, no. 3 (1999): 67-80. See also Walter E. Rast, "Bab edh-Dhr'a and the Origin of the Sodom Saga," in *Archaeology and Biblical Interpretation: Essays in Memory of D. Glenn Rose*, eds. Leo D. Perdue, Lawrence E. Toombs, and Gary L. Johnson (Atlanta: John

Knox Press, 1987), 185-201, with further bibliography; Walter E. Rast, "Bronze Age Cities along the Dead Sea," *Archaeology* 40, no. 1 (1987): 42-49; Michael D. Coogan, "Numeira 1981," *Bulletin of the American Schools of Oriental Research* 255 (1984): 75-81; Walter E. Rast and R. Thomas Schaub, *The Southeastern Dead Sea Plain Expedition: An Interim Report of the 1977 Season (Annual of the American Schools of Oriental Research)*, vol. 46 (Cambridge, MA: ASOR, 1981); R. Thomas Schaub, "Bab edh-Dhra," *The Oxford Encyclopedia of Archaeology in the Near East*, vol. 1, ed. Eric N. Meyers (New York: Oxford University Press, 1997), 248-251; R. Thomas Schaub, "Southeast Dead Sea Plain," *The Oxford Encyclopedia of Archaeology in the Near East*, vol. 5, ed. Eric N. Meyers (New York: Oxford University Press, 1997), 62-64; R. Thomas Schaub, "Bab edh-Dhra," *The New Encyclopedia of Archaeological Excavations in the Holy Land*, vol. 1, ed. Ephraim Stern, Ayelet Lewinson-Gilboa, and Joseph Aviram (Jerusalem: Carta, 1993), 130-136.

48   *One of the excavators* Coogan, "Numeira 1981," 76; Rast, "Bronze Age Cities," 47-48.

48   *In June 1980* See Rast and Schaub, "Expedition to the Southeastern Dead Sea," 16-17.

49   *As Rast pointed out* See Rast, "Bab edh-Dhr'a and the Origin," 193.

49   *Rast also mentioned* See Rast, "Bab edh-Dhr'a and the Origin," 186.

50   *Ron Wyatt, the nurse anesthetist* For these claims about Sodom and Gomorrah, see the official Wyatt Archaeological Research Web site: http://www.wyattmuseum.com/cities-of-the-plain.htm and linked pages, especially http://www.wyattmuseum.com/cities-of-the-plain-02.htm (accessed on January 5, 2007).

50   *Wyatt's claims are baseless* See Elizabeth H. Gierlowski-Kordesch, review of Ron Wyatt's "Discovered: Sodom and Gomorrah! A Video," *Biblical Archaeology Review* 24, no. 5 (1998): 60-62; Ron W. Pritchett, "Recognizing Junk Science," *Professional Geologist*, December 1997.

51   *Similarly, Michael S. Sanders* For more on Sanders's Dead Sea diving expedition, see Christopher Goodwin, "Satellite Sleuth Finds Sodom and Gomorrah," *Sunday Times*, October 18, 1998; Jonathan Leake, "Dead Sea Sub Dives for Lost City of Sodom," *Sunday Times*, November 21, 1999; Jonathan Petre, "Sodom and Gomorrah are 'Found at Bottom of Dead Sea,'" *London Telegraph*, March 26, 2000; Peter Sheridan, "Finder of the Lost Ark . . . and the Garden of Eden, Sodom and Gomorrah, the Tower of Babel and the 10 Commandments," *Daily Express*, March 15, 2001. See also Sanders's own Web site, http://www.biblemysteries.com (accessed on January 5, 2007).

52   *For instance, as early as 1936* See Frederick G. Clapp, "The Site of Sodom and Gomorrah," *American Journal of Archaeology* 40 (1936): 323-344; Frederick G. Clapp, "Geology and Bitumens of the Dead Sea Area, Palestine and Transjordan," *Bulletin of the American Association of Petroleum* 20 (1936): 881-909. See also various suggestions

provided by Harland, "Sodom and Gomorrah. Part I," 17-32; Harland, "Sodom and Gomorrah. Part II," 41-54; as well as the summaries presented by David Howard, Jr., "Sodom and Gomorrah Revisited," especially 394-399.

53 *More recently, in 1995* See David Neev and K. O. Emery, *The Destruction of Sodom, Gomorrah, and Jericho* (Oxford: Oxford University Press, 1995). For the brief—and harsh—reviews, see Amos Nur's review in *Earth Sciences History* 16, vol. 1 (1997): 57-58 and Ronald Hendel's review in *Biblical Archaeology Review* 23, no. 4 (1997): 70.

53 *As they and others have pointed out* See Graham M. Harris and Anthony P. Beardow, "The Destruction of Sodom and Gomorrah: A Geotechnical Perspective," *Quarterly Journal of Engineering Geology* 28 (1995): 349-362.

53 *Harris and Beardow also suggested* See Harris and Beardow, "The Destruction of Sodom and Gomorrah," 349. For a discussion of "liquefaction failure" in layman's terms, see Jeanne B. Perkins, et al., "The REAL Dirt on Liquefaction: A Guide to the Liquefaction Hazard in Future Earthquakes Affecting the San Francisco Bay Area," February 2001, http://www.abag.ca.gov/bayarea/eqmaps/liquefac/Lq_rept.pdf (accessed January 5, 2007).

53 *Most recently, in 2001* See BBC News, "Scientists Uncover Sodom's Fiery End," August 18, 2001, http://news.bbc.co.uk/2/hi/middle_east/1497476.stm (accessed January 5, 2007). See also the longer discussion by Jessica Cecil, "The Destruction of Sodom and Gomorrah," http://www.bbc.co.uk/history/ancient/cultures/sodom_gomorrah_01.shtml (accessed January 5, 2007).

54 *Maxwell Miller and John Hayes* For a succinct discussion that includes the now-discounted "Amorite Hypothesis" proposed by William F. Albright and others, see J. Maxwell Miller and John H. Hayes, *A History of Ancient Israel and Judah*, 2nd ed. (Louisville, Ky.: Westminster John Knox Press, 2006), 51-53. See also Iaian Provan, V. Philips Long, and Tremper Longman III, *A Biblical History of Israel* (Louisville, Ky.: Westminster John Knox Press, 2003), 108-121. On the suggested dates for Abraham, see Jack Finegan, *Handbook of Biblical Chronology: Principles of Time Reckoning in the Ancient World and Problems of Chronology in the Bible,* rev. ed. (Peabody, MA: Hendrickson Publishers, 1998), 196-206.

56 *The debates concerning Abraham* For a summary of the various suggestions, see Israel Finkelstein and Neil Asher Silberman, *The Bible Unearthed: Archaeology's New Vision and the Origin of Its Sacred Texts* (New York: Free Press, 2001), 319-325.

56 *there is no proof, however, that these two sites are one and the same* For further discussion, see Finkelstein and Silberman, *The Bible Unearthed,* 312-313; Molly Dewsnap Meinhardt, "Abraham's Ur: Did Woolley Excavate the Wrong Place?" *Biblical Archaeology Review*

26, no. 1 (2000): 20-25, 60; Alan R. Millard, "Where Was Abraham's Ur? The Case for the Babylonian City," *Biblical Archaeology Review* 27, no. 3 (2001): 52-53, 57.

57　*In addressing the first question*　See Rast, "Bab edh-Dhr'a and the Origin," 186.

57　*Other scholars have suggested*　For a brief discussion of scholars who have suggested a possible Canaanite origin for the story of Sodom and Gomorrah, see Rast, "Bab edh-Dhr'a and the Origin," 188-190 (also see page 189 for a possible Iron Age date for the story).

59　*short-lived carbon-14 dates*　R. Thomas Schaub, personal communication, February 17, 2007.

59　*In* The Oxford Companion to the Bible　Joseph A. Greene, "Sodom and Gomorrah," in *The Oxford Companion to the Bible*, eds. Bruce M. Metzger and Michael D. Coogan (New York: Oxford University Press, 1993), 707.

59　*Steven Collins*　See Tall el Hammam Excavation Project (TeHEP), "Digging the Past," April 2006, http://www.trinitysouthwest.com/uploads/hammam_hi.pdf (accessed January 5, 2007). The article mentions an additional monograph published by Collins, *The Search for Sodom and Gomorrah* (Albuquerque, NM: TSU Press, 2003-2006).

60　*Frankly, though*　Originally quoted by Andrew L. Slayman in "Sodom and Gomorrah Update," *Archaeology* 49, no. 4 (July/August 1996), and reprinted in *Secrets of the Bible* (New York: Hatherleigh Press, 2004), 56.

CHAPTER 4

65　*the parting of the Red (Reed) Sea*　See Bruce M. Metzger and Roland E. Murphy, eds., *New Oxford Annotated Bible, with the Apocryphal/Deuterocanonical Books* (New York: Oxford University Press, 1991), 86-87OT.

65　*Let us begin by considering precisely when*　On the date of Joseph in Egypt, see James K. Hoffmeier, *Israel in Egypt: The Evidence for the Authenticity of the Exodus Tradition* (Oxford: Oxford University Press, 1997), 77-98, with further bibliography; see also Jack Finegan, *Handbook of Biblical Chronology: Principles of Time Reckoning in the Ancient World and Problems of Chronology in the Bible,* rev. ed. (Peabody, MA: Hendrickson Publishers, 1998), 206-213, 220-221, 223-224; Iaian Provan, V. Philips Long, and Tremper Longman III, *A Biblical History of Israel* (Louisville, Ky.: Westminster John Knox Press, 2003), 121-125.

66　*well-known wall paintings at Beni Hasan*　See Eric H. Cline, "Trade and Exchange in the Levant," in *Near Eastern Archaeology: A Reader:* 360-366, ed. Suzanne Richard (Winona Lake, Ind.: Eisenbrauns, 2003), 362 and figure 94. On both the wall paintings and the larger question of Semites in Egypt, see Hoffmeier, *Israel in Egypt,* 52-68, with further bibliography. On connecting the Joshua story to the Hyksos period, see Baruch Halpern, "The Exodus from Egypt: Myth or Reality?" in *The Rise of Ancient Israel*, ed. Hershel Shanks (Washington, D.C.: Biblical Archaeology Society, 1992), 99-101. On the Hyksos in Egypt, see Donald B. Redford, *Egypt, Canaan, and Israel in Ancient Times* (Princeton: Princeton University Press, 1992), 98-122.

67   *it is not unique among the annals of ancient stories*   On parallels for the story of the birth and childhood of Moses, see Hoffmeier, *Israel in Egypt*, 136-143, with further bibliography; Provan, Long, and Longman, III, *A Biblical History*, 125-126.

67   *the myth of Romulus and Remus*   See Livy, *The Early History of Rome*, 1.3-1.5.

70   *the great Persian ruler and conqueror, Cyrus the Great*   See Herodotus, *The Histories*, 1.107-122.

70   *I am Sargon, the mighty king—king of Akkad*   Translation follows Mark W. Chavalas, *The Ancient Near East: Historical Sources in Translation* (Oxford: Blackwell Publishing, 2006), 22-24. See also James B. Pritchard, ed., *Ancient Near Eastern Texts Relating to the Old Testament*, 3rd ed. (Princeton: Princeton University Press, 1969), 119.

74   *Maxwell Miller and John Hayes*   For a brief discussion on the numbers given and the problems that they cause in trying to interpret the story of the Exodus, see J. Maxwell Miller and John H. Hayes, *A History of Ancient Israel and Judah*, 2nd ed. (Louisville, Ky.: Westminster John Knox Press, 2006), 72.

74   *600 families or clans*   See discussion by Nahum M. Sarna, "Israel in Egypt: The Egyptian Sojourn and the Exodus" (revised by Hershel Shanks), in *Ancient Israel: From Abraham to the Roman Destruction of the Temple*, rev. and exp. ed., (New York: Prentice Hall, 1999), 45, 306, and footnote 40.

75   *Not all scholars are prepared to accept these dates*   For arguments about the date of the Exodus, see John J. Bimson and David Livingston, "Redating the Exodus," *Biblical Archaeology Review* 13, no. 5 (1987): 40-53, 66-68; Baruch Halpern, "Radical Exodus Redating Fatally Flawed," *Biblical Archaeology Review* 13, no. 6 (1987): 56-61; John J. Bimson, "Redating the Exodus: A Reply to Baruch Halpern," *Biblical Archaeology Review* 14, no. 4 (1988): 52-55; Alan Millard, "How Reliable Is Exodus?" *Biblical Archaeology Review* 26, no. 4 (2000): 50-57; see also John J. Bimson, *Redating the Exodus and Conquest*, 2nd ed. (Sheffield: Almond Press, 1981), passim; Jack Finegan, *Handbook of Biblical Chronology: Principles of Time Reckoning in the Ancient World and Problems of Chronology in the Bible*, rev. ed. (Peabody, MA: Hendrickson Publishers, 1998), 202-203, 225-245; Sarna, "Israel in Egypt," 33-54; Provan, Long, and Longman, *A Biblical History*, 131-132.

77   *On the stele*   Translation following Pritchard, *Ancient Near Eastern Texts*, 378. See also Miller and Hayes, *A History of Ancient Israel*, 39-41. There have been many discussion of this

inscription over the years. Some of the most recent include Itamar Singer, "Merneptah's Campaign to Canaan and the Egyptian Occupation of the Southern Coastal Plain of Palestine in the Ramesside Period," *Bulletin of the American Schools of Oriental Research* 269 (1988): 1-10; Michael G. Hasel, "Israel in the Merneptah Stela," *Bulletin of the American Schools of Oriental Research* 296 (1994): 45-61; Frank J. Yurco, "Merneptah's Canaanite Campaign," *Journal of the American Research Center in Egypt* 23 (1986): 189-215; Frank J. Yurco, "Merneptah's Wars, the Sea Peoples' and Israel's Origins," in *Ancient Egypt, the Aegean and the Near East: Studies in Honour of Martha Rhoads Bell,* vol. 2, ed. Jacke Phillips, Lanny Bell, Bruce B. Williams, James Hoch, and Ronald J. Leprohon (San Antonio, TX: Van Siclen Books, 1997), 497-506.

77   *There is, however, also a third possibility*   See Halpern, "The Exodus from Egypt," 105. See also Avraham Malamat, "Let My People Go and Go and Go and Go," *Biblical Archaeology Review* 24, no. 1 (1998): 62-66, 85.

78   *textual mention of the Israelites' existence*   On the "Habiru" (or "'Apiru") who are mentioned in Canaanite texts from the 14th and 13th centuries B.C., and their possible relationship to the biblical Hebrews, see most recently Miller and Hayes, *A History of Ancient Israel,* 37, 113, 115, 117; see also Nadav Na'aman, "The 'Conquest of Canaan' in the Book of Joshua and in History," reproduced in Nadav Na'aman, *Canaan in the Second Millennium B.C.E. Collected Essays,* vol. 2 (Winona Lake, Ind.: Eisenbrauns, 2005), 317-392.

78   *what route would (or could) Moses and the Hebrews have followed*   On the possible geographical routes taken by the Hebrews during the Exodus, see the very detailed and useful discussions by Hoffmeier, *Israel in Egypt,* 176-222, with full bibliography, maps, and photographs; see also Hoffmeier, *Ancient Israel in Sinai: The Evidence for the Authenticity of the Wilderness Tradition* (Oxford: Oxford University Press, 2005), 35-109, with full bibliography, maps, and photographs. Similarly, see the discussion by Kenneth A. Kitchen, *On the Reliability of the Old Testament* (Grand Rapids, Mich.: William B. Eerdmans Publishing Company, 2003), 254-274, and contrast the views presented by Israel Finkelstein and Neil A. Silberman, *The Bible Unearthed: Archaeology's New Vision of Ancient Israel and the Origin of Its Sacred Texts* (New York: Free Press, 2001), 58-64.

79   *the question of the location of Mount Sinai*   On the various locations which have been suggested for Mount Sinai, and the arguments for and against each, see James K. Hoffmeier, *Ancient Israel in Sinai,* 111-148, with full bibliography; Kitchen, *On the Reliability,* 269-272 and table 20. See also Finkelstein and Silberman, *The Bible Unearthed,* 326-328.

80 *the so-called Negative Confession* Translation following W. K. Simpson, ed., *The Literature of Ancient Egypt*, 3rd ed. (New Haven: Yale University Press, 2003), 267-277.

81 *The Ten Commandments were not the only laws* For a recent discussion of the laws received by Moses at Mount Sinai, with full bibliography, see Hoffmeier, *Ancient Israel in Sinai*, 177-192.

81 *the Sumerian and other law codes of Ur-Nammu, Eshnunna, and Lipit-Ishtar* For an early Sumerian law code and for the translations from Hammurabi's Law Code, which are followed here, see Pritchard, *Ancient Near Eastern Texts*, 163-180, 525-526. See Jacob J. Finkelstein, *The Ox That Gored* (Philadelphia: American Philosophical Society, 1981), for a fascinating comparison of biblical laws that are also found in earlier law codes in the ancient Near East.

82 *the same punishments into the Hebrew Bible* See the brief discussion by Peter Enns, *Inspiration and Incarnation: Evangelicals and the Problem of the Old Testament* (Grand Rapids, Mich.: Baker Academic, 2005), 31-34.

82 *As the late Samuel Noah Kramer* See Samuel Noah Kramer, *History Begins at Sumer: Thirty-Nine "Firsts" in Recorded History* (Philadelphia, PA: University of Pennsylvania Press, 1981).

83 *when turning to archaeological evidence* On Hoffmeier's excavations at Tell el Borg, see especially Hoffmeier, *Ancient Israel in Sinai*; Hoffmeier, "The North Sinai Archaeological Project's Excavations at Tell el-Borg (Sinai): An Example of the 'New Biblical Archaeology,'" in *The Future of Biblical Archaeology: Reassessing Methodologies and Assumptions*, ed. James K. Hoffmeier and Alan Millard (Grand Rapids, Mich.: William B. Eerdmans Publishing Company, 2004), 53-55; see also the official Web site at www.tellelborg.org (accessed on January 18, 2007).

85 *no such evidence at the supposed time of the Exodus* See Finkelstein and Silberman, *The Bible Unearthed*, 62-63.

85 *to identify the famous ten plagues* See Robert R. Stieglitz, "Ancient Records and the Exodus Plagues," *Biblical Archaeology Review* 13, no. 6 (1987): 46-49; Siro I. Trevisanato, *The Plagues of Egypt: Archaeology, History, and Science Look at the Bible* (Piscataway, N.J.: Gorgias Press, 2005). See also the detailed discussions by Hoffmeier, *Israel in Egypt*, 144-155, with further bibliography; Kitchen, *On the Reliability*, 249-254.

85 *One of the favorite suggestions* See Christos G. Doumas, "High Art from the Time of Abraham: Was this the Lost Continent of Atlantis? Did a Volcano Part the Red Sea?" *Biblical Archaeology Review* 17, no. 1 (1991): 40-51; Hershel Shanks, "The Exodus and the Crossing of the Red Sea, According to Hans Goedicke," *Biblical Archaeology Review*

7, no. 5 (1981): 42-50; Charles R. Krahmalkov, "A Critique of Professor Goedicke's Exodus Theories," *Biblical Archaeology Review* 7, no. 5 (1981): 51-54; Eliezer D. Oren, "How Not to Create a History of the Exodus–A Critique of Professor Goedicke's Theories," *Biblical Archaeology Review* 7, no. 6 (1981): 46-53; Trevisanato, *The Plagues of Egypt.* On the revised date of the Santorini eruption, see the full discussion in Sturt W. Manning, *A Test of Time: The Volcano of Thera and the Chronology and History of the Aegean and East Mediterranean in the Mid Second Millennium BC* (Oxford: Oxbow Books, 1999); see also Sturt W. Manning, et al., "Chronology for the Aegean Late Bronze Age 1700-1400 B.C.," *Science* 312, no. 5773 (2006): 565-569; Michael Balter, "New Carbon Dates Support Revised History of Ancient Mediterranean," *Science* 312, no. 5773 (2006): 508-509; Walter L. Friedrich, et. al, "Santorini Eruption Radiocarbon Dated to 1627-1600 B.C.," *Science* 312, no. 5773 (2006): 548. On Jacobovici's television extravaganza on the Exodus, which aired in August 2006, see the subsequent debate between Jacobovici and Hershel Shanks, editor and publisher of *Biblical Archaeology Review,* posted at http://www.bib-arch.org/bswbOOexodus.html, and an additional debate between Jacobovici and Professor Ron Hendel of UC Berkeley, following Hendel's review of the film, posted at http://www.bib-arch.org/bswbOOexodusbeware.html; see also the review by Dr. Bryant G. Wood, director of the Associates for Biblical Research, posted at http://abr.christiananswers.net/articles/article58.html; and the official "Exodus Decoded" Web site, maintained by Jacobovici's company Associated Producers: http://www.theexodusdecoded.com (all sites accessed on January 5, 2007).

86   *the Egyptian expulsion of the Hyksos*   See the brief discussion by Finkelstein and Silberman, *The Bible Unearthed,* 56-57; see also Halpern, "The Exodus from Egypt," 87-113.

86   *the story was fabricated*   See Thomas L. Thompson, *The Mythic Past: Biblical Archaeology and the Myth of Israel* (New York: Basic Books, 2000) and Keith Whitelam, *The Invention of Ancient Israel* (Boston: Routledge, 1997), as compared to Redford, *Egypt, Canaan, and Israel* and Finkelstein and Silberman, *The Bible Unearthed,* 65-71.

87   *Finkelstein refers to himself as a "centrist"*   See the interview by Hershel Shanks, "A 'Centrist' at the Center of Controversy: BAR Interviews Israel Finkelstein," *Biblical Archaeology Review* 28, no. 6 (2002): 38-49, 64-68.

87   *Finkelstein and Silberman point out*   Finkelstein and Silberman, *The Bible Unearthed,* 65.

91   *an interview with the Israeli newspaper* Ha'aretz   Aviva Lori, "Grounds for Disbelief," *Ha'aretz,* http://www.haaretz.com/hasen/pages/ShArt.jhtml?itemNo=291264andcontrassID=2and subContrassID=14andsbSubContrassID=0andlistSrc=Y (accessed on January 5, 2007).

CHAPTER 5

96   *Legend of Keret*   Translation following James B. Pritchard, ed., *Ancient Near Eastern Texts Relating to the Old Testament*, 3rd ed. (Princeton: Princeton University Press, 1969), 142-149.

97   *Numerous scholars have already commented*   See Theodor Gaster, *Myth, Legend and Custom in the Old Testament* (New York: Harper and Row, 1969), 412; Steven E. Loewenstamm, "The Seven Day Unit in Ugaritic Epic Literature," *Israel Exploration Journal* 15, no. 3 (1965): 121-133; Foster R. McCurley, Jr., "'And After Six Days' (Mark 9:2): A Semitic Literary Device," *Journal of Biblical Literature* 93, no. 1 (1974): 67-81; Daniel E. Fleming, "The Seven-Day Siege of Jericho in Holy War," in *Ki Baruch Hu: Ancient Near Eastern, Biblical, and Judaic Studies in Honor of Baruch A. Levine*, eds. Robert Chazan, William W. Hallo, and Lawrence H. Schiffman (Winona Lake, Ind.: Eisenbrauns, 1999), 211-228, with extensive bibliography. Fleming also gives additional examples of military campaigns involving seven days which are found in the Hebrew Bible, including 1 Samuel 11:3, 13:8; and 2 Kings 3:9.

97   *accounts of armies marching around cities*   See Yigael Yadin, *The Art of Warfare in Biblical Lands* (New York: McGraw-Hill, 1963), 99-100; Theodor Gaster, *Myth, Legend and Custom in the Old Testament* (New York: Harper and Row, 1969), 412-413; Daniel E. Fleming, "The Seven-Day Siege of Jericho in Holy War," in *Ki Baruch Hu: Ancient Near Eastern, Biblical, and Judaic Studies in Honor of Baruch A. Levine*, eds. Robert Chazan, William W Hallo, and Lawrence H Schiffman (Winona Lake, Ind.: Eisenbrauns, 1999), 219 and footnote 26; Avraham Malamat, "Israelite Conduct of War in the Conquest of Canaan," in *Symposia Celebrating the Seventy-Fifth Anniversary of the Founding of the American Schools of Oriental Research (1900-1975)*, ed. Frank M. Cross (Cambridge, MA: ASOR, 1979), 47-48.

99   *a lot more archaeological data available*   For full bibliographic references and an excellent summary of the earlier excavations and the problems involved with the archaeological evidence, see Bryant G. Wood, "Did the Israelites Conquer Jericho? A New Look at the Archaeological Evidence," *Biblical Archaeology Review* 16, no. 2 (1990): 44-58. See earlier research as well: Ernst Sellin and Carl Watzinger, *Jericho: Die Ergebnisse der Ausgrabungen (Jericho)* (Leipzig: J. C. Hinrichs, 1913); Carl Watzinger, "Zur Chronologie der Schichten von Jericho," *Zeitschrift der Deutschen Morgenländischen Gessellschaft* 80 (1926): 131-136; John Garstang and J. B. E. Garstang, *The Story of Jericho*, rev. ed. (London: Marshall, Morgan and Scott, 1948); Kathleen M. Kenyon, "Some Notes

on the History of Jericho in the Second Millennium B.C.," *Palestine Exploration Quarterly* (1951): 101-138; Kathleen M. Kenyon, *Digging Up Jericho* (London: Ernest Benn, 1957); Thomas A. Holland, ed., *Excavations at Jericho Volume 3: The Architecture and Stratigraphy of the Tell* (London: British School of Archaeology in Jerusalem, 1981); Kathleen M. Kenyon and Thomas A. Holland, *Excavations at Jericho Volume 4: The Pottery Type Series and Other Finds* (London: British School of Archaeology in Jerusalem, 1982); Kathleen M. Kenyon and Thomas A. Holland, *Excavations at Jericho Volume 5: The Pottery Phases of the Tell and Other Finds* (London: British School of Archaeology in Jerusalem, 1983). See also John R. Bartlett, *Jericho* (Grand Rapids, Mich.: William B. Eerdmans Publishing Company, 1982); Piotr Bienkowski, *Jericho in the Late Bronze Age* (Warminster: Aris and Phillips, 1986); Kathleen M. Kenyon, "Jericho," in *The New Encyclopedia of Archaeological Excavations in the Holy Land,* vol. 2, eds. Ephraim Stern, Ayelet Lewinson-Gilboa, and Joseph Aviram (Jerusalem: Carta, 1993), 674-681; Thomas A. Holland, "Jericho," in *The Oxford Encyclopedia of Archaeology in the Near East,* vol. 3, ed. Eric M. Meyers (New York: Oxford University Press, 1997), 220-224.

100 *The city was essentially uninhabited after that date*   See the brief discussion and description in Bryant G. Wood, "Dating Jericho's Destruction: Bienkowski Is Wrong on All Counts," *Biblical Archaeology Review* 16, no. 5 (1990): 45-49, 68-69.

101 *Bryant G. Wood, director of the Associates for Biblical Research*   The Web site for the Associates for Biblical Research can be found at http://abr.christiananswers.net/home. html. Their mission statement and philosophy of ministry can be found at http://abr. christiananswers.net/abr-ministry.html (both accessed on January 5, 2007).

101 *Piotr Bienkowski, former curator of Near Eastern and Egyptian antiquities*   Piotr Bienkowski is currently head of collections and academic development at the Manchester Museum at the University of Manchester, England. He is also an honorary research fellow at the School of Archaeology, Classics, and Egyptology at the University of Liverpool.

101 *Wood argued*   See Wood, "Did the Israelites Conquer Jericho?" 44-58; Wood, "Dating Jericho's Destruction," 45-49, 68-69.

101 *Bienkowski, however, stood firm with Kenyon*   See Piotr Bienkowski, "Jericho Was Destroyed in the Middle Bronze Age, Not the Late Bronze Age," *Biblical Archaeology Review* 16, no. 5 (1990): 45-46; see also Piotr Bienkowski, *Jericho in the Late Bronze Age* (Warminster: Aris and Phillips, 1986).

102 *The scholarly arguments between Bryant Wood and Piotr Bienkowski*   Randall Price's book *The Stones Cry Out: What Archaeology Reveals about the Truth of the Bible* (Eugene, Ore.: Harvest House Publishers, 1997), 152-153, presents Wood's arguments and conclusions

about Jericho, stating, "Wood has shown that once the destruction is correctly dated, the archaeological evidence harmonizes perfectly with the biblical record" (p. 152). However, Price never mentions Bienkowski in his chapter, nor does he present to his readers Bienkowski's very valid objections, nor does he cite—in either his footnotes or bibliography—the article in which Bienkowski presented his objections, even though he cites (in footnote 12 on page 413) both Wood's original article and Wood's subsequent response to Bienkowski's criticisms.

103 *An earthquake at Jericho that occurred less than a century ago* See Amos Nur, "And the Walls Came Tumbling Down: Old Testament Writings of Doom and Destruction Are Now Providing Researchers with a Record of Earthquakes Spanning 4,000 Years," *New Scientist,* July 6, 1991, 45-48; Amos Nur, "The End of the Bronze Age by Large Earthquakes?" in *Natural Catastrophes During Bronze Age Civilisations: Archaeological, Geological, Astronomical and Cultural Perspectives,* eds. Benny J. Peiser, Trevor Palmer, and Mark E. Bailey (Oxford: Archaeopress, 1998), 142-143, 146, and figure 6. See also Amos Nur and Christopher MacAskill, *The Walls Came Tumbling Down—Earthquakes in the Holy Land, a Video Documentary* (Stanford, Calif.: ESI Productions, 1991); Amos Nur and Hagai Ron, "Earthquake! Inspiration for Armageddon," *Biblical Archaeology Review* 23, no. 4 (1997): 48-55; Bryant G. Wood, "Did the Israelites Conquer Jericho? A New Look at the Archaeological Evidence," *Biblical Archaeology Review* 16, no. 2 (1990): 44-58.

104 *However, in 1993, a team of earthquake specialists* See now A. Shapira, R. Avni, and A. Nur, "Note: A New Estimate for the Epicenter of the Jericho Earthquake of 11 July, 1927," *Israel Journal of Earth Sciences* 42, no. 2 (1993): 93-96; R. Avni, D. Bowman, A. Shapira, and A. Nur, "Erroneous Interpretation of Historical Documents Related to the Epicenter of the 1927 Jericho Earthquake in the Holy Land," *Journal of Seismology* 6 (2002): 469-476. See previously John Garstang, *Joshua-Judges* (London: Constable and Co., 1931), 136-139.

107 *The book also gives us a summary of Joshua's southern campaign* See Kenneth A. Kitchen, *On the Reliability of the Old Testament* (Grand Rapids, Mich.: William B. Eerdmans Publishing Company, 2003), 173-174.

108 *Obviously, there are two tales within the biblical account* That there is more than one tale contained within this biblical account is by no means a new observation; biblical scholars using textual criticism have long proposed that there are a number of different stories concerned with the conquests of Joshua intertwined within the books of Joshua and Judges. It is likely that these stories were written at different times and by different groups (that is, the various tribes of Israelites may each have had their own

version), but that they were eventually redacted by later editors to form the single account that we possess today. See, for instance (each with extensive bibliography), J. Alberto Soggin, *Joshua: A Commentary* (Philadelphia: Westminster Press, 1972); Robert G. Boling, *Joshua: A New Translation with Notes and Commentary* (New York: Doubleday and Company, 1982); E. John Hamlin, *Inheriting the Land: A Commentary on the Book of Joshua* (Grand Rapids, Mich.: William B. Eerdmans Publishing Company, 1983); Yehezkel Kaufmann, *The Biblical Account of the Conquest of Canaan* (Jerusalem: Magnes Press, 1985); Carolyn Pressler, *Joshua, Judges, and Ruth* (Louisville, Ky.: Westminster John Knox Press, 2002). See also Kitchen, *On the Reliability,* 159-190.

109   *the site of et-Tell*   See Joseph Callaway, "Ai," in *The Anchor Bible Dictionary*, vol. 1, ed. David Noel Freedman (New York: Doubleday, 1992), 125-130; Joseph Callaway, "Ai," in *The New Encyclopedia of Archaeological Excavations in the Holy Land,* vol. 1, eds. Ephraim Stern, Ayelet Lewinson-Gilboa, and Joseph Aviram (Jerusalem: Carta, 1993), 39-45; William G. Dever, *Who Were the Early Israelites and Where Did They Come From?* (Grand Rapids, Mich.: William B. Eerdmans Publishing Company, 2003), 47-48; Kitchen, *On the Reliability,* 188-189.

110   *the nearby site of Khirbet el Maqatir*   Several of the preliminary reports written by Bryant Wood are available on the Internet; see http://bibleplaces.com/bolen/ai2000. htm (2000 season), http://bibleplaces.com/bolen/maqatir.htm (1999 season), and http://bibleplaces.com/bolen/maqatirdetailed.html (1998 season) (all accessed on January 5, 2007).

111   *As for the other cities*   For a brief and up-to-date summation of some of these (and other) sites, see Dever, *Who Were the Early Israelites,* 49-50, 54-64, 68-71; see also Kitchen, *On the Reliability,* 182-190; John J. Bimson, *Redating the Exodus and Conquest,* 2nd ed. (Sheffield: Almond Press, 1981), 106-214; Provan, Long, and Longman, *A Biblical History,* 174-189.

111   *Excavations were first conducted at Lachish*   Quotation and specific details taken from the very useful article by David Ussishkin, "Lachish—Key to the Israelite Conquest of Canaan?" *Biblical Archaeology Review* 13, no. 1 (1987): 18-39. See also, in much greater detail, the five-volume publication on his excavations at Lachish: *The Renewed Archaeological Excavations at Lachish (1973-1994),* vol. 1-5 (Tel Aviv: Institute of Archaeology, Tel Aviv University, 2005). See also his earlier articles, "Lachish," in *The New Encyclopedia of Archaeological Excavations in the Holy Land,* vol. 3, ed. Ephraim Stern, Ayelet Lewinson-Gilboa, and Joseph Aviram (Jerusalem: Carta, 1993), 897-911, and "Lachish," in *The Oxford Encyclopedia of Archaeology in the Near East,* vol. 3, ed. Eric M. Meyers (New York: Oxford University Press, 1997), 317-323.

112 *characteristics of an Israelite settlement* This brings up the interesting question of how to tell a Canaanite city from an Israelite city, from an archaeological point of view. On this topic, see William G. Dever, "How to Tell an Israelite from a Canaanite," in *The Rise of Ancient Israel,* ed. Hershel Shanks (Washington, D.C.: Biblical Archaeology Society, 1992) 27-56; Israel Finkelstein, *The Archaeology of the Israelite Settlement* (Jerusalem: Israel Exploration Society, 1988).

112 *Yigael Yadin, professor of archaeology* See Amnon Ben-Tor and Maria T. Rubiato, "Excavating Hazor, Part Two: Did the Israelites Destroy the Canaanite City?" *Biblical Archaeology Review* 25, no. 3 (1999): 22-39; Amnon Ben-Tor, "The Fall of Canaanite Hazor–The 'Who' and 'When' Questions," in *Mediterranean Peoples in Transition: Thirteenth to Early Tenth Centuries BCE,* eds. Sy Gitin, Amihai Mazar, and Ephraim Stern (Jerusalem: Israel Exploration Society, 1998), 456-468. See also the earlier Yigael Yadin, *Hazor: The Rediscovery of a Great Citadel of the Bible* (New York: Random House, 1975); Yigael Yadin, *Hazor: The Schweich Lecture Series of the British Academy 1970* (Oxford: Oxford University Press, 1972); Yigael Yadin and Amnon Ben-Tor, "Hazor," in *The New Encyclopedia of Archaeological Excavations in the Holy Land,* vol. 2, eds. Ephraim Stern, Ayelet Lewinson-Gilboa, and Joseph Aviram (Jerusalem: Carta, 1993), 594-606; Amnon Ben-Tor, "Hazor," in *The Oxford Encyclopedia of Archaeology in the Near East,* vol. 3, ed. Eric M. Meyers (New York: Oxford University Press, 1997), 1-5.

115 *the German journalist Werner Keller* See Werner Keller, *The Bible as History: A Confirmation of the Book of Books* (New York: William Morrow, 1956). While it is fun to read, with good descriptions of some archaeologists and their discoveries, it is certainly a stretch–and overly optimistic–for Keller to say that the discoveries had proven the Bible, or that they even showed that it is historically accurate. See the more recent books from the nonspecialists discussing such topics, including Jeffery L. Sheler, *Is the Bible True? How Modern Debates and Discoveries Affirm the Essence of the Scriptures* (San Francisco: HarperSanFrancisco, 1999); Amy D. Marcus, *The View from Nebo: How Archaeology Is Rewriting the Bible and Reshaping the Middle East* (Boston: Little, Brown and Company, 2000).

115 *several alternate hypotheses were put forward* For these various theories, including Albright's, see previous discussions summarized in Israel Finkelstein and Neil Asher Silberman, *The Bible Unearthed: Archaeology's New Vision of Ancient Israel and the Origin of Its Sacred Texts* (New York: Simon and Schuster, 2001), 72-122, 329-339; Dever, *Who Were the Early Israelites,* 37-74; Neil Asher Silberman, "Who Were the Israelites?" *Archaeology* 45, no. 2 (1992): 22-30; Provan, Long, and Longman, *A Biblical History,* 138-148; David

Merling, Sr., *The Book of Joshua: Its Theme and Role in Archaeological Discussions* (Berrien Springs, Mich.: Andrews University Press, 1996), with full references and bibliography. On the "Conquest" model, see William F. Albright, "The Israelite Conquest of Canaan in the Light of Archaeology," *Bulletin of the American Schools of Oriental Research* 74 (1939): 11-23; Paul W. Lapp, "The Conquest of Palestine in the Light of Archaeology," *Concordia Theological Monthly* 38 (1967): 495-548; Yigael Yadin, "Is the Biblical Conquest of Canaan Historically Reliable?" *Biblical Archaeology Review* 8 (1982): 16-23; Israel Finkelstein, *The Archaeology of the Israelite Settlement* (Jerusalem: Israel Exploration Society, 1988), 295-302. On the "Peaceful Infiltration" model, see Albrecht Alt, *Essays on Old Testament History and Religion* (Oxford: Oxford University Press, 1966), 135-139; Martin Noth, *The Deuteronomistic History* (Sheffield: JSOT Press, 1981). On the "Revolting Peasants" model, see George E. Mendenhall, "The Hebrew Conquest of Palestine," *Biblical Archaeologist* 25 (1962): 66-87; George E. Mendenhall, *The Tenth Generation: The Origins of the Biblical Tradition* (Baltimore: Johns Hopkins University Press, 1973); Norman K. Gottwald, *The Tribes of Yahweh: A Sociology of the Religion of Liberated Israel 1230-1050 B.C.E.* (Maryknoll, N.Y.: Orbis, 1979). On the "Invisible Israelites" model, see Finkelstein and Silberman, *The Bible Unearthed,* 105-118, with references.

116   *was an outcome of the collapse of the Canaanite culture, not its cause*   See Finkelstein and Silberman, *The Bible Unearthed,* 118.

117   *Of the major suggestions that have been made*   See also Dever, *Who Were the Early Israelites,* for discussions on why these various suggestions do not work particularly well.

118   *These Sea Peoples*   On the Sea Peoples, see most recently Eric H. Cline and David O'Connor, "The Mystery of the 'Sea Peoples,'" in *Mysterious Lands,* eds. David O'Connor and Stephen Quirke (London: UCL Press, 2003), 107-138, with further references. See also the earlier Lawrence E. Stager, "The Impact of the Sea Peoples in Canaan (1185-1050 BCE)," in *The Archaeology of Society in the Holy Land,* ed. Thomas E. Levy (New York: Facts on File, 1995), 332-348; and the full discussions in Eliezer D. Oren, ed., *The Sea Peoples and Their World: A Reassessment,* University Museum Monograph 108, University Museum Symposium Series 11 (Philadelphia: University Museum, University of Pennsylvania, 2000). See also Eric H. Cline, "The Sea Peoples' Possible Role in the Israelite Conquest of Canaan," in *Festschrift for Spyros E. Iakovidis,* ed. Vassiliki Pliatsika (Athens: publisher and date forthcoming).

119   *the Book of Judges may give a slightly more accurate historical account*   See the discussion in Joseph A. Callaway, "The Settlement in Canaan: The Period of the Judges" (revised by J. Maxwell Miller), in *Ancient Israel: From Abraham to the Roman Destruction of the Temple,*

rev. and exp. ed., ed. Hershel Shanks (New York: Prentice Hall, 1999), 56-58; Provan, Long, and Longman, *A Biblical History,* 148-168.

120   *I agree completely with William G. Dever*   See Dever, *Who Were the Early Israelites,* 227-228.

120   *Esteemed scholar Nadav Na'aman*   See Nadav Na'aman, "The 'Conquest of Canaan' in the Book of Joshua and in History," reproduced in Nadav Na'aman, *Canaan in the Second Millennium B.C.E. Collected Essays, Volume 2* (Winona Lake, Ind.: Eisenbrauns, 2005), 347, with many additional references and extensive bibliography.

CHAPTER 6

121   *The ark is mentioned numerous times in the Hebrew Bible*   The ark is mentioned in the following passages in the Hebrew Bible: Exodus 25-26, 30-31, 35, 37, 39-40; Leviticus 16; Numbers 3-4, 7, 10, 14; Deuteronomy 10, 31; Joshua 3, 4, 6-8; Judges 20; I Samuel 3-7, 14; II Samuel 6-7, 15; I Kings 2, 3, 6, 8; I Chronicles 6, 13, 15-17, 22, 28; 2 Chronicles 1, 5, 6, 8, 35; Psalm 132; Jeremiah 3. It is also mentioned in II Maccabees 2:4-5 and 2 Esdras 10 in the Apocrypha, and in Revelation 11 in the New Testament.

122   *the craftsmen Bezalel and Oholiab*   Bezalel and his qualifications, as well as his helper Oholiab, are described in Exodus 31:1-5.

123   *The subsequent history of the ark*   See also the discussion in Ephraim Isaac, "From Israel to Ethiopia: The Journey of the Ark," in *Mysteries of the Bible: From the Garden of Eden to the Shroud of Turin,* ed. Molly Dewsnap Meinhardt (Washington, D.C.: Biblical Archaeology Society, 2004), 113-121. For scholarly disputes regarding the biblical account, see the book by eminent scholars J. Maxwell Miller and John Hayes, *A History of Ancient Israel and Judah,* 2nd ed. (Louisville, Ky.: Westminster John Knox Press, 2006), 127-128 and 130-134, with additional references and bibliography. The book points out some of the conflicts and contradictions concerning the travels and history of the ark as found in the account in the Book of Joshua and the Book of Judges. These include the role of Shiloh itself as a religious center as well as additional problems with the so-called Ark Narrative found in I Samuel 4:1-7:2 and II Samuel 6. These conflicts and contradictions may well render some or all of the biblical account's early history of the ark moot, but I present it here in brief anyway, since it is the account most usually followed both by scholars and the general populace. Technically, it matters little to us if the biblical account of the early history and travels of the ark is factually accurate, since we are more concerned with what happened to it after the time of Solomon—but we should also keep in mind the problematic nature of this biblical material when considering the ark's later history.

124   *The ark remained at Shiloh for an unspecified period* How long this length of time lasted depends upon when we believe Joshua and Samuel, respectively, lived. Many biblical scholars, ancient historians, and archaeologists suggest that Joshua was active in the very late 13th and early 12th centuries B.C. (from 1210 B.C. onward) and that Samuel was a child in the mid-11th century B.C. (circa 1050 B.C.). This would place the ark at Shiloh for just over a century at the most. Note, however, that in his book *Searching for the Ark of the Covenant: Latest Discoveries and Research* (Eugene, Ore.: Harvest House Publishers, 2005), evangelical biblical maximalist Randall Price states that the ark was at Shiloh for more than 300 years. In his table on page 72, Price has an entry which says: "c. 1385-1050 B.C.: The Ark is housed with the Tabernacle at Shiloh," in between entries which state "c. 1446 B.C.: Bezalel constructs the Ark" and "c. 1050 B.C.: The Ark is captured by the Philistines." Also note that on page 62 he minimizes this length of time by saying only: "For over 100 years it remained at Shiloh and at other sites until King David restored its central status by installing it at Jerusalem." Placing the ark at Shiloh for more than 300 years, instead of only 100 years, is one of the few ways that biblical maximalists link a hypothesized 1450 B.C. date for the Exodus with the more definite 1050 B.C. date for the battle against the Philistines during which the ark was taken, and Eli's two sons were killed.

126   *the Ark of the Covenant had possibly been removed during the rule of King Manasseh* See Menahem Haran, "The Disappearance of the Ark," *Israel Exploration Journal* 13 (1963): 46-58. See also the further discussions based on Haran's suggestions by Leen Ritmeyer, *The Quest: Revealing the Temple Mount in Jerusalem* (Jerusalem: Carta, 2006), 309-310; Jacob M. Myers, *II Chronicles: Translation and Notes,* the Anchor Bible (New York: Doubleday and Company, 1965), 196-197; Stuart Munro-Hay and Roderick Grierson, *The Ark of the Covenant: The True Story of the Greatest Relic of Antiquity* (London: Weidenfeld and Nicholson, 1999), 112-114; Price, *Searching for the Ark,* 81-84.

126   *the Book of Jeremiah also mentions the ark* See the brief discussion of this passage in John Bright, *Jeremiah: Introduction, Translation, and Notes,* the Anchor Bible (New York: Doubleday and Company, 1965), 26-27; Price, *Searching for the Ark,* 70-71, 122.

126   *took from Jerusalem during their attacks on the city* While it is unlikely that Nebuchadnezzar also attacked the city in 605 B.C., as suggested in the Book of Daniel, we may note that even here there is no mention of the Ark of the Covenant being taken back to Babylon. The biblical account simply says: "The Lord let King Jehoiakim of Judah fall into his [Nebuchadnezzar's] power, as well as some of the vessels of the house of God. These

he brought to the land of Shinar [Babylon], and placed the vessels in the treasury of his gods" (Daniel 1:2). On Nebuchadnezzar's attacks on Jerusalem in 598, 597, and 587/586 B.C., see the full discussion in Eric H. Cline, *Jerusalem Besieged: From Ancient Canaan to Modern Israel* (Ann Arbor: University of Michigan Press, 2004), 50-65, 320-321, footnote 39.

128   *As Bezalel Porten, professor of Jewish history* See Bezalel Porten, "From Jerusalem to Egypt: Did the Ark Stop at Elephantine?" in *Mysteries of the Bible: From the Garden of Eden to the Shroud of Turin*, ed. Molly Dewsnap Meinhardt (Washington, D.C.: Biblical Archaeology Society, 2004), 128.

129   *In the Book of II Maccabees* See the brief discussion of this passage in Jonathan A. Goldstein, *II Maccabees: A New Translation with Introduction and Commentary*, the Anchor Bible (New York: Doubleday and Company, 1983), 182-183; Price, *Searching for the Ark*, 123-124.

130   *the treasures kept in Solomon's Temple were plundered* See my original publication of this list and my discussion in *Jerusalem Besieged*, 129, 331, and especially footnote 97. See also Price, *Searching for the Ark*, 78-81, 168-169.

131   *the ark is only mentioned in a few extra-biblical sources* In addition to those discussed in the main text, there are a few more extra-biblical sources that are late and of dubious quality and therefore will not be considered here; these include the *Life of Jeremiah*, the *Paralipomena of Jeremiah*, and the *Apocalypse of Baruch*. For discussions of these, see Munro-Hay and Grierson, *The Ark of the Covenant*, 117-120; Price, *Searching for the Ark*, 124-126.

131   *The first reference* The translation follows Michael L. Rodkinson, trans., *The Babylonian Talmud*, book 2, vols. 3 and 4 (1918), available at http://www.sacred-texts.com/jud/t02/shk10.htm (accessed on January 8, 2007). See also the discussion in Price, *Searching for the Ark*, 142-148.

132   *The second reference* For a translation of the entire debate, see Rodkinson, *The Babylonian Talmud*, at http://www.sacred-texts.com/jud/t03/yom10.htm. See also the discussion in Price, *Searching for the Ark*, 142-148.

133   *we are told* Quotation following http://www.chabad.org/holidays/3weeks/insights/article.asp?AID=144580 (accessed January 8, 2007), which cites the Mishneh Torah, *Laws of the Holy Temple* 4:1.

133   *the Ethiopian* Kebra Nagast For a partial translation, see Gerald Hausman, ed., *The Kebra Nagast: The Lost Bible of Rastafarian Wisdom and Faith from Ethiopia and Jamaica* (New York: St. Martin's Press, 1997), 103-119, 144-149. See also the earlier translation by

E. A. Wallis Budge, *The Queen of Sheba and Her Only Son Menyelek (I)* (London: Kegan Paul, 2001); David A. Hubbard, *The Literary Sources of the Kebra Nagast,* Ph.D. thesis (St. Andrews: University of St. Andrews, 1957); Don Stewart, *In Search of the Lost Ark: The Quest for the Ark of the Covenant* (Murrieta, Calif.: AusAmerica Publishers, 1992), 136-139, also available online at www.cvc.tv/resources/2_InSearchOfTheLostArk.pdf (accessed on January 12, 2007); Munro-Hay and Grierson, *The Ark of the Covenant,* 195-291; Price, *Searching for the Ark,* 42-43, 101-103, 106; Stuart Munro-Hay, *The Quest for the Ark of the Covenant: The True History of the Tablets of Moses* (London: I. B. Tauris, 2005), passim.

134   *the house of Abinadab in the city of Kiriath-jearim*   See Price, *Searching for the Ark,* 192-194, for a discussion of the "Our Lady Ark of the Covenant Church," which is built "on top of the hill where tradition locates the house of Abinadab, the priest who tended the Ark."

134   *The closest that we get to such excavations*   On the various explorations and excavations of and near the Temple Mount, see Ritmeyer, *The Quest,* passim.

135   *From the early amateur explorations*   On the early explorers and the underground cisterns and reservoirs, including the famous and ill-fated Parker expedition, led by British Lt. Montague Parker and the Swedish (or Danish) mystic Walter Juvelius in 1911, see Leen Ritmeyer, *The Quest,* chapters 1 and 4; Neil Asher Silberman, "In Search of Solomon's Lost Treasures," *Biblical Archaeology Review* 6, no. 4 (1980): 30-41; Price, *Searching for the Ark,* 92-95.

135   *they do provide circumstantial evidence that Solomon's Temple was located there*   Note the finds from the First (and Second) Temple Period that have been discovered by the team led by Gabriel Barkai and Tzachi Zweig in sifting through the debris dumped by the Islamic Waqf after its illegal digging on the Temple Mount. See Nadav Shragai, "First Temple Artifacts Found in Dirt Removed from Temple Mount," *Ha'aretz,* October 19, 2006, available at http://www.haaretz.com/hasen/spages/776922.html (accessed on January 9, 2007).

135   *claims that can be dismissed outright*   See Cline, *Jerusalem Besieged,* chapter 5, with full references and bibliography.

135   *Leen Ritmeyer, an architect*   See the discussion in Ritmeyer, *The Quest,* 241-277, especially 268-277. See also the earlier Ritmeyer, "The Ark of the Covenant: Where It Stood in Solomon's Temple," *Biblical Archaeology Review* 22, no. 1 (1996): 46-55, 70-72, and the debates between Ritmeyer, Asher Kaufman, and David Jacobson over the precise location of the Temple itself upon the Temple Mount in *Biblical Archaeology Review* 9, no. 2 (1983): 40-59; 18, no. 2 (1992): 24-45, 64-65; 25, no. 4 (1999): 41-53, 62-64; 25, no. 5 (1999): 54-63; 26, no. 2 (2000): 52-59.

136   *resembles other such containers found in the ancient Near East*   On the chest found in King Tut's tomb, see Munro-Hay and Grierson, *The Ark of the Covenant,* 294-297; Randall Price, *The Stones Cry Out: What Archaeology Reveals about the Truth of the Bible* (Eugene, Ore.: Harvest House Publishers, 1997), 206, figure 46; Graham Hancock, *The Sign and the Seal: A Quest for the Lost Ark of the Covenant* (New York: Crown Publishers, 1993), 288-289, figure 56; Price, *Searching for the Ark,* 48-49.

136   *the ark was a transmitter*   See Erich von Däniken, *Chariots of the Gods* (New York: Bantam Books, 1969), 40-41; Stewart, *In Search of the Lost Ark,* 36-38, 42; Price, *Searching for the Ark,* 25-26, 35, 38-43.

137   *the ark is presently in a secret chamber deep within the Temple Mount*   See full arguments and discussion in Price, *Searching for the Ark,* 138-151. Just before this book went to press, Professor Eilat Mazar, who is currently excavating a structure that she identifies as David's palace, was asked by a reader of the *Jerusalem Post,* "Is it true that the Ark of the Covenant is buried under the mount?" Mazar replied: "There is a very high probability that the most important ancient remains are inside the compound in the massive underground halls. This includes the Ark of the Covenant." See "Q and A on the Temple Mount with Dr. Eilat Mazar," *Jerusalem Post,* January 14, 2007, also available online at http://www.jpost.com/servlet/Satellite ?cid=1170359857094andpagename=JPost/JPArticle/ShowFull (accessed January 14, 2007).

137   *the Temple Institute, an ultra-Orthodox Jewish group*   See the Temple Institute's Web site, www.templeinstitute.org, specifically the statements quoted from www.templeinstitute.org/ark_of_the_covenant.htm (both accessed on January 12, 2007). See also Stewart, *In Search of the Lost Ark,* 11-12, 147-148.

138   *digs have been conducted under the Temple Mount in search of the ark*   See Ritmeyer, *The Quest,* 311. See also the Web page of the Temple Institute, www.templeinstitute.org/ark_of_the_covenant.htm, which notes, "An attempt was made some few years ago to excavate towards the direction of this chamber. This resulted in widespread Moslem unrest and rioting" (accessed on January 12, 2007). For a more complete version of the stories, see Stewart, *In Search of the Lost Ark,* 11-12, 147-148, available at www.cvc. tv/resources/2_InSearchOfTheLostArk.pdf (accessed on January 12, 2007); see also Price, *Searching for the Ark,* 151-163 and 184-188, who reiterates the stories in detail and includes quotations from personal interviews conducted with several rabbis in Jerusalem, some of whom were reportedly involved in the secret excavations.

140   *According to the Wyatt Archaeological Research Web site*   See www.wyattmuseum.com/ark-of-the-covenant-02.htm and linked pages (all page accessed on January 12, 2007). See also the lengthy discussion and critique in Price, *Searching for the Ark,* 178-184.

141 *Menahem Haran, a respected biblical scholar* See again Haran, "The Disappearance of the Ark," 46-58, and the further discussions by Ritmeyer, *The Quest*, 309-310; Myers, *II Chronicles*, 196-197; Munro-Hay and Grierson, *The Ark of the Covenant*, 112-114; Price, *Searching for the Ark*, 81-84.

143 *Graham Hancock, a former journalist who used to write for the London* Economist See Hancock, *The Sign and the Seal;* Isaac, "From Israel to Ethiopia," 113-121; Porten, "From Jerusalem to Egypt," 123-147; Stewart, *In Search of the Lost Ark;* Price, *Searching for the Ark*, 101-115, 167-177. See also the effective rebuttal to Hancock by Munro-Hay in his book *The Quest for the Ark*.

143 *One proponent, however, was Bob Cornuke* See Robert Cornuke and David Halbrook, *In Search of the Lost Ark of the Covenant* (Nashville, Tenn.: Broadman and Holman Publishers, 2002); see also http://www.baseinstitute.org/covenant.html and linked pages (accessed on January 17, 2007). See also Price, *Searching for the Ark*, 101-115, 167-177, where he critiques both Hancock and Cornuke.

143 *an article in the* Los Angeles Times See Michael A. Hiltzik, "Does Trail to Ark of Covenant End Behind Axum Curtain?" *Los Angeles Times*, June 9, 1992; see also Stewart, *In Search of the Lost Ark*, 140-141; Price, *Searching for the Ark*, 176-177. See Edward Ullendorff's books on Ethiopia, including *The Ethiopians: An Introduction to Country and People* (London: Oxford University Press, 1965); *Ethiopia and the Bible* (Oxford: Oxford University Press, 1968); *The Two Zions: Reminiscences of Jerusalem and Ethiopia* (New York: Oxford University Press, 1988).

144 *Tom Crotser, founder of the Institute for Restoring Ancient History* See Hershel Shanks, "Tom Crotser Has Found the Ark of the Covenant—Or Has He?" *Biblical Archaeology Review* 9, no. 3 (1983), 66-69; Anis A. Shorrosh, *The Exciting Discovery of the Ark of the Covenant* (Spanish Fort, Ala.: Anis Shorrosh Evangelsitic Association, 1984), 19-32. See also the earlier publications Antonia F. Futterer, *Palestine Speaks* (Los Angeles: A. F. Futterer, 1931), 536-556; Stewart, *In Search of the Lost Ark*, 127-133. Finally, see discussion in Vendyl Jones, *A Door of Hope: My Search for the Treasures of the Copper Scroll* (Springdale, Ark.: Lightcatcher Books, 2005), 159-163.

145 *Vendyl Jones, a longtime enthusiast of biblical archaeology from Texas* See Jones, *A Door of Hope*, 74-75, 171-181, 187-207; see also the Web site and linked pages of the Vendyl Jones Research Institute: http://www.vendyljones.org.il/ (accessed on January 11, 2007); Stewart, *In Search of the Lost Ark*, 177-178. On the quotation for when he was to find the ark, see "Kabbalist Blesses Jones: Now's the Time to Find Holy Lost Ark," *Arutz Sheva*, May 20, 2005, available at http://www.israelnationalnews.com/

news.php3?id=82226 (accessed on January 11, 2007); for the correction on the home Web page of the Vendyl Jones Research Institute, see http://www.vendyljones.org.il/ (accessed on January 11, 2007). On the Copper Scroll, see P. Kyle McCarter, "The Mysterious Copper Scroll: Clues to Hidden Temple Treasure?" *Bible Review* 8 (1992): 34-41, 63-64.

145 *Andis Kaulins, a German lawyer with a law degree from Stanford University* See the links from Kaulins's Web site http://www.lexiline.com/lexiline/civilization.htm and specifically the pages found at http://www.lexiline.com/lexiline/lexi000.htm (accessed on January 11, 2007). On the chest in King Tut's tomb, see again the discussions in Price, *The Stones Cry Out,* 206, figure 46; Hancock, *The Sign and the Seal,* 288-289, figure 56; Munro-Hay and Grierson, *The Ark of the Covenant,* 294-297; Price, *Searching for the Ark,* 48-49.

147 *let alone captured it* See discussion in Eric H. Cline, *Jerusalem Besieged,* 39-41, with full references and bibliography.

147 *Nevertheless, Michael S. Sanders* See Jon Ungoed-Thomas, "Is Lost Ark Buried in Terrorist Camp?" *Sunday Times,* September 6, 1998. See also McGraw, "Thou Shalt Search," March 3, 2001; Peter Sheridan, "Finder of the Lost Ark . . . and the Garden of Eden, Sodom and Gomorrah, the Tower of Babel and the 10 Commandments," *Daily Express,* March 15, 2001. Note, however, that Sanders apparently does not equate Shishak with Shoshenq, as most mainstream biblical archaeologists and Egyptologists do; see his Web site, http://www.biblemysteries.com, with relevant linked pages (accessed on January 12, 2007). For a lengthy discussion about Shishak and the possibility that he took the Ark of the Covenant, see Price, *Searching for the Ark,* 78-81; see also 95-98 for a discussion, critique, and ultimately a debunking of Sanders's theory.

148 *Herbert G. May, professor of Old Testament language and literature* See Herbert G. May, "The Ark—A Miniature Temple," *American Journal of Semitic Languages and Literatures* 52, no. 4 (1936): 220; see also Price, *Searching for the Ark,* 81, who cites and quotes May's statement. Note that May's earliest suggested date of 621 B.C. for the possible disappearance of the ark has been followed by enthusiasts such as Ron Wyatt, who (apparently) claims to have found this date himself: http://www.wyattmuseum.com/ark-mary-nell-special-04.htm (accessed January 14, 2007).

148 *Nebuchadnezzar and the Neo-Babylonians* See Price, *Searching for the Ark,* 84-90, for an account by someone who disagrees with this possibility.

150 *The biblical minimalists* For a quick entrée into the world of the biblical minimalists, see Hershel Shanks, "The Biblical Minimalists: Expunging Ancient Israel's Past," *Bible Review* 13, no. 3 (1997): 32-39, 50-52; Hershel Shanks, "Face to Face: Biblical

Minimalists Meet Their Challengers," *Biblical Archaeology Review* 23, no. 4 (1997): 26-42, 66. On the Tel Dan inscription, see William M. Schniedewind, "Tel Dan Stela: New Light on Aramaic and Jehu's Revolt," *Bulletin of the American Schools of Oriental Research* 302 (1996): 75-90, with full references. On David and Solomon, see Baruch Halpern, *David's Secret Demons: Messiah, Murderer, Traitor, King* (Grand Rapids, Mich.: William B. Eerdmans Publishing, 2001); Jonathan Kirsch, *King David: The Real Life of the Man Who Ruled Israel* (New York: Ballantine Books, 2001); Steven L. McKenzie, *King David: A Biography* (New York: Oxford University Press, 2000); Israel Finkelstein and Neil A. Silberman, *David and Solomon: In Search of the Bible's Sacred Kings and the Roots of the Western Tradition* (New York: Free Press, 2006).

CHAPTER 7

155 *The first time the fighting occurred was during the reign of Menahem* See discussion, with additional references, in J. Maxwell Miller and John Hayes, *A History of Ancient Israel and Judah,* 2nd ed. (Louisville, Ky.: Westminster John Knox Press, 2006), 361, 376-377; K. Lawson Younger, Jr., "The Deportations of the Israelites," *Journal of Biblical Literature* 117, no. 2 (1998): 201-202; Bob Becking, *The Fall of Samaria: A Historical and Archaeological Study* (Leiden: E. J. Brill, 1992), 1-6.

155 *Tiglath-pileser III attacked Israel during the reign of Pekah* See discussion, with additional references, in Miller and Hayes, *A History of Ancient Israel,* 365, 370, 378-383; Younger, "The Deportations of the Israelites," 202; Becking, *The Fall of Samaria,* 6-13.

155 *The account in I Chronicles provides more information* See Younger, "The Deportations of the Israelites," 207 and footnotes 29-31. See also Jacob M. Myers, *I Chronicles: Introduction, Translation and Notes,* the Anchor Bible (New York: Doubleday and Company, 1965), 34, 38-39.

156 *He apparently attacked the northern kingdom of Israel twice* See discussion, with additional references, in Miller and Hayes, *A History of Ancient Israel,* 385-387.

157 *To replace the deportees* For a brief series of archaeological and historical clues for the presence of the Israelites in Samaria after the Neo-Assyrian resettlement, see Israel Finkelstein and Neil A. Silberman, *The Bible Unearthed: Archaeology's New Vision of Ancient Israel and the Origin of Its Sacred Texts* (New York: Free Press, 2001), 220-221; Nadav Na'aman, "Population Changes in Palestine Following Assyrian Deportation," reproduced in Nadav Na'aman, *Ancient Israel and Its Neighbors: Interaction and Counteraction, Collected Essays, Volume 1* (Winona Lake, Ind.: Eisenbrauns, 2005), 204-208, with

further references and bibliography. For the origins of these resettled peoples, see these references and K. Lawson Younger, Jr., "Recent Study on Sargon II, King of Assyria: Implications for Biblical Study," in *Mesopotamia and the Bible: Comparative Explorations*, eds. Mark W. Chavalas and K. Lawson Younger, Jr. (Sheffield: Sheffield Academic Press, 2002), 301-312; K. Lawson Younger, Jr., "The Repopulation of Samaria (2 Kings 17:24, 27-31) in Light of Recent Study," in *The Future of Biblical Archaeology: Reassessing Methodologies and Assumptions,* eds. James K. Hoffmeier and Alan Millard (Grand Rapids, Mich.: William B. Eerdmans Publishing Company, 2004), 254-280; Becking, *The Fall of Samaria,* 95-104.

158   *Tiglath-pileser III's own inscriptions*   Translations following James B. Pritchard, ed., *Ancient Near Eastern Texts Relating to the Old Testament,* 3rd ed. (Princeton: Princeton University Press, 1969), 283-284. See also Hayim Tadmor, *The Inscriptions of Tiglath-pileser III King of Assyria: Critical Edition, with Introductions, Translations and Commentary* (Jerusalem: Israel Academy of Sciences and Humanities, 1994), 68-69, 106-107, 141; Younger, "The Deportations of the Israelites," 202-203, 206-207; Miller and Hayes, *A History of Ancient Israel,* 370, 382-383.

158   *Tiglath-pileser claimed that he spared only the city of Samaria*   See Finkelstein and Silberman, *The Bible Unearthed,* 215-216; Younger, "The Deportations of the Israelites," 202-203, 206-207, 210-211, with additional references; Hayim Tadmor, *The Inscriptions of Tiglath-pileser III King of Assyria,* 81-83, 188-189, 280-281; Na'aman, "Population Changes in Palestine," 201-202, with full references; Nadav Na'aman, "Tiglath-pileser III's Campaigns Against Tyre and Israel (734-732 BCE)," reproduced in Nadav Na'aman, *Ancient Israel and Its Neighbors: Interaction and Counteraction. Collected Essays, Volume 1* (Winona Lake, Ind.: Eisenbrauns, 2005), 60-63, with full references; Younger, "Recent Study on Sargon II," 294-295; Becking, *The Fall of Samaria,* 1-20.

159   *biblical scholars consider it more likely*   See Younger, "The Deportations of the Israelites," 207 and footnote 31; Mordechai Cogan and Hayim Tadmor, *II Kings: A New Translation with Introduction and Commentary,* the Anchor Bible (Garden City, N.Y.: Doubleday, 1988), 197.

159   *we have been left with no inscriptions of Shalmaneser V*   See Miller and Hayes, *A History of Ancient Israel,* 384, with discussion; Younger, "The Deportations of the Israelites," 211, 214-215.

159   *Fortunately, we do have the Babylonian Chronicles*   Translations following Miller and Hayes, *A History of Ancient Israel,* 384, with discussion; see also Younger, "The Deportations of the Israelites," 211, 214-215; Nadav Na'aman, "The Historical Background to the

Conquest of Samaria (720 BCE)," reproduced in Nadav Na'aman, *Ancient Israel and Its Neighbors: Interaction and Counteraction. Collected Essays, Volume 1* (Winona Lake, Ind.: Eisenbrauns, 2005), 79; K. Lawson Younger, Jr., "The Fall of Samaria in Light of Recent Research," *Catholic Biblical Quarterly* 61, no. 3 (1999): 464-467; Becking, *The Fall of Samaria*, 22-25; Cogan and Tadmor, *II Kings: A New Translation*, 199.

160   *At Sargon's palace in Khorsabad*   Translation following Miller and Hayes, *A History of Ancient Israel*, 386, text 10 and discussion, with further references and bibliography, on pages 387-388; see also Na'aman, "Population Changes in Palestine," 203; Younger, "The Deportations of the Israelites," 215-219. On where the "distant Arabs" came from, see discussion in Nadav Na'aman and Ran Zadok, "Sargon II's Deportations to Israel and Philistia (716-708 BCE)," *Journal of Cuneiform Studies* 40 (1988) 36-46; Younger, "The Deportations of the Israelites," 226-227. On the possible depictions of the Samarians, see Norma Franklin, "The Room V Reliefs at Dur-Sharrukin and Sargon II's Western Campaign," *Tel Aviv* 21 (1994): 255-275; Younger, "The Fall of Samaria," 475-476.

161   *In eight separate inscriptions*   See discussion in Miller and Hayes, *A History of Ancient Israel*, 388-389; Younger, "The Deportations of the Israelites," 215-219; see also Younger, "Recent Study on Sargon II," 290-295; Younger, "The Fall of Samaria," 468-473; Bob Becking, *The Fall of Samaria: An Historical and Archaeological Study* (Leiden: E. J. Brill, 1992), 25-33.

162   *many possible suggestions have been put forward*   For a good summary and discussion of all the suggestions, see Younger, "The Fall of Samaria," 461-482; Becking, *The Fall of Samaria*, 21.

162   *The first suggests that while the biblical account*   On this first possibility, see Miller and Hayes, *A History of Ancient Israel*, 384-388. See also the discussion in Finkelstein and Silberman, *The Bible Unearthed*, 217-220; Younger, "The Deportations of the Israelites," 214-215; Younger, "Recent Study on Sargon II," 289-290; Younger, "The Fall of Samaria," 482; Becking, *The Fall of Samaria*, 34-45.

162   *Eminent scholars Mordechai Cogan and Hayim Tadmor*   See Cogan and Tadmor, *II Kings: A New Translation*, 197, 199-210.

163   *It posits*   See the suggestion by Gershon Galil, "The Last Years of the Kingdom of Israel and the Fall of Samaria," *Catholic Biblical Quarterly* 57, no. 1 (1995): 52-65; countered by Younger, "The Fall of Samaria," 479.

163   *The third hypothesis gives the Bible the most credit*   See Na'aman, "The Historical Background," 76-93. Na'aman also explains away the brief mention in the Babylonian Chronicle that Shalmaneser besieged Samaria and argues (on page 88) that the passage

in II Kings 18:9-11 (which says that "King Shalmaneser of Assyria came up against Samaria, besieged it, and at the end of three years took it") is a mistake made by a later redactor of the biblical text trying to make sense of the earlier passage in II Kings 17:1-6. This is a suggestion that has been made previously by other scholars as well.

165　*an elegant solution to a complex problem*　Alert readers will note that in my 2004 book, *Jerusalem Besieged: From Ancient Canaan to Modern Israel* (Ann Arbor, Mich.: University of Michigan Press, 2004), 44-45, I followed the standard line that Shalmaneser V laid siege to Samaria, conquered it after three years, and then deported the conquered population. I would now consider revising my earlier statement to conform with Na'aman's suggestion, despite Galil's and Younger's arguments against it; see Galil, "The Last Years of the Kingdom," 52-65; Younger, "The Fall of Samaria," 464-467.

165　*the deported members of the Ten Tribes were sent off into exile*　On the location of these specific places, see discussions in Miller and Hayes, *A History of Ancient Israel,* 389; Finkelstein and Silberman, *The Bible Unearthed,* 220; Na'aman, "Population Changes in Palestine," 203, with further references and bibliography; Younger, "The Deportations of the Israelites," 221-224; Younger, "Recent Study on Sargon II," 294-296; K. Lawson Younger, Jr., "'Give Us Our Daily Bread': Everyday Life for the Israelite Deportees," in *Life and Culture in the Ancient Near East,* eds. Richard E. Averbeck, Mark W. Chavalas, David B. Weisberg (Bethesda, Md.: CDL Press, 2003), 269-288; K. Lawson Younger, Jr., "Israelites in Exile: Their Names Appear at All Levels of Assyrian Society," *Biblical Archaeology Review* 29, no. 6 (2003): 36-45, 65-66; Becking, *The Fall of Samaria,* 61-93; Rivka Gonen, *To the Ends of the Earth: The Quest For the Ten Lost Tribes of Israel* (North Bergen, N.J.: Book-Mart Press, 2002), 20-23; Cogan and Tadmor, *II Kings: A New Translation,* 197.

166　*The Prophet Isaiah was active*　On the dates, see the discussion in Bruce M. Metzger and Roland E. Murphy, eds., *New Oxford Annotated Bible, with the Apocryphal/Deuterocanonical Books* (New York: Oxford University Press, 1991), 866OT, 960OT, 1057OT.

166　*One of these is found in the Book of Tobit*　On the dates, see the discussion in the *New Oxford Annotated Bible,* pages 1AP and 3AP.

167　*they may have identified some of the deported Samarians in Neo-Assyrian records*　See Younger, "The Deportations of the Israelites," 219-220, with full references and additional bibliography; Younger, "Recent Study on Sargon II," 296-301; Younger, "'Give Us Our Daily Bread,'" 269-288. For earlier editions, see Stephanie Dalley, "Foreign Chariotry and Cavalry in the Armies of Tiglath-pileser III and Sargon II," *Iraq* 47 (1985): 31-48; I. Eph'al, "The Samarian(s) in the Assyrian Sources," in *Ah, Assyria . . . : Studies in Assyrian History and Ancient Near Eastern Historiography Presented to Hayim Tadmor,* ed. Mordechai Cogan and Israel Eph'al (Jerusalem: Magnes Press, 1991), 36-45.

167   *The other passage within the Apocrypha*   See discussion in the *New Oxford Annotated Bible,* page 300AP.

168   *the excavations at the site of Samaria itself*   See discussion in Miller and Hayes, *A History of Ancient Israel,* 302-303; see also earlier books including G. A. Reisner, C. S. Fisher, and D. G. Lyon, *Harvard Excavations At Samaria, 1908-1910* (Cambridge, MA: Harvard University Press, 1924); J. W. Crowfoot, K. M. Kenyon, and E. L. Sukenik, *The Buildings at Samaria (Samaria-Sebaste 1)* (London: Palestine Exploration Fund, 1942). See also Ron E. Tappy, *The Archaeology of Israelite Samaria, I: Early Iron Age through the Ninth Century BCE* (Atlanta: Scholars Press, 1992); Ron E. Tappy, *The Archaeology of Israelite Samaria, II: The Eighth Century BCE* (Winona Lake, Ind.: Eisenbrauns, 2001); Norma Franklin, "Samaria: From the Bedrock to the Omride Palace," *Levant* 36 (2004): 189-202; Na'aman, "The Historical Background," 78; Nahman Avigad, "Samaria," in *The New Encyclopedia of Archaeological Excavations in the Holy Land,* vol. 4, eds. Ephraim Stern, Ayelet Lewinson-Gilboa, and Joseph Aviram (Jerusalem: Carta, 1993), 1300-1310; Ron E. Tappy, "Samaria," in *The Oxford Encyclopedia of Archaeology in the Near East,* vol. 4, ed. Eric M. Meyers (New York: Oxford University Press, 1997), 463-467; Younger, "The Fall of Samaria," 473-475.

169   *Even though there is clear evidence of Neo-Assyrian occupation at the site*   See Tappy, "Samaria," 465; Tappy, *The Archaeology of Israelite Samaria, II;* Daniel Master, review of Ron E. Tappy, *The Archaeology of Israelite Samaria,* in *Journal of Near Eastern Studies* 63, no. 2 (2004): 136-138.

170   *Megiddo and other major sites that were occupied by the Neo-Assyrians*   See Magen Broshi and Israel Finkelstein, "The Populations of Palestine in Iron Age II," *Bulletin of the American Schools of Oriental Research* 287 (1992): 55; Younger, "The Deportations of the Israelites," 212-214.

170   *the city of Megiddo IVA*   See most recently and completely Jennifer Peersman, "Assyrian Magiddu: The Town Planning of Stratum III," in *Megiddo III: The 1992-96 Seasons,* eds. Israel Finkelstein, David Ussishkin, and Baruch Halpern (Tel Aviv: Tel Aviv University, 2000), 524-534; also Eric H. Cline, *The Battles of Armageddon: Megiddo and the Jezreel Valley from the Bronze Age to the Nuclear Age* (Ann Arbor, Mich.: University of Michigan Press, 2000), 89, with further references and bibliography; Younger, "The Deportations of the Israelites," 213 and note 43, with further bibliography and references.

171   *Israel was not decimated by the Neo-Assyrians*   See Broshi and Finkelstein, "The Populations of Palestine," 47-60; Finkelstein and Silberman, *The Bible Unearthed,* 221-222; see also Na'aman, "Population Changes in Palestine," 200-219; Younger, "The Deportations of the Israelites," 211, 213-214.

171   *the excavations that have been carried out in the city of Jerusalem itself*   See Magen Broshi, "The Expansion of Jerusalem in the Reigns of Hezekiah and Manasseh," *Israel Exploration Journal* 24 (1974): 21-26; Broshi and Finkelstein, "The Populations of Palestine," 47-60; Dan Bahat, "Was Jerusalem Really That Large?" in *Biblical Archaeology Today, 1990: Proceedings of the Second International Congress on Biblical Archaeology, Jerusalem, June-July 1990,* eds. Avraham Biran and Joseph Aviram (Jerusalem: Israel Exploration Society, 1993), 581-584; Jane M. Cahill, "Jerusalem at the Time of the United Monarchy: The Archaeological Evidence," in *Jerusalem in Bible and Archaeology: The First Temple Period,* eds. Andrew G. Vaughn and Ann E. Killebrew (Atlanta: Society of Biblical Literature, 2003), 70-71; Hillel Geva, "Western Jerusalem at the End of the First Temple Period in Light of the Excavations in the Jewish Quarter," in *Jerusalem in Bible and Archaeology: The First Temple Period,* eds. Andrew G. Vaughn and Ann E. Killebrew (Atlanta: Society of Biblical Literature, 2003), 183-208; Ann E. Killebrew, "Biblical Jerusalem: An Archaeological Assessment," in *Jerusalem in Bible and Archaeology: The First Temple Period,* eds. Andrew G. Vaughn and Ann E. Killebrew (Atlanta: Society of Biblical Literature, 2003), 336-337; Roni Reich and Eli Shukron, "The Urban Development of Jerusalem in the Late Eighth Century B.C.E.," in *Jerusalem in Bible and Archaeology: The First Temple Period,* eds. Andrew G. Vaughn and Ann E. Killebrew (Atlanta: Society of Biblical Literature, 2003), 209-218; Israel Finkelstein, "The Rise of Jerusalem and Judah: The Missing Link," in *Jerusalem in Bible and Archaeology: The First Temple Period,* eds. Andrew G. Vaughn and Ann E. Killebrew (Atlanta: Society of Biblical Literature, 2003), 81-101. Quotations are from Finkelstein and Silberman, *The Bible Unearthed,* 243-245.

172   *with the welcome exception of Rivka Gonen*   See Gonen, *To the Ends of the Earth;* see also Tudor Parfitt, *The Lost Tribes of Israel: The History of a Myth* (London: Weidenfeld and Nicolson, 2002). For an article in which archaeologists and biblical scholars respond as reviewers, see Hershel Shanks, Rivka Gonen, Ronald S. Hendel, and Hillel Halkin, "The Tribe of Manasseh: Found in India?" in *Mysteries of the Bible: From the Garden of Eden to the Shroud of Turin,* ed. Molly Dewsnap Meinhardt (Washington, D.C.: Biblical Archaeology Society, 2004), 101-109.

173   *Josephus is also one of the first authors*   Translation following William Whiston, *The New Complete Works of Josephus,* rev. ed. (Grand Rapids, Mich.: Kregel Publications, 1999), 368.

173   *The tradition continued thereafter*   See Gonen, *To the Ends of the Earth,* 31-37; see also Parfitt, *The Lost Tribes,* 4-6.

173   *the descendants of the Ten Tribes can be found*   A sample of books that have been published in the fairly recent past include David A. Law, *From Samaria to Samarkand: The Ten Lost Tribes of Israel* (Lanham: University Press of America, 1992); R. Clayton Brough, *The Lost Tribes: History, Doctrine, Prophecies and Theories about Israel's Lost Ten Tribes* (Bountiful, Utah: Horizon Publishers, 1999); Hillel Halkin, *Across the Sabbath River: In Search of a Lost Tribe of Israel* (Boston: Houghton Mifflin, 2002); Magdel le Roux, *The Lemba: A Lost Tribe of Israel in Southern Africa?* (Unisa, South Africa: Unisa Press, 2003); Joshua M. Benjamin, *The Mystery of Israel's Ten Lost Tribes and the Legend of Jesus in India* (New Delhi: Mosaic Books, 2001); Simcha Shtull-Trauring, ed., *Letters From Beyond the Sambatyon: The Myth of the Ten Lost Tribes* (New York: Maxima New Media, 1997); Charles Even, *The Lost Tribes of Israel or the First of the Red Men* (New York: Arno Press, 1977); Tudor Parfitt, *The Thirteenth Gate: Travels Among the Lost Tribes of Israel* (London: Weidenfeld and Nicolson, 1987); Tudor Parfitt, *Journey to the Vanished City: The Search for a Lost Tribe of Israel* (New York: St. Martin's Press, 1992); Tudor Parfitt and Yulia Egorova, *Genetics, Mass Media and Identity: A Case Study of the Genetic Research on the Lemba and Bene Israel* (London: Routledge, 2006).

174   *a corruption of two Hebrew words*   Gonen, *To the Ends of the Earth,* 30.

175   *I . . . approached Qarqa*   Translation following Miller and Hayes, *A History of Ancient Israel,* 293 (text 3) and see also discussion, with further references and bibliography, on pages 292, 308, 310; see also A. K. Grayson, *Assyrian Rulers of the Early First Millennium BC, II (858-745 BC)*, RIMA 3 (Toronto: University of Toronto Press, 1996); Moshe Elat, "The Campaigns of Shalmaneser III Against Aram and Israel," *Israel Exploration Journal* 25 (1975): 25-35.

175   *Tribute of Iaua [Jehu]*   Translation following Miller and Hayes, *A History of Ancient Israel,* 307 (text 5) and see also discussion on pages 292, 330-331. See also Grayson, *Assyrian Rulers.*

175   *This deportation and repopulation*   See Finkelstein and Silberman, *The Bible Unearthed,* 215; see also discussion in Na'aman and Zadok, "Sargon II's Deportations," 36-46; Younger, "The Deportations of the Israelites," 219-220, 224-226; Bustenay Oded, *Mass Deportations and Deportees in the Neo-Assyrian Empire* (Wiesbaden: Reichert, 1979); Miller and Hayes, *A History of Ancient Israel,* 389.

176   *several different variations of deportation and repopulation tactics*   Na'aman, "Population Changes in Palestine," 214. See also Younger, "The Deportations of the Israelites,"

214, 224-226, who agrees that the deportations of Tiglath-pileser III were "one-way" and those of Sargon II were "two-way"—or, as Younger puts it, "unidirectional" and "bidirectional"; Younger, "Recent Study on Sargon II," 294, 301; Becking, *The Fall of Samaria*, 61; Oded, *Mass Deportations and Deportees*, 28-30.

177 *The Neo-Assyrians have a well-deserved reputation for cruelty* See the Neo-Assyrian treatment of the peoples of Lachish, in southern Judah, when they captured it in 701 B.C.: Erika Bleibtreu, "Five Ways to Conquer a City," *Biblical Archaeology Review* 16, no. 3 (1990): 37-44; Erika Bleibtreu, "Grisly Assyrian Record of Torture and Death," *Biblical Archaeology Review* 17, no. 1 (1991): 52-61, 75.

177 *whose descendants may still live in Israel today* See Peidon Shen, et al., "Reconstruction of Patrilineages and Matrilineages of Samaritans and Other Israeli Populations From U-Chromosome and Mitochondrial DNA Sequence Variation," *Human Mutation* 24 (2004): 248-260.

179 *Thus, I believe that the archaeological and textual evidence indicates* See Finkelstein and Silberman, *The Bible Unearthed*, 243-245; also Miller and Hayes, *A History of Ancient Israel*, 390; Hershel Shanks, "Lost and Found: Evidence of Tribes Discovered Close to Home," in *Mysteries of the Bible: From the Garden of Eden to the Shroud of Turin*, ed. Molly Dewsnap Meinhardt (Washington, D.C.: Biblical Archaeology Society, 2004), 97-100.

179 *only a portion of the population was exiled* On the "Myth of the Empty Land" situation in Judah after 586 B.C., see the discussions by Hans M. Barstad, *The Myth of the Empty Land* (Oslo: Scandinavian University Press, 1996); Hans M. Barstad, "After the 'Myth of the Empty Land': Major Challenges in the Study of Neo-Babylonian Judah," in *Judah and the Judeans in the Neo-Babylonian Period,* eds. Oded Lipschits and Joseph Blenkinsopp (Winona Lake, Ind.: Eisenbrauns, 2003), 3-20; Oded Lipschits, "Demographic Changes in Judah between the Seventh and the Fifth Centuries B.C.E.," in *Judah and the Judeans in the Neo-Babylonian Period*, eds. Oded Lipschits and Joseph Blenkinsopp (Winona Lake, Ind.: Eisenbrauns, 2003), 323-376; Finkelstein and Silberman, *The Bible Unearthed*, 305-308; see also Cline, *Jerusalem Besieged*, 64-65.

180 *As for Hezekiah, the Judaean* Translation following Miller and Hayes, *A History of Ancient Israel*, 418-419 (text 12). On Sennacherib's deportations in 701 B.C., see Na'aman, "Population Changes in Palestine," 209-211, among many other possible references.

180 *probably a gross exaggeration* For a brief discussion of the accuracy of the reported number, including one suggestion that the number should be amended to read 2,150 people deported, rather than 200,150, see Broshi and Finkelstein, "The Populations of Palestine," 54-55. Na'aman suggests in "Population Changes in Palestine," in footnote

5 on page 211: "It is hardly conceivable that thousands of Judahites were deported to Nineveh (or other major Assyrian cities), in light of the absence of Hebrew names in the onomastica. Instead, we may assume that the people of Judah were transferred to some remote area(s), rather than the royal cities of Assyria."

Epilogue

184   *the modern Greek poet Constantine Cavafy*   Translation follows Rae Dalven, trans., *The Complete Poems of Cavafy* (New York: Harcourt Brace Jovanovich, 1976), 36-37.

185   *Hershel Shanks, the editor and publisher of* Biblical Archaeology Review   Hershel Shanks, "Nor Is It Necessarily Not So," *Ha'aretz,* November 5, 1999.

185   *Robert Eisenman, professor of biblical archaeology*   Quoted in Peter Sheridan, "Finder of the Lost Ark . . . and the Garden of Eden, Sodom and Gomorrah, the Tower of Babel and the 10 Commandments," *Daily Express,* March 15, 2001.

186   *Randall Younker, director of the Institute of Archaeology*   See Randall W. Younker, "Integrating Faith, the Bible, and Archaeology: A Review of the 'Andrews University Way' of Doing Archaeology," in *The Future of Biblical Archaeology: Reassessing Methodologies and Assumptions,* eds. James K. Hoffmeier and Alan Millard (Grand Rapids, Mich.: William B. Eerdmans Publishing Company, 2004), 43-52.

INDEX

BIBLE INDEX

About the Author

ERIC H. CLINE holds degrees in classical archaeology, Near Eastern archaeology, and ancient history from Dartmouth, Yale, and the University of Pennsylvania. He currently serves as chair of the department of classical and Semitic languages and literatures at the George Washington University, where he has won both national and local teaching awards. His book *The Battles of Armageddon: Megiddo and the Jezreel Valley from the Bronze Age to the Nuclear Age* won a Biblical Archaeology Society Publication Award for "Best Popular Book on Archaeology" and was a main selection of the Natural Science Book Club. Also among his seven books and more than seventy other published works are *Jerusalem Besieged: From Ancient Canaan to Modern Israel* (selected by the AAUP for Public and Secondary School Libraries in June 2005) and *Sailing the Wine-Dark Sea: International Trade and the Late Bronze Age Aegean.* He was co-editor of *Amenhotep III: Perspectives on His Reign, The Aegean and the Orient in the Second Millennium BC,* and *Thutmose III: A New Biography* and co-author, with Jill Rubalcaba, of a book for young adults entitled *The Ancient Egyptian World.* He is the associate director (USA) of the ongoing excavations at Megiddo (biblical Armageddon) in Israel and served as a consultant to the National Geographic Channel's television series *Science of the Bible.*